C A N A D A
NA
NORTH DAKOTA
MINNESOTA
SOUTH DAKOTA
YOMING
Independence Rock
North Platte River
Joel Hembree Grave
water River
Ayres Natural Bridge
evil's Gate
Register Cliff
Fort Laramie NHS
Scotts Bluff NM (Mitchell Pass)
IOWA
NEBRASKA
Chimney Rock NHS
Lake McConaughy
Ash Hollow
North Platte River
Platte River
South Platte River
Big Blue River
George Winslow Grave
Rock Creek Station
Little Blue River
St. Joseph
Independence
COLORADO
KANSAS
MISSOURI
W MEXICO
TEXAS
OKLAHOMA
AR

GHOSTS *of the* PIONEERS

GHOSTS of the PIONEERS

A Family Search for the Independent Oregon Colony of 1844

TWAIN BRADEN

LP

The Lyons Press
Guilford, Connecticut
An imprint of The Globe Pequot Press

The Lyons Press is an imprint of The Globe Pequot Press.

10 9 8 7 6 5 4 3 2 1

Printed in the United States of America

Illustrations by Jim Sollers

ISBN 978-1-59921-041-4

Library of Congress Cataloging-in-Publication Data is available on file.

CONTENTS

PROLOGUE

THE WESTERN MIGRATION DURING THE 1840S was a family migration, a unique time in American history and in the history of the West in particular, in which groups of families, not solitary adventurers, attempted to forge a new life together. Prior to this period, fur trappers—rough, hard-living men—traveled the Western wilderness in small bands, scouring the forests and mountains for beavers. The mountain men of the 1820s and '30s were solitary adventurers skilled in trapping and shooting. They lived out of doors for years at a time, enduring the hardship of weather extremes without benefit of modern Polartec fleece, Gore-Tex, or even a modicum of the comforts outdoor adventurers now enjoy. Their knowledge of the West was passed on by word of mouth: the mountain passes, the water sources, and the best places to graze stock were experienced firsthand and shared in campfire gatherings. The land was not mapped in any real sense, and a fragile peace between American and European fur trappers and the Indians was based on mutual interest, bemused curiosity, and some rousing, debauched gatherings during which any number of half-breed children were given life. The Indians knew the land; the trappers brought items to trade. The groups were on equal footing and mingled freely. Fur trappers often took Indian "wives" who bore the trappers' children, yet these mixed-race families retained the same reckless free-spirited wanderings typical of both the Indian and trapper archetype, rarely, if ever, immersing themselves in the founding of American settlements or towns. Unlike their pioneer counterparts, whose westward travels would be immortalized as symbols of American chutzpah and doggedness, the Indian-trapper families, if they could even be called families in any modern sense, would remain cultural enigmas.

The fur trappers were motivated in part by the spirit of adventure. What red-blooded youth would not want to travel a vast, lawless wilderness in pursuit of wild animals? But they were also motivated by immediate profit, since they were well paid by the ever-hungry Eastern and European conglomerates that were feeding the appetites of cities for fashionable fur hats and coats.

But by 1840 the beaver stock was severely diminished and, more significantly, fashion tastes had changed. Beaver-felt hats, a sign of sophistication since the 1600s, were passé, silk hats being the new rage. The fur business faded rapidly, leaving bands of former trappers wandering the edge of the wilderness—the spotty half-towns along the Missouri River in western Missouri and Iowa—seeking the next big thing. Which came along soon enough: the Gold Rush of 1849, when young men once again had a chance to seek adventure and riches in the western wilderness. But sandwiched in between these two periods was a distinct movement motivated by something besides a quest for individual adventure—a familial urge. The families that went West from 1842 to 1848 were not led by a desire for immediate profit, although they were inspired by the prospect that the reportedly fertile land in Oregon would ultimately yield a measure of return. They were really after something more elusive: the opportunity to start a new life, the chance to define their world for themselves, to start fresh in land that was truly wild and bountiful. Which isn't to say life back East was all that bad for most of these people, who were neither destitute nor wealthy, but mostly prosperous, middle-class farmers and tradesmen who were driven by restlessness and the thought that free, fertile land was available, just over the horizon, for them and their families merely for the taking. But why would these otherwise-comfortable families attempt to take such a risk? What is it about the American character that legitimizes the pursuit of dreams that seem, particularly in hindsight, to be utter foolishness? In an interview in an article in *The New Yorker* in May 2006, Robert B. Reich, former secretary of labor, described the Americanness of seeking new chances despite one's relative comfort: "American culture is uniquely prone to the 'too good to miss' fallacy. 'Opportunity' is our favorite word. What may seem reckless and feckless and hapless to people in many parts of the world seems a justifiable risk to Americans."

He was referring to the subject of the article, a late-middle-age family man, by all appearances a conservative, straight-up type, who was bamboozled by the notorious Nigerian Internet scam that offered millions to anyone who would shelter money in an American bank account. In reality, the perpetrators would empty the victim's accounts and repeatedly ask for, and often get, more money. But Reich could just as easily have been speaking about the people who went west in the 1840s, spurred by newspaper editorials and romantic reports from the dashing explorer John Charles Frémont, who had just completed his first of several western mapping journeys. They were crazy to have gone: there was no viable route for wagons; water was scarce; grass and other forage scarcer; no real civilization awaited them once they arrived. Yet good land was available, and it was free. All you had to do was get to it!

This is what brought me to this period in American history and to this particular period in the chapter of American expansion. I'd emerged from the self-absorption of my twenties into the uncharted zone of my thirties with a sense of dread. I was a "dad," the sexless, emasculated figure who, according to popular conception, for the next ten years had nothing to look forward to but a growing pastiness, perhaps baldness, and Saturday T-ball games. I would pull sweat socks up to the middle of my calves, push a lawnmower, pick up dried dog turds like Neil Young's Ordinary Average Guy. In a last-ditch effort to stave off the inevitable, some would shave their heads or grow a goatee. I would live in the suburbs because I could have a yard for my kids to play in, although I would long to be connected to the city for the energy and hipness. As a father, as a husband, and as an educated male seeking to make the most of my experiences to forge a meaningful life, I was drawn to these men of similar age who, in the 1840s, loaded their belongings into a wagon, often over the protestations of their wives, or at least with their silent and grim resignation, and headed west. The men in this brief period—lasting only seven or eight years—were who I was at this stage in my life, restless, able to see the next decade too clearly, dull yet necessary in its commitments, and I wanted to see what they sought and what they found in Oregon: ultimately, whether it brought fulfillment. We, in the twenty-first century, still imagine ourselves as individualists, as pioneering spirits who, whether we live in suburban tract housing or in city apartments, are aware that our history was built upon the inuring hardship of self-invention. From the Pilgrims to the pioneers, our history is infused with this sense of ourselves as somehow capable of forging our own destiny if we only explore the right opportunities. (An image that makes everyone else in the world, at least recently, hate our guts.) Can we believe this view of ourselves? Can we take credit for the accomplishments of our ancestors and gain sustenance and identity from it? Or is this image really just so much bullshit, a misty view of ourselves seen through a forgiving lens that is really just a self-serving response to an urge to make sense of our past?

These families of the Oregon Trail would have an answer, if one was to be had at all. My family and I would reexamine the Trail—the route of the Independent Oregon Colony of 1844—as it exists today, searching for signs of emigrant ghosts, for traces of this mass migration in the remaining wagon ruts; the abandoned, dried-up, and collapsed prairie buildings that served as outposts; and the roadside plaques bearing messages of hardship endured and unlikely triumph. Nothing like this period has existed since for American families. We bucked up against the Pacific and realized that was it. All the land was gone. And as American dad-ness goes, it's been downhill ever since.

In *Democracy in America*, Alexis de Tocqueville presaged this particular western movement in a chapter entitled, "Why the Americans are so Restless in the Midst of their Prosperity." He had traveled the American continent, at least that portion that was then considered the United States, in 1831, just a dozen years before the mass migration, and had been amazed to see otherwise thriving families "brooding" over opportunities elsewhere that would be missed if not acted on. He described an American character obsessed with seizing opportunity not out of greed but out of a sense that time was short and life was to be seized with a passionate energy. "A native of the United States . . . is so hasty in grasping at all within his reach that one would suppose he was constantly afraid of not living long enough to enjoy them," he reflected after his return to France—to scribble his ruminations while holed up in his parents' attic. He described talented, successful men building houses and selling them "before the roof is on," and tilling a verdant garden only to leave "other men to gather the crops; he embraces a profession and gives it up; he settles in a place, which he soon afterwards leaves to carry his changeable longings elsewhere." (Or as Calvin Trillin put it in his recent book, *Travels with Alice*, "Americans drive across the country as if someone's chasing them.")

The travel writer Pico Iyer picked up this same theme in his introduction to the *Best American Travel Writing of 2004*: "Restlessness is part of the American way—it's part of what brought many of the rest of us to America, in fact—and it's no coincidence that Americans invented the car culture." He then quoted Henry James who, explaining the American predilection for finding meaning in one's travels, said that Americans are "passionate pilgrims." Iyer elaborated: "From its earliest colonial origins, America has been a country for pilgrims longing to draw closer to their God." Whether we actually draw closer to our God during travels is not answered—the emigrants, suffused with their evangelical Protestantism, probably thought so—but the urge to move and find meaning along the way is real, as real today in America, where the average family spends no more than four years in one place, as it was in the nineteenth century.

Tocqueville was describing these emigrants of the 1840s precisely: their motivations, their economic circumstances, and their feverish passion for devouring opportunity until, exhausted, their time on earth expired. And he was doing it twelve years before the Westward Migration, the most ambitious family journey in American history (at least the early European settlers were brought to these shores by professional seamen!). Tocqueville's next remark carried particular sting, considering that my wife, Leah, and I, inspired by these 1840s families, would load the kids into the family wagon and set off in search of their ghosts on a summer break between terms at law school: "[A]nd if at the end of a year of unremitting labor he finds he has a few days' vacation, his eager curiosity whirls him over the vast extent of the United States, and he will travel fifteen hundred miles in a few days to shake off his happiness." Indeed. In three months, we would travel more than ten thousand miles.

The Independent Oregon Colony of 1844 included at least three contrasting figures who embody distinct American character archetypes.

On the one hand is emigrant Henry Sager: charming, reckless, a dreamer; he was victim to his own folly of heading west into the harsh territories with a very pregnant wife when he lacked the basic conservative instincts to keep himself and his family safe. He was defeated by his fatal flaw: an insatiable thirst for adventure that overpowered his otherwise sensible nature, before he even reached the Rockies. He was buried in a hastily dug grave alongside the trail, on the banks of the Green River in what is now southwestern Wyoming. A few weeks later, his wife, Naomi, died, too, and their surviving seven children, the youngest a newborn infant, continued with the train to Oregon, only to fall prey to further tragedy.

William Shaw and Robert W. Morrison, on the other hand, were tempered and laconic, quiet leaders who earned the respect of the emigrants because of their ability to manage risk with steadiness and aplomb. Together they became leaders of the Independent Oregon Colony after the original leader, a poorly organized, moody former slave chaser named Cornelius "Neal" Gilliam, resigned following a vote of no-confidence. Both Shaw and Morrison were well liked and conscientious, helpful to each of the families. Shaw was a former military leader; he grasped the subtleties of commanding an ill-prepared group through arduous circumstances. He was alternately kind and firm; he had considerable skills in horsemanship and with firearms. He and his wife Sally brought their teenage sons—and then the Sager orphans—safely to Oregon, faithfully delivering the Sager children to a mission for adoption by a white family, in accordance with Henry Sager's dying wishes. The Shaws led an almost charmed life in the territory, establishing a successful farm. Shaw even became one of the first members of the Oregon territorial legislature. He lived to the age of ninety-two and upon his death was eulogized in the state newspaper.

The other person to take over leadership after Gilliam resigned was Robert Wilson Morrison, whose wife Martha was also a considerable presence on the journey. Morrison was a wealthy Missouri landowner, who began the two-thousand-mile journey as prepared as anyone could be, taking two loaded wagons, several hired hands, a large herd of cattle and several horses, and huge loads of supplies. When he assumed command, he also took personal responsibility for every person on the journey, such that his supplies were entirely exhausted by the time his family reached the Blue Mountains of Oregon. His wife and their daughters were barefoot—literally starving—by the time they arrived at the Columbia River. They'd given everything away to others in need.

The Sagers, Shaws, and Morrisons took the same risks and sought the same goals; both Sagers died in the process, and the others, whether by good fortune or careful judgment, not only survived but thrived, becoming well-loved pillars of their respective communities. Incredibly, they achieved what the hyperbolic editorials of the 1840s had predicted.

The Sager family is one of the most famous and notorious of the emigrant families of the 1840s. Henry Sager was a blacksmith and farmer, known for his ingenuity but not, apparently, for his good sense. He had itchy feet, was a wanderer and a good-hearted schemer who imagined his chance to succeed lay over the horizon to the west. When I first read of Sager I thought of Bo Mason in Wallace Stegner's *Big Rock Candy Mountain*, a character whose yearning for success always collapsed because of an inability to manage his passions. I also thought of the restless Gus McCrae in Larry McMurtry's *Lonesome Dove*, whose insatiable joy of riding the open prairie—"I wanna see that country before the bankers and lawyers all git it"—cost him his life. (The Sager family's misfortune served as inspiration for Honoré Morrow's 1926 bestseller, *On to Oregon!* and even a hard-to-watch 1970s movie, *Seven Alone*, which bore little semblance to reality. The story was also told in the 1984 young adult book, *Stout-Hearted Seven*, which was an attempt to set much of the murky record of Morrow's book and the subsequent movie straight.)

Sager moved his family to various farms and small towns in Ohio and Missouri, four times in two years, inching his way to St. Joseph, Missouri, like a moth to the flame, hoping his wife, Naomi, would suddenly be stricken with the same itch he had to go west. She had forebodings. Besides, they had six children, and by 1844 she was pregnant again. Finally, when Henry had set up shop in St. Joseph, the very edge of the wilderness, she could no longer resist his belligerence and relented. In April 1844, they outfitted a prairie schooner and joined the Independent Oregon Colony.

The tragic facts of the Sager journey are simple enough and have been told several times over the past one hundred years: Henry Sager's fatal flaw was a bombastic recklessness. He would charge off on horseback when herds of buffalo crossed the path, whooping with abandon, leaving his pregnant wife to drive the oxen, the children to fend for themselves. The children—described as mannerless and almost feral by later historians—had free rein and were frequently injured, sometimes seriously. Catherine Sager, the oldest daughter who would go on to publish an account of her family's travails, was run over by the family wagon when she jumped off the tongue of the wagon between the oxen and her dress caught. Her leg was crushed by a wheel before her father could stop the team. Another child, a boy, was playing with fire and gunpowder; the explosion incinerated his eyebrows and burnt all the hair off his head. He was lucky to have not been seriously injured. Another accident caused severe burns on one of the other daughter's legs. Naomi Sager gave birth in eastern Kansas, on the side of the "trail," just open grassland. Record-setting rainfall that summer had turned the prairie to virtual swampland; the tents, crude shelter for a birth to begin with, were defenseless against the torrents. The convoy stopped for seventy-two hours waiting for her to deliver the baby, a girl, before pressing on. By the time Henry Sager contracted typhoid from drinking contaminated water, no one was all that surprised. He lingered for weeks, lying in the back of the family wagon, suffering from intestinal hemorrhage and severe abdominal pain. He died in the rocky wastelands of southwestern Wyoming and was buried on the banks of the Green River. The train moved on. Three weeks later, Naomi Sager was dead, the result of a nasty combination of both typhoid and scarlet fever, likely contracted while caring for her dying husband.

The children eventually made it—after six months on the trail—to the Whitman Mission in what is now Walla Walla, Washington. They were adopted by the Whitmans and lived happily for three years until a band of abject Cayuse Indians, convinced the whites had been somehow spreading measles as a way to wipe out the natives, slaughtered them and their adoptive parents on their farm. Only the girls survived. The event was one of the lowest points in Anglo-Indian interactions in the West and would precipitate numerous such encounters in the years that followed.

But the more complete story—the one this book is about—must include the stories of the other members of the Independent Oregon Colony, the ones who balance the Sager tragedy. In the process this story sketches the striking contrast between the two conflicting American personalities, one tragic and the other alluringly successful. Where Sager was reckless, William Shaw and Robert Wilson Morrison were sober and reflective. Where Sager was loose tongued and prone to bombast, Shaw and Morrison were deliberate and reflective. Sager died young, defeated by what seems in retrospect a foolish dream. Shaw and Morrison became successful Oregon pioneers and statesmen. Each man chased the same dream. One died in pursuit of his and the others flourished. What happened? Was it luck? While there may have been some luck involved, there is an essential balancing act taking place in the psyche of every American who pursues fleeting opportunity, decided one way or another by an ounce more or less of something called judgment. Shaw and Morrison possessed sound judgment; it's what saved their lives and the lives of their wives and young children and allowed them to build their dreams in Oregon. Sager possessed an ounce less and died as a result. And that's what made one dream foolish and the other realistic. But what a fine line it was. The 1840s Westward Migration was an essential period of time in American history, a national pilgrimage still, in many ways, being pursued, which gave rise to an enduring image of ourselves that has defined our national psyche. "The West was where the forces of order met the forces of chaos," in the words of curator John Carter in the PBS docudrama, *The Way West*. The era established the notion of the rugged individualist, the optimist, who set out in search of a new beginning and was willing to make the ultimate sacrifice in order to try, risking everything.

These inward questions come at a time when our image of ourselves is in crisis. We're reviled abroad as arrogant cowboys. Unlike the 1840s pioneers, we're no longer seen as pictures of health and strength: our national image is associated more accurately with the excesses of McDonald's—induced obesity, violent video games, and a vapid mall culture. Yet we retain an unflappable optimism and entrepreneurial spirit, which is rooted in our historical notion of ourselves because of people like Henry and Naomi Sager, William and Sally Shaw, Robert and Martha Morrison, and the dozens of other members of the Independent Oregon Colony.

Twain Braden
Charleston, South Carolina
May 2007

1

AN INAUSPICIOUS BEGINNING

I WAS SITTING ON THE FRONT STEPS of the North Charleston Methodist Church in the late afternoon sunshine—the light slanting through the Spanish moss and live oak canopy in a soothing greenish haze. Temperature and humidity were conspiring in that uniquely soporific way of the Low Country summer. Birds trilled. Cars rumbled by slowly: churchgoers, picnickers, softball players headed home after a game. I was enjoying a quiet reverie, forcing my body to store this sense of peaceful relaxation, while waiting for my two oldest sons, Finn and Jonah, ages eight and ten, to begin their piano recital.

Oakley, impervious to the somnolence affecting everyone else, was spiritedly running to and fro through the hedges at the edge of the church like a deranged pig snuffling for truffles. He'd pop into the bushes and disappear around the corner of the church, scamper along the low masonry walls on either side of the entrance as parents filed inside, and then back into the hedges. Then he'd emerge to check that I was still following his movements, hoping I wasn't. So I couldn't sit for long. I would follow him, back and forth, to be sure he didn't run away, around the back of the church and into the neighborhoods beyond. He was pretending to ignore me, pretending that the whole of his interest was captured by the hedges and the front steps and not—as I knew better—by anywhere else that was not under my direct supervision. He was toying with me, looking for his chance, and then, when something diverted my attention, he would make his escape. It was a pattern he had perfected in the less than two years since he'd learned to walk (and, unfortunately, run). Oakley, not quite three years old, was a miniature Cool Hand Luke—hard-wired for escape, disinterested in abiding by the laws of parental authority, and, worst of all, unaffected by discipline—with the only exception being that he had the body, however small, of a doped-up running back. His little thigh and calf muscles, the size and feel of unripe tangerines, made him capable of great bursts of speed; his shoulders, improbably square and muscled, had once prompted an admiring comment at the swimming pool by a jealous father. "Golly!" he'd exclaimed, pointing to a bare-chested Oakley. "Look at the shoulders on that kid." Oakley, understanding the spirit of the comment if not the actual words, grinned up at him. I often surmised that the pharmaceuticals he'd been given in his first year and a half of life, to treat the ill effects of premature birth—lung steroids in particular—were to blame for creating this uncannily agile, powerful, and wholly defiant toddler.

As I caught up with him and was herding him back to the front of the church after one halfhearted escape attempt, he must have sensed a soft spot in my defense because he started running, willingly going the direction I was leading him, too willingly, I noticed, but too late. He rounded the corner at a run, dropping his shoulder into the turn, leapt the low wall without breaking stride, and made it up the front steps in a flash, cutting in front of someone who was opening the heavy church doors, and bolting inside the church. I followed more slowly with a forced nonchalance, waiting for the people to pass through before ducking around them in the vestibule and craning my neck to get a glimpse of blond hair. He could by now be anywhere inside the large church. Not surprisingly, he had disappeared, not inhibited as I was by the formality of the place. As I moved through the church and looked calmly down the rows of pews, I heard nervous titters from the front. I caught sight of a flash of yellow hair at the altar, and there he was:

wandering peacefully around the raised sanctuary and inspecting the brightly colored piano and organ trophies that had been set out on display. The scene was tranquil, yet brimming with portent. The altar was draped in satin. An enormous wooden cross hung above. A pipe organ, its keys uncovered and gleaming, was off to the right of the apse—beckoning. He was casually striding amongst it all, no doubt considering his options. I knew his next move if I didn't hurry: hopping up on the organ bench and mashing the keys with his little fingers (or fists!). I imagined the discordant, deafening blast from the pipes that would give him a visceral thrill and captivate his senses: The power! The joy! The horror! He wouldn't believe his luck as he brought forth, from his ten little fingers, a hellish cacophony, the Devil's own scream inside a packed church! He would be in ecstasy and would be impossible to remove without a dramatic fit of kicking and thrashing. I prayed the organ wasn't turned on, activated, engaged, or however such an instrument is readied for thunderous action.

I moved up the aisle swiftly, although still walking so as not to alert him of my approach. As I got near, however, he saw me and flashed me the grin he uses when he knows he has an advantage and is prepared to press it further. I cut off his route to the organ, but he ducked behind the altar out of sight. As I went one way, feeling the eyes of the two hundred guests at my back, I realized he had me. I couldn't exactly run after him at full tilt. The sanctuary was a delicate maze of candleholders and other religious paraphernalia requiring my respect, and even then, in the small space he would have the advantage because of his uncanny ability to duck and weave like a rabbit on the run from a fox. After two turns around the altar—"Oakley, stop!" I hissed several times—Oakley keeping perfect distance with the altar between us, he broke for the choir seats at the back of the apse, gaining distance as he made it behind the chairs.

The performance was about to start; I felt like an unwilling vaudevillian, a farcical opening act, and the audience was delighted. The fathers, wearing their Sunday-dad polo shirts, were smirking at my misfortune (*they'd been there before*); the women, hair coiffed—they had obviously come from church earlier in the day—and sitting pertly in their pews, were smiling warmly at him. I knew they were all rooting for him; they always do. "He's *such* a little doll," the Southern women always coo when he flashes his orblike blue eyes at them. This could go on for some time unless I thought of something to distract him. I suddenly remembered Kipling's Elephant's Child—whose "satiable curtiosity" drew him to the water's edge and into the jaws of the wily crocodile. The same curiosity that brought Oakley to this sanctuary could prove his demise.

"Oakley," I said, feigning lack of interest in catching him, "What's that?" I pointed to the ceiling—at nothing—and looked up, open-mouthed, eyebrows raised in mock surprise. Oakley paused and looked up, too, and in that split second of distraction must have known he'd been tricked, since he squealed in frustration—like a doomed rabbit (or elephant's child with his trunk in a croc's jaws)—and tried to bolt, his legs a blur of churning action, his torso twisting like a fish on a line, but I had him. I picked him up, clutching him tightly to my chest to restrain his thrashing, and broke headlong for the side door of the sanctuary, hoping it wasn't locked so that I wouldn't have to walk through the church and face the congregation. As the doorknob turned I enjoyed a flush of relief, my ears burning in embarrassment. As I let out my breath and closed the door behind me, I heard scattered applause.

The piano recital was the last domestic act we needed to participate in before starting our trip. The house had been rented; bills paid for the month, checkbook and paperwork for the next three months tucked in the car's already stuffed glove box. The car was packed, stuffed like a grotesque toad—we would soon dub it the "Road Toad"—and parked out back in the church lot, in the shade for the benefit of the dog, our miniature dachshund Balloo. We were about to depart on a ten thousand–mile journey across America and back as we retraced the journey of an 1844 Oregon Trail emigrant colony. But first we had to listen to our eldest sons, Finn and Jonah, play "The Tempest" and "Messy Day," which they'd been diligently preparing for the past several months. (I wouldn't appreciate the irony those two titles offered until much later.) As we waited for the performance to begin, the boys were sweltering in their clip-on ties, dress shoes, and button-down shirts, the tails already half untucked. Leah had drawn the long straw and so could sit in the audience with Raven, our six-year-old daughter. (We also call her "Thistle," a nickname bestowed by her brothers when she was a baby because of her curly hair.) Oakley, his aplomb restored, was now on the fenced-in playground, with me guarding the gate, but would soon be bribed with gum (to keep him briefly quiet and distracted) so I could at least hear the boys' performance from the church vestibule.

It had taken us many months to get to this point. What had started out as a vague knowledge of the Oregon Trail—*It goes to Oregon, right?*—had given way to particulars. The Trail in the 1840s, before the Gold Rush precipitated a virtual free-for-all of routes west, followed a very specific path along Western rivers and key mountain passes. From Independence and St. Joseph, Missouri, the usual "jumping off" places, I learned from my readings that travelers crossed what is now northeastern Kansas and into Nebraska, where they picked up the Platte River—"The Great Platte River Road," as it would come to be called by National Park Service historian Merrill J. Mattes—and followed, upstream, its meandering path northwest to its source in the Rockies into the Sweetwater Valley in central Wyoming, south of what is now Casper. From the Sweetwater the emigrants, now surrounded by rugged, barren hills and on a route that was now more than a mile high, trekked westward and ever upward to the edge of the Rockies, where South Pass offered a relatively easy passage to the "waters of the Pacific." South Pass, one of many key geographical features that allowed this trip to be made at this particular time in history, was a smooth low saddle between the impossibly steep and jagged Wind River Range to the north, more than nine thousand feet high, capped in snow the year-round, and the badlands of the Antelope Hills to the south—a geologic anomaly that ushered the wagons smoothly through the Rockies. The second half of the journey—drier, dustier, more awful in every way than the first half—took the emigrants across southern Idaho along the aptly named Snake River Plain to the steep and closely forested Blue Mountains, and then to the home stretch across eastern Oregon and the mighty Columbia River Gorge. The emigrants of the 1840s then scattered, mostly in the fertile and mild Willamette Valley where they established farms and towns.

What I came to discover as I studied the lives of these early pioneers (in an effort to catch a glimpse of some essence of the American family experience) was that the whole Trail was a puzzle, a perfect, lineal assemblage of water sources, mountain passes, and smooth travel surfaces trod first by animals and Indians, that ultimately allowed rolling caravans to travel from the Missouri River Valley to the Pacific Ocean. I had originally surmised that these pioneers had departed with little more than their wagons, their innate American bravado, and crude navigational devices to be sure they traveled in a fairly straight line west much as Columbus followed the parallels. Did they take compasses and sextants? How would a Missouri farmer know how to use these things, which in those days required a fair amount of mathematical prowess? I discovered, however, that they were actually standing on the shoulders of numerous others. The animals had shown the Indians the water sources; the Indians showed the early explorers and fur trappers; the fur trappers became guides and showed the emigrants. And the American government kept apace. John Charles Frémont's explorations of 1842 (and those that came later in the 1840s) would produce the most accurate maps and narrative guide to date, documenting the pieces of this puzzle for anyone who was reasonably literate and equipped with a modicum of good sense.

Most of the original pieces of the puzzle still existed for us to explore. While rivers had been dammed, cities built, and roads paved over, the mountains beckoned and many hundreds of miles of *swales*—ruts—could still be discerned from the pathway of the original trail. The graves of the thousands of emigrants who died along the way—one-tenth of all who started, estimated to be over 500,000 people—may have largely disappeared, if ever they were marked, but other ghosts remained. The towns and villages they built, the farms they cultivated, even the ruts their oxen and wagons cut into the earth were still in evidence. I discovered books that documented each mile of the Trail, replete with compass directions, surveyed grids, and notations of prominent, lasting landmarks. I found the exact maps and books that the emigrant families had used as their guides so I could attempt to envision, with a blurring of my eyes, what sort of an experience it may have been. "The unseen exists," wrote novelist Richard Ford in *The*

Lay of the Land, "and has properties." Along with the ruts and trails and watering holes, the unseen was really what we'd be after.

We would search for signs of the passing of a single group of families, the Independent Oregon Colony, who, from May to October of 1844, only the fourth year that such an organized migration occurred, left their prosperous farms and middle-class homes in Missouri, packed their wagons, and left for Oregon. As described in the book's prologue, the Independent Oregon Colony, and the other wagon trains of 1844, included some of the most notorious and well-known characters of the early northwest emigration: Henry and Naomi Sager, who would die of typhoid on the trail and leave their seven children orphaned; James Marshall, who in 1848 would discover gold at Sutter's Mill in California; Cornelius "Neal" Gilliam, who started out as the expedition's leader but was soon voted out because of his poor leadership style and bad judgment; William "Uncle Billy" Shaw, who, with his wife Sally, turned west when they saw the opportunities on the Missouri frontier fading and hoped Oregon would offer success for their young sons—when Gilliam resigned, Shaw would assume leadership of the expedition with a quiet confidence, while, at the same time, he and Sally cared for the Sager children for the duration of the journey; Robert Wilson Morrison, with his wife Martha, a wealthy Missouri farmer who lost everything on the journey west because of his willingness to help others less prepared than he and who assumed leadership with Shaw; Moses "Black" Harris, a garrulous former mountain man who parlayed his knowledge of the Western wilderness, earned during decades spent as a fur trapper, into a successful career as an emigrant guide; and the ebullient, always-singing Scottish immigrant, John Minto, who, at the age of twenty went west as a hired hand to Robert W. Morrison and on arriving in Oregon eventually became one of the most prominent members of the state's fledgling legislature.

The Independent Oregon Colony, made up of some forty-eight families and led by the flighty and moody Neal Gilliam, was one of six groups to depart in the summer of 1844. With our four children and dog, as foolishly naïve and intent on our own adventure of self-discovery, we would pick up the traces of their trail in St. Joseph, Missouri, and follow it west—and wherever else it led.

After the recital, Finn and Jonah tore off their ties, pulled off their shiny shoes and their Oxford shirts, and threw the whole ensemble in a box that we would drop in the mail to our neighbor at the next opportunity to save for us until we returned. Where we were going, we wouldn't have use for such clothing. As I pulled the car onto U.S. Route 26 West, Leah turned in her seat to share with the kids the iced tea she had saved for herself. She gave careful instructions to all that each person was to have "two sips apiece." Almost immediately, controversy erupted.

"Thistle had five!" Jonah shouted.

"No!"

"Pass it back!" Finn said, a desperate edge to his voice. And then, as gurgling sounds ushered from the rear: "She finished it!"

"I only had three sips!"

"We're supposed to have only two!"

And so on. The odometer read 3.2 miles.

2

ST. JOSEPH, MISSOURI

The Edge of the Wilderness

WHILE ST. JOSEPH, MISSOURI, could properly be called a town in May 1844—it had achieved that status the year before—it was hardly so in any physical sense. It was still dominated by Joseph Robideaux, an enterprising French-Canadian fur trapper who had won the government contract to establish a trading post at this spot in 1839, but who had been a powerful presence in the area since 1826 when he set up an exclusive ferry service across the Missouri River. Named for Robideaux's patron saint, St. Joseph featured a handful of businesses by 1844: a saddle and harness shop, a general merchandise store, a meat market, and a shoemaker. A Methodist church opened early in 1844, perhaps as a peremptory defensive measure against the corrupting influence of the now-numerous mountain men. Most of the buildings of any permanence were built of red brick; others were modest wood structures. The streets were packed earth or mud, depending on the season. "But the town was built on river bottom, so the river had a tendency to wash through the town quite a bit," Jackie Lewin, the town's historian and most prominent Oregon Trail enthusiast, told me. The permanent population, if such a thing could be said of a town of transients, was a little over two hundred.

As a town St. Joseph was more of an emerging idea, a place that hadn't quite caught up with itself as the growing epicenter of westward expansion. A few years later, St. Joseph was feeling the full effects of its growth as a boomtown, as one observer, Agnes Stewart, piously observed in April 1853: "Was quite disappointed at the appearance of this place. I had expected to find log houses and frame shanties, but instead I find brick houses and plenty of whiskey. Every man I meet looks like an ale cask himself." The market for beaver pelts had all but collapsed, leaving hundreds of fur trappers suddenly with no gainful employment, and St. Joe was the geographical ground zero for their career-slump shufflings. Just across the river from the Indian territory of the grassy plains that are now Kansas, St. Joseph was uniquely poised to capitalize on the emerging market of supporting the Westward Expansion. St. Joe was north of Independence, a full two days' journey by steamship, and thus that much shorter by wagon. Newspapers across the country were heralding the Oregon question, guiding people to these half-towns along the frontier—or in the case of New York editor Horace Greeley and other naysayers, warning against such a proposition.

In the previous two years, two prominent men, independent of each other, had passed through the area on steamers, using the landing as a resting place—a final chance to resupply in civilization—prior to their exploration of the Missouri River and beyond. The visits were typical of the budding interest in the area and would presage the bursting of the edge of the wilderness that began just across the brown waters of the Missouri River. Both men were bastard children of French extraction, unlikely geniuses who defied the social confines of their times; and both were passionate explorers and chroniclers of the American wilderness. John James Audubon and John Charles Frémont navigated the Missouri River, taking steamers from St. Louis to St. Joseph and then northward, in the early 1840s, documenting the area in highly detailed journals and illustrations. Each, in his own way, would represent to the outside world the nature of the area that, as a result, became the subject of a focused cultural spotlight.

Audubon was almost sixty years old, enjoying the height of his fame with the publication of *Birds of America* the year before, and making his last adventure in pursuit of his last opus, *The Viviparous Quadrupeds of North America*, when he explored the upper reaches of the Missouri River. (His notebooks were eventually published as *Missouri River Journals*.) Audubon's legacy today is largely equated with amateur ornithologists and conservationists, an aging, largely white population that brings to mind oversized binoculars, wide-brimmed Tilley hats shading puffed pink cheeks, and the kinds of breathable-fabric trousers that allow the wearer to unzip at the knees to make shorts. But Audubon's true nature, which likely appalls his modern devotees, was more in line with other explorers of the time. He was an avid hunter and regarded all living things as potential subjects of his work. The *Journals* intimately describe his expedition as the killing spree it was, a chronicle of death after death of countless species of birds and mammals. Audubon and his companions, most notably his friends Edward Harris and John G. Bell, blasted everything that moved with their arsenal of rifles and shotguns so that Audubon could then retire to his tents, configure the dozens of carcasses in fetching poses, and then sketch them at his leisure. The near-virgin wilderness, never before catalogued by western science, presented an overwhelming number of opportunities for Audubon. And the more exotic the species, the more fanatically Audubon would shoot. The following passage, describing a stop near St. Joseph, Missouri, is typical: "We started a couple of Deer, which Bell and I shot at, and a female Turkey flying fast; at my shot it extended its legs downwards as if badly wounded, but it sailed on, and must have fallen across the muddy waters. Bell, Harris, and myself shot running exactly twenty-eight Rabbits, *Lepus sylvatucus*, and two Bachmans [a kind of warbler, now believed extinct, named for Audubon's coauthor of the *Quadruped* book, Rev. John Bachman], two *Sciurus macrourus* of Say [fox squirrel], two *Arctomys monax* [marmot], and pair of *Tetrao umbellus* [ruffed grouse]." In another passage Audubon marveled at the discovery of a species that he had never before seen: "I heard the note of a bird new to me, and as it proceeded from a tree above our heads, I looked up and saw the first Yellow-headed Troupial alive that ever came across my own migrations." Audubon admitted in his journals that the captain of the steamer "thought me probably crazy" when, without hesitation, he lifted his gun and blasted the bird midflight. He lustily killed three more before the day was out. Day after day, from March to November 1843, as Audubon and his friends ascended the river to the mouth of the Yellowstone through what is now South and North Dakota and eastern Montana, piles of birds and mammals were slaughtered, carefully catalogued, and sketched for later study.

Had Audubon been in better health—his senility quickly accelerated, and he died eight years later—he would no doubt have been among the first to sojourn fully into the newly opening West, all the way to the Pacific and along its shores, to catalogue (and slaughter) the countless unknown species of birds and mammals, further fanning the flash of interest in the West.

But it was John Charles Frémont, whose vigorous youth, masterful skills as a surveyor, and fortuitous marriage to a leading senator's daughter, would provide the elemental key to opening the West to emigrants through his writings and maps.

Frémont became who he was through a cunning exploitation of his innate bootstrap sagacity combined with good fortune. He grew up in Charleston, South Carolina, the illegitimate product of a union between a hotheaded French rogue, Charles Fremon (as the name was then spelled), whose earlier dalliances with a prostitute had purportedly provoked an angry defense of "I will do as I please!", and a married Virginia debutante, the former Anne Whiting. Whiting had been married at sixteen to Maj. John Pryor, a man in his sixties who owned a fashionable amusement park on the James River in Virginia. Fremon was hired as her French tutor, but the pair soon fell in love and fled to Charleston, producing John Charles along the way. Frémont, a brilliant if distractible youth, attended the College of Charleston (with the likes of such notables as Charles Cotesworth Pinkney, son of a signer of the U.S. Constitution) but was kicked out for repeated absences just three months prior to graduation. Following the name "JC Frémont" in the college's logs, the notes of professors show his continuous absences indicated by a lowercase "a"—with such notes as "engaged in teaching in the country." He invariably did well in the subjects that interested him and, apparently, did not require his presence in class. Even with his frequent and extended absences, he earned top marks in his oral examinations, particularly in astronomy and mathematics. But even as a young man, Frémont, despite his churlish nature, had a unique ability to endear himself to people of consequence. He would use this quality, his disinterest in sedentary jobs, and a brilliance in mathematics to full effect by becoming a Western surveyor, exploring and mapping tens of thousands of miles of rivers, trails, dead ends, cutoffs, and prominent landmarks. Frémont's observation skills, coupled with his interest in the natural world, lend particular readability to his journals, which are full of accounts of unusual bird sightings, scrupulous reference to plant and animal life, and geology of the terrain. "What was new in Frémont's reports was their scientific maps and measurements, and their literary voice, transcending the prosaic flatness of previous Western tour books," wrote Tom Chaffin, Frémont's biographer, in *Pathfinder*. Frémont's lyrical style—his observation of the natural world coupled with the telling of a story—Chaffin wrote, would be borrowed by other writers and artists who were inspired by the American outdoors, from Walt Whitman, John Wesley Powell, and Willa Cather, to Jack Kerouac, Robert Pirsig, and Wallace Stevens. "Indeed, Frémont's voice sang with the same sense of enchantment with American landscapes that would later resonate in the works of [others]."

Not surprisingly, Frémont married well. Jessie Benton Frémont was the daughter of Missouri senator Thomas Hart Benton, whose outspoken interest in expanding the westward frontier, along with the movement's other main champion Senator Lewis F. Linn, would become his life's work. In later years, John Charles Frémont would ultimately become a controversial figure, often accused of self-promotion and braggadocio. And Jessie would be accused by Frémont's detractors of exaggerating Frémont's published reports to draw attention to her husband's accomplishments. Chaffin, Frémont's biographer, however, maintains that the level of detail provided in his reports strongly suggests that Fremont's own hand is responsible for the fascinating *Report of the Exploring Expedition*, which I would come to rely on myself in search of the 1844 Independent Oregon Colony, since they likely had a copy, as it was widely reprinted in newspapers around the country following Frémont's return to the East in 1843. While Jessie no doubt edited his work (and served as his amanuensis), and her father nudged the book's wide distribution, Frémont's accomplishments, his numerous expeditions and subsequent reports, serve as carefully documented glimpses directly into this place and time in our history. As someone following his footsteps, I was simply amazed at Fremont's work ethic: how he managed to survey and record as much as he did, replete with comments on his adventures, is a true wonder. Charles Preuss, a stammering, nervous little German artist, was hired to distill Frémont's mathematical notes and calculations into two-dimensional drawings. Preuss quickly learned cartography under Frémont's direction, although he was no scholar, so Frémont alone was responsible for every mathematical detail of the navigation. No one in the company had the requisite skills to even check his work. On our trip I often had little time for anything except cooking, caring for the children, and setting up and taking down our camp. Granted, Frémont didn't have his kids along, but still, he was the leader of two dozen rough-hewn men (and Creole and Canadian *voyageurs* at that). On his first expedition in 1842, when he was charged by Congress as a lieutenant in the U.S. Army Bureau of Topographical Engineers to survey and map the "main emigrant route" west of the Missouri through the Rockies, he was just twenty-nine years old. Like Ernest Shackleton, he never lost a man—at least not on his exploring expeditions.

One other character in Frémont's company bears mentioning: Christopher "Kit" Carson, who would serve as guide. Carson, thirty-three years old, had already gained fame as a mountain man, and was an accomplished guide. Frémont wrote: "He was a man of medium height, broad-shouldered and deep chested, with a clear steady blue eye and frank speech and address; quiet and unassuming." Fremont was also impressed by his abilities with horses: "Mounted on a fine horse, without a saddle, and scouring bare-headed over the prairies, Kit was one of the finest pictures of a horseman I have ever seen." But Carson lacked the comprehensive knowledge of the backcountry in any systematic way. It was this void that Frémont would fill.

In March 1843 Frémont and Preuss reported back to Congress in Washington, D.C. The immediate result was that Congress authorized his narrative for distribution: one thousand bound copies would be disseminated to the public. Numerous newspapers excerpted the *Report,* and the maps, professionally redrawn and compiled onto a single page, circulated widely. While there is no definitive record to prove its existence in the hands of Henry Sager and the rest of the Independent Colony of 1844, Frémont's *Report* was very much in circulation. Along with the many diaries of the emigrants of the Independent Colony we discovered, the *Report* would serve to guide my family and me westward from St. Joseph, Missouri.

Henry Sager, average height but well muscled, was not quite forty years old when, on waking before dawn one cool morning in April 1844, he rose from the makeshift bunk in his crude log cabin on the outskirts of St. Joseph, Missouri, to build a fire in the hearth. His six children, between the ages of three and fourteen, slept; his wife, Naomi, eight months pregnant, stirred. The night before, prior to getting into bed, Sager had covered the coals in ash so that this morning, when he stooped and blew on them, they glowed red. Taking a length of kindling from the stack on the dirt floor, Sager used his knife to shave strips of soft wood onto the coals, which ignited in yellow flame. After he'd built up the fire, crackling and snapping in the morning quiet, he stepped outside in the spring darkness to feed and harness the team of four oxen. The covered wagon, its oak tongue resting on the grass, stood—a looming shadow—outside the door along the dirt road that led to town. It was loaded, weighing some thirty-five hundred pounds, with the most precious of the family's furnishings: a cherry chest of drawers that was a wedding gift to Naomi from her mother; a handmade rag carpet wrapped in canvas; linens and extra clothing; a set of fine china, white and "sprinkled with tiny pink rosebuds" painted on the face, which Naomi had purchased with money earned over the previous five years for her embroidery and sewing; a three-legged iron skillet that would serve as stewpot; a Dutch oven; and a canvas buckaroo tent that Sager and the boys would use (while Naomi and the girls slept in the front of the wagon). All was packed together in the four-by-eight-foot wagon with supplies for the next six months: slabs of bacon and half a dozen hams; sacks of flour, cornmeal, sugar, beans, dried peas; and bags of dried fruit, including apricots, peaches, pears, and raisins. The oxen teams (Jake and Ike; Buck and Barney) were hobbled close by, huffing their steamy breath in the morning chill.

Sager had never owned oxen before these. He had owned and worked only horses and mules.

Sager had hoped to go west the previous spring, having devoured the newspaper reports of the fertile land available in Oregon, influenced more by the encouraging stories, however varnished in hyperbole, than the more cautionary or anti-expansionist ones. Both sides had merit: The journey west, while it had been completed by ox-and-wagon teams by overland emigrants for the past few years, was two thousand miles long and across what was then known as the Great American Desert—almost all of it considered Indian land and populated only by whites at a handful of tiny fur-trading forts. A public debate amongst prominent statesmen and columnists raged in newspapers throughout the country in 1842 and 1843. Horace Greeley, editor of the *New York Daily Tribune* and future founder of the Republican Party, was vociferously opposed to the attempts of American families to head west by ox and wagon and believed the best prospects for a trade route west lay across Mexico or Panama. Greeley would go on to see the benefits of the journey and is often credited with the phrase, "Go West, young man" (although it was first penned by *Terre Haute Express* editor John Soule).

Yet in these early days, when the viability of overland travel was still an open question, perhaps due to his own humble beginnings as a farm boy in rural New Hampshire, Greeley had dubbed the transcontinental journey by covered wagon "palpable homicide." He cited the financial impossibilities of furthering the Union to the Pacific shores, calling upon both the American and British governments to cede their tenuous claims to a fledgling effort aimed at establishing a new nation. Greeley was responding to the Cincinnati *Chronicle*, and others, that had asserted its belief that overland trade, from St. Louis across the Rockies, was indeed viable. By late 1843, presidential candidate James K. Polk, who was campaigning on the pivotal Oregon question, was promising, if elected in November 1844, to set up safety and resupply stations along the Oregon route. An estimated one thousand emigrants had reached Oregon in 1843, and positive reports had been trickling east all winter—the most tangible and, to Sager, the most convincing evidence. Yet the 1843 migration included the deaths of eight emigrants who expired before they even reached the Rockies. Greeley suggested that this accomplishment (the success of the nine hundred and ninety-two others) wore an "aspect of insanity" and asserted that those who had left behind their communities—churches, businesses, bridges, roads, indeed, civilization itself—were succumbing to a "cherished delusion." He published a letter from one of the 1843 emigrants, Thomas J. Farnham, who, notwithstanding his own success at reaching Oregon, found it "remarkable" that so few had died. Greeley wrote: "For what, then, do they brave the desert, the wilderness, the savage, the snowy precipices of the Rocky Mountains, the weary summer march, the storm-drenched bivouac, and the gnawings of famine? Only to fulfill their destiny!" His next line was probably most prescient, certainly so for Sager: "There is probably not one among them whose outward circumstances will be improved by this perilous pilgrimage."

Yet Sager had also no doubt read of a newspaper's characterization of John Charles Frémont's recently published *Report*, in which the existence of a wagon road through the Rockies, was compared—more favorably—with the wilderness of the Allegheny Mountains back East. Rep. David A. Stark of Ohio had publicly quipped that the Western states (those that lay west of the Alleghenies) would still be the province of savages and wild animals if Daniel Boone had shrunk from his urges and heeded words of caution.

According to British historian Frank McLynn, the 1840s, in economic terms, was an "odd decade" in American history, "wedged between the fur trade bonanza years of 1820–40 and the gold rush of 1849." McLynn declared that "the year of decision" was not 1846 (which historian Bernard De Voto had asserted in a book that declared the 1846 annexation of the American West territory from Great Britain and Mexico as the defining moment in American history), but was in fact 1844, since the real groundwork was done that year: the spirited public debate followed by the election of expansionist Polk to the presidency. By December 1845 the editor of the New York *Morning News*, John O'Sullivan, was writing confidently about the "manifest destiny" of the United States "to overspread and to possess the whole of the continent which Providence has given us for the development of the great experiment of liberty and federated self-government entrusted to us." But by this time the great experiment stage was over, and it was a faît accompli: thousands of emigrants had decided for themselves by outfitting wagons and pouring west each spring. O'Sullivan was merely commenting on a phenomenon that was already in full effect.

But for Henry Sager in April 1844, the journey was to be the achievement of several years' effort. He was already possessed of the uniquely American wanderlust that would prove fertile turf for the spawning of such an adventure. Six years before, he had moved the family—there were five children at the time—to Green River, Missouri, from Ohio, and then, edging closer to the famed "jumping off" places of Independence and St. Joseph, to Platte County, the very edge of the United States at the time. Across the river in Kanzas, Indian territory, the only white settlements were "stations"—places where Indians could learn farming and market principles, earn credit for livestock and other homestead supplies. (The reality was that these stations were welfare offices, frequented by Indians who had grown dependent on the federal handouts.)

Catherine Sager, just three years old, would remember an event from the move that would presage their later emigration across the continent and offer a glimmer of Sager's tragic flaw. While traveling from Ohio to Missouri, by way of Indiana to visit Naomi's sister, the team of horses, which was hitched to the wagon bearing the five children and the family's belongings, spooked and dashed off at a sprint, running uncontrollably for some time before Sager brought in the reins. None of the family was hurt, but a traveling companion was "somewhat injured," Catherine said. And these events, seemingly capable of happening to anyone, would haunt Sager, who was as practical and sensible as any American of the time—if restless and prone to acting on his passions—and possessed of the same can-do spirit of his Swiss-German great-grandparents who had emigrated to Philadelphia in 1738. Yet repeated evidence of runaway wagons, errant children, and a seemingly endless string of ill luck suggests a soft spot in Sager's prudence. Nonetheless, Sager was a skilled blacksmith and lay doctor, well liked and respected in his community. He could build just about anything: spinning wheels, harnesses, wagon hardware, and even coffins when his neighbors asked him to, according to Catherine, who in later years would describe his workshop as a "resort" for the community, a place where their mechanical (or medical) troubles could find capable assistance.

For his medical knowledge, Sager relied on Dr. John C. Gunn's popular medical text, *Gunn's Domestic Medicine*, to administer medicine to farmers' families when no trained doctor was available. The tome, also called *Poor Man's Friend*, was almost 450 pages long and was wildly popular on the frontier in those days, first published in Tennessee in 1830 and by the 1840s was in its nineteenth edition. (It is still printed in facsimile by the University of Tennessee as a historical curiosity.) The book's florid subheading provides the best insight into the kind of medical advice it, and lay practitioners like Henry Sager who relied on it, offered:

> In the Hours of Affliction, Pain and Sickness. This Book Points out, in Plain Language, Free from Doctor's Terms the Diseases of MEN, WOMEN, AND CHILDREN, and the Latest and Most Approved Means Used in Their Cure, and is Expressly Written for the Benefit of FAMILIES in the Western and Southern States. It Also Contains Descriptions of the Medicinal Roots and Herbs of the Western and Southern Country, and How They Are To Be Used in the Cure of DISEASES: Arranged on a New and Simple Plan, By Which the Practice of Medicine is Reduced TO PRINCIPLES OF COMMON SENSE.

The last line serves further as a glimpse into the minds of small-town farmers working land on the edge of the American frontier at the time when professional medical attention was days away, or wholly unavailable: "Why should we conceal from mankind that which relieves the distresses of our fellow-beings?" Such a sales pitch, according to the book's modern editor, is indicative of the suspicion most people had for the academic world, of which professionally trained doctors were squarely a part. Reflecting this sentiment, Dr. Gunn wrote: "Three fourths of medicine as now practiced and imposed upon the common people amounts to nothing but fudge and mummery." Lay people who could read and understand these titles were regarded with the same acceptance as country doctors back East.

The editor, Charles Rosenberg, a University of Pennsylvania professor of the history of medicine, also admired Gunn's aggressive approach to lay doctoring: "Violent and unpredictable symptoms demanded violent countermeasures; in retrospect such measures may seem irrational, even dangerous, but at least they reassured family and friends that something was in fact being done. Drastic bleeding, puking, and purging left no doubt that the physician was intervening in a frightening and possibly fatal situation."

Gunn typically suggested "lancets" (bleeding) as a "purgative"—a violent remedy for just about every internal ailment, from "bilious fever" ("if you will divest yourself of irresolution and timidity in the commencement of the attack . . . "and then, "*bleed freely*"), to "inflammation of the brain" ("bleed as largely in quantity as the strength of your patient will possibly admit"), to "inflammation of the intestine" ("The only *hope of* relief, is from the immediate and free use of the LANCET; for without its instrumentality, you may abandon every hope of saving your patient").

In short, Henry Sager, with his homegrown remedies, his practical German-stock ingenuity, and equipped with an easy charm, was the ideal candidate to head west, and he was as prepared as he could hope to be. Gunn's book was packed in the wagon alongside the family Bible.

The most convincing evidence of the viability of the overland journey for Sager, however, was the story of Dr. Marcus Whitman's 1836 overland journey, on which he had brought his young wife Narcissa, and his friends, fellow missionaries, Henry and Eliza Spalding. The Whitmans had since established a successful mission, Waiilatpu, on the fertile plains just over the Blue Mountains in the Oregon Territory. And most recently, Dr. Whitman had returned to the East and reported to Congress on the success of the overland migration and of the mission (and also asked for funding). In 1843, the year that the Sagers had hoped to venture west, Whitman had led another, larger company of emigrants west. Sager had read of Whitman's journeys as letters published in newspapers as early as 1838, when he and Naomi were still living in Ohio, where both had been raised. As a self-educated lay doctor, whose homegrown remedies were sought by farmers throughout Platte County, Missouri, Sager likely associated himself with Dr. Whitman, whose enthusiastic reports were also reproduced in newspapers throughout the country during the winter of 1842–43. If he, Dr. Whitman, could complete the journey—twice!—why couldn't Sager?—especially since he had so much proven mechanical skill.

The Sagers had actually planned to join Dr. Whitman's 1843 journey but had demurred when a mysterious infection in their daughter Matilda's knee, a curious lump, refused to heal. When Sager's own remedies failed to have an effect, they had sought treatment and were advised to stay put in Missouri until the following spring. Sager agreed, waiting until the summer (of 1843) to sell the farm. By fall he had rented a log cabin, just five miles from St. Joseph, living throughout the winter on what he earned as a blacksmith, supplemented by savings and stores of food.

Naomi Sager, a school teacher who was also born in Virginia but raised in Ohio, seemed only to tolerate her husband's dream of going west. This attitude was not uncommon. The women of this migration were largely opposed to the migration, following their husband's lead only from a sense of duty or helplessness. "Less than one-quarter of women who kept journals on the trail agreed with the decision to emigrate, but simply acquiesced," wrote historian and author Frank McLynn in *Wagons West: The Epic Story of America's Overland Trails*, "with fully one-third obeying their husbands only reluctantly or sullenly." Repeatedly, entries in Catherine Sager's journals—written when she was a young woman and living in the West—show tension between Henry and Naomi Sager even just prior to their departure in St. Joseph. He wanted more than anything to head to Oregon, for the free land and open spaces, for the fresh start and for the sheer adventure of the prospect. She thought of the children, of her successful, if middling, life in Missouri and Ohio: her home, her family, and her friends. Now that she was pregnant with their seventh child, due to arrive in early June when they would be on the trail, the tension had turned to abject fear of what lay ahead. Yet, as pregnant as she was, she was also likely feeling vulnerable and not capable of a spirited defense against her husband's impassioned dream. According to Catherine, on the morning they were to cross the Missouri River into Kansas and begin their journey, Henry Sager responded to her protestations with the sort of trick husbands everywhere would recognize: *I'm doing it for you, dear!* Supposedly, his actual words were: "Naomi, it is for you I want to go. Dr. Whitman said that in Oregon nobody has the chills and fever the way you do every year. Wouldn't you like to feel well?" He promised that when they got to Oregon they would never move again. To sweeten the deal, he also promised that once they were in Oregon he would buy an iron, wood-fired "cookstove," the latest contraption that would allow a woman to be released from the chore of cooking over an open fire in a fireplace. To the children, he said that like all Sagers before them, they were "stout-hearted"—"brave and determined to finish what you begin."

Whether Naomi Sager was fooled, too defeated or helpless to resist, or whether she truly saw the benefits of the Oregon climate as outweighing the risks associated with the journey is unclear. Catherine Sager knew her mother would have preferred to stay in Missouri and stop rambling. In retrospect, that she acquiesced to such a trip—two thousand miles by covered wagon while pregnant!—seems unfathomable. But it was a fact that Sager had sold the family farm, fully equipped a wagon with six months' supplies, and was at that moment, on that early spring morning as the sun's rays slanted through the cottonwoods, securing the heavy yokes around the broad shoulders of his four oxen.

3

THE OX WHISPERER

THE FIVE-MILE RIDE TO TOWN would have taken less than three hours. It was no doubt an exciting morning: the six children running alongside the slow-moving oxen as their father walked, switch in hand, with an awkward yet determined bearing. Driving oxen was still a new skill to him. Naomi, hugely pregnant, must have ridden at least part way, although on the overland journey most people chose to walk. It would have been a devilish choice for her either way: sit atop an unsprung wagon, lurching and jerking with the dirt track's every imperfection, or trudging through the dust. Either way, the Sager family arrived at the river's edge in St. Joseph by noon—the dank smell of the river wafting in the spring breeze—and queued up for the flatboat ferry that would take their wagon across. The oxen would swim, accompanied by Sager in a hired rowboat, their horns lashed loosely together with rope to form a chain of swimming animals. Naomi and the children would ride the flatboat.

Sager drove the oxen into the ferry queue, just north of St. Joseph at Amazonia, and into a teeming snarl of dozens of wagons, lowing and shuffling livestock, running and shouting children, and men attempting to keep order. He was given a numbered card by the ferry crew. When the number was called several hours later, Sager separated the oxen from the tongue, and then led the yoked animals to the back end of the wagon. He then lashed ropes to their horns and secured the other ends of the ropes to the back end of the wagon, and then slowly eased the wagon down the steep bank with the animals acting as brakes. Once the wagon was safely aboard, with Naomi and the four girls inside, the wheels were chocked, and Sager released the team. The crossing made a considerable impression on the young girls sitting in the wagon—the teetering wagon motion exacerbated by their emotions, as it was the last they would see of friends and family who saw them off at the eastern bank of the Missouri. The crossing was not without peril. On May 3, 1853, emigrant Agnes Stewart wrote of an incident she witnessed the previous day: "The ferry ran onto a root of a tree in the water and upset. All the men were drowned, and the cattle, although yoked together, swam out and were recovered next morning. The men had been drinking too much and were reckless."

The flatboat itself, nothing more than an assemblage of heavy planks joined together at the edges with heavy iron rods, crossed the swift current by means of a heavy rope, which was used to guide the boat, and its load of a single wagon, with the current as power, the half-mile distance across. One emigrant, Gustavus C. Pearson, explained his 1849 crossing at St. Joseph thus: "The motive power of the scow-shaped, flat-bottomed boat was the strong current of the river. A large hawser was fastened to a tree on the bank some distance up stream from the point of crossing, and was attached by a smaller rope to both ends of the boat." The current would then carry the laden boat down-stream, diagonally across the river, where it could be retrieved with the use of the lighter line. Pearson paid five dollars per wagon.

Today the river is deeper and narrower at St. Joseph than it was in the 1840s, since its banks have been retained through the efforts of the U.S. Army Corps of Engineers. "Before the Corps' work, the river meandered back and forth in its five-mile valley between the bluffs. During a flood, the river might seek a new channel, cutting off one of its many loops," reads St. Joseph historian Jackie Lewin's book,

The St. Joe Road. And: "That is why today you have to go into Kansas to get to the St. Joseph, Missouri, airport."

Once Sager released the team from the wagon, he led the team to the rowboat he had rented for the occasion. Tying the horns of Jake, apparently the most trusted of the four, to the stern of the skiff, Sager started out into the stream as the three other oxen, and the family's milk cow Bossy, plunged, one by one, into the brown water. Watching from a peephole in the wagon, the girls recalled that only the milk cow needed prodding. John and Francis Sager jumped from the ferry, ran to the cow, and slapped her on the rump, and she too followed the skiff into the water. The wagon crossed swiftly and without incident and on the opposite bank was pushed off to the side by the two Sager boys and the ferry crew for the team to retrieve later, but it took several hours for Sager to pilot his little craft and the stream of oxen across the swift current without getting swept downstream. This little adventure alone would not have been for the faint of heart, especially since handling a rowboat in a swift current is tricky enough, let alone with five frightened animals—one of whom, weighing three thousand pounds, is tied to your stern—pawing their way along behind. But Sager made it across by late afternoon and was just leading the team up the riverbank toward the wagon, to the shouts and laughter of the Sager children, when a little dog charged up, yapping and snarling at the legs of the oxen. Jake, led by Sager with his switch, put his head down and snorted and kicked at the dog, pawing at the earth. But the dog persisted. Jake suddenly tossed his head and turned back toward the river, charging full speed back into the water. Almost immediately, the other three oxen retreated as well, scattering from the yipping dog, and all four oxen swam together back to the Missouri side, leaving Sager helplessly shouting and cursing from shore. Only Bossy the cow remained on the Kansas side.

It's hard to imagine a more suitable animal for crossing the two thousand miles of American plains and mountain passes than the ox. If the Oregon Trail were a puzzle—incomplete and impossible to achieve without certain essential factors—then the use of the oxen was as elemental as the availability of rivers and a smooth pass through the Rocky Mountains. Like camels in Africa, elephants in India, and *burros* in Mexico, the ox's evolutionary design predestined it for overland travel, hauling unbelievably heavy loads at the same rate as a strolling human being, all the while being nourished by the scrubby plant life found along the dusty trail.

The popular image of overland travel has been symbolized most effectively by the stagecoach or Conestoga wagon and team of eight or ten galloping horses (with a band of arrow-slinging Indians giving chase). The reality was that early overland travel—in the 1830s and 1840s, before the Gold Rush of '49 and before the Overland Trail opened with the advent of evenly spaced "stages" where horses could be fed and watered each night—all travel involved the use of slow-moving oxen. Teams of four oxen, yoked two-by-two along the wagon's tongue, would haul a single wagon loaded with thirty-four hundred pounds of gear along the two thousand-mile, six-month trek. They would be led by a single drover who, walking to the left of the lead pair, typically carried a light hickory-and-leather switch in one hand.

Unlike horses, oxen are not picky about what they eat. To be efficient and healthy, horses require daily feedings of grain in addition to nutritious grasses. Horses move faster, to be sure, but they are nervous animals and burn their energy quickly. It is not uncommon to read in Western diaries of horses dropping dead from exhaustion or malnutrition. Oxen, on the other hand, because of their efficient digestion—four stomachs!—can eat and be fully nourished by all manner of meager grasses, leaves, weeds, cottonwood bark and twigs, and even sagebrush, which covers the Western plains and Rocky Mountains like a veritable carpet, more common than any other forage plant. Sagebrush has the same high protein as alfalfa grass, provided you have the stomach capability to extract the nutrients. The only other animal, native or otherwise, that can effectively extract the nutrients from sagebrush is the prong-horned antelope, which is believed to have this ability because it evolved on the North American continent at the same time as sagebrush. Not even deer can digest sagebrush.

To learn more about the handling of these beasts, to get a sense of what Sager and others faced that summer of 1844, I turned to Dixon

Ford, the preeminent oxen drover in the West today. Ford, whose great-grandfather was among the Mormon emigrants who came to Utah in the 1850s by pushing handcarts and driving oxen, lives just north of Salt Lake City. A retired inventor of products for the medical industry, Ford regards oxen with an awe and respect akin to a Hindu, although, as a fifth-generation Mormon, he would likely bridle at the comparison. His manner is hushed and restrained, and he projects the sort of quiet command of a ship captain; perhaps it's the presence required to control the movement of heavy objects. Although a lean man, Ford himself has the same centered presence of an ox—the same mellow strength. Taught to drive oxen by his grandfather when just ten years old, Ford keeps eight animals that range in weight from twenty-eight hundred pounds to more than thirty-four hundred pounds. Several of them stand six feet tall at the shoulders and have chests as broad as mature cottonwoods. He uses the oxen for reenactments all over Utah, Wyoming, Idaho, and Nebraska, and has even traveled as far away as Oregon and Missouri to participate in historic events. In 2004 he had his team haul a twenty-thousand-pound block of stone through the streets of Salt Lake City in celebration of the one hundredth anniversary of the laying of the Mormon Temple's cornerstone. In 2002 he and his team "performed" during the opening ceremony of the Salt Lake City Olympics.

Oxen are the "poor man's beasts of burden," Ford told me in his raspy and measured whisper. In the 1840s, a team of oxen cost $25. Horses, on the other hand—whose prices were driven up by the cavalry needs of the Mexican-American War—cost $125 apiece; mules $150. While horses were used for early overland travel, it was mostly for saddle use, and the oxen often hauled extra horse feed in the wagons.

"Horses burn gas," Ford said, "and oxen burn diesel." In other words, horses go fast and are lively animals, but when heavy, monotonous work needs doing, oxen are the unquestionable preference. They put their heads down and lean into the weight in the yoke with the slow-churning power of a diesel locomotive. Unlike horses, though, cattle don't sweat and rely instead on their lungs to cool their immense bodies. "When oxen breathe in, their breath only cools the front portion of their bodies, whereas horses' sweat cools their whole bodies." As a result, in the choking dust of the trail, an ox can become overheated more easily than a horse. Ford likes to point to this fact as validation of the belief that women were better drovers than the men. "Women were gentler and more compassionate with the animals, more tuned in to their rhythms," he said. Men tended to get frustrated and resort to beating the animals to get them to move. When an ox begins to overheat, it pants heavily and begins to roll its head to one side. "It's a very loud and obvious sign," Ford said. Nonetheless, the men, perhaps distracted and frustrated by their own desperate condition, were more inclined than women to drive the animals beyond even their considerable capacities to their deaths.

Any member of the cattle family can be an ox, provided it has horns (to secure ropes for occasional towing, particularly in river crossings and steep ascents), is at least three years old, and is trained for the yoke. Bulls are castrated when they reach six to nine months, and then they become steers. The castrated bulls continue to grow until they reach their full size, sometimes well over three thousand pounds, by age nine. A cow ox, which can also double as a dairy animal if it's been bred recently, won't get as large as a bull, but since the emigrants had two goals—not just getting to Oregon but also setting up farms on arrival—having dairy cattle was desirable. Fifty percent of the Oregon emigrants' stock was dairy cattle, according to Ford.

Ford likes to compare the haphazard Oregon emigration with that of the Mormons, whose fleeing of the lands east of the Mississippi and Missouri Rivers in 1847 is credited with being swifter and leaner than the trek of Oregon-bound Gentiles. Mormons followed the north bank of the Platte River, for example, which allowed less contact with Gentiles and had the added benefit of being less trod and therefore providing more virgin grassland. "The Mormons were better organized," he would say again and again in our interviews. "They had a lower percentage of dairy cattle, more like 30 percent, and they would keep them separate from the wagons when they were moving on the trail. They'd have the deacons, teachers, and priests go out ahead of the rest of the company early in the morning to graze the stock, and then they would milk the herd. The rest of the wagons would catch up to where they were later in the morning." That way, the dairy herd wouldn't mix with the wagons and cause confusion among the yoked animals. "There was a lot of bickering and fighting amongst the Oregon Trail groups," Ford said. "Because it was every man for himself, they had to drive the herds alongside the wagons. There was not much overall organization like the Mormons had." True as this is, it's not an altogether fair comparison, since the Oregon Trail emigrants were motivated for different reasons, seeking individual goals—fertile, inexpensive land in unspoiled country—while the Mormons were collectively fleeing persecution and united in a common goal of reaching Great Salt Lake.

A full team of oxen consists of two pairs, the "leaders" and the "wheelers." The leaders were selected for their attentiveness to commands and for their bravery in going through rivers. The "nigh" ox is the animal closest to the drover, who always stands to the left of the team; the "off" ox stands opposite the nigh. The wheelers, positioned between the leaders and the wagon, were the dumb muscle of the operation. They did not need to be particularly attentive animals, since they were merely following the leaders, but they needed to be stout, since they were the ones that would hold back the wagon going down steep slopes.

The basic commands to drive oxen are simple enough: "Gee" (turn right), "Haw" (turn left), "Come up" (move forward), "Whoa" (stop), and "Back" (move backward). The drover can also use the whip for the same signals, tapping the nigh ox's forelegs or respective shoulders to indicate direction. The off ox follows the nigh ox's lead. A well-trained team needs no tapping or even verbal commands, however, and such signals merely serve as encouragement or a reminder if a team is tired. After each command is followed, a quiet "good boy" is offered by the drover. Dixon Ford leads his team without words and without tapping, the leaders following his every move. When he starts to walk, they move forward. When he stops, they stop. If he turns, they turn. "They're incredibly perceptive," Ford told me. "They just watch you silently with those huge eyes. Drover body position is very important. Both oxen key in on this and will obey his position first, even if he gives a different verbal command or whip signal. To them, the body positions mean what the drover intends to do or where he intends to go." This is consistent with how animals communicate with one another, according to Ford. "Posturing is 95 percent of the way animals interact with each other. 'Moo' only means 'I am of the bovine family, what are you?' But pawing the earth is pretty expressive behavior that gets a clear message across."

Backing a team of oxen can be a tricky affair. Straight back is hard enough, especially so that the wagon and tongue don't jackknife and bind against the back legs of the wheeler team. But turning and backing—"Back haw" and "Back gee"—is accomplished with the animals moving at a different rate from one another, like the treads of a bulldozer. Backing to the left—which backs the wagon in the opposite direction—involves the nigh ox, tapped once on the forelegs by the drover, slowly moving backward, and the off ox moving also backward but more slowly. The whole effect is a potentially a calamity for the beginner, especially on steep, rough, or loose terrain. Anyone who has ever backed a vehicle with a trailer knows the feeling. Imagine backing a bulldozer attached to a trailer, the treads of which are four independent animals each weighing three thousand pounds. Except that your trailer is exceedingly top-heavy and is loaded with your life's savings and all the gear needed to establish a new life for you and your family in the years ahead.

While any breed of cattle suffices to serve as an ox, red Durhams, also called milking shorthorns, are the preferred breed and were the most commonly used on the Oregon Trail. The horns are good-sized without being excessively long like those of Texas longhorns; the cows provide a good quantity of milk; they are docile yet strong; and they make excellent draft animals because of their heartiness and willingness to work, according to Ford.

Numerous emigrant diaries refer to the love that developed between a drover and his team of oxen. When I asked Ford about this, he said it is more than a love borne of necessity. He paused a few moments before replying in a burst: "You have to see a team like mine to appreciate it. They're so gentle. They watch everything you do and are so attentive," he said. "I've had quite a few horses before, too. But I think you can develop a better relationship with an ox; they're more loving, I think, because they're not as nervous."

Training an ox, as Henry Sager discovered to his considerable annoyance when his team, after successfully crossing the Missouri River, turned around and swam back to the eastern shore, can be frustrating to the uninitiated. Sager's oxen likely sensed his inattention, Ford said, and simply returned to their familiar winter feeding grounds. With the distraction of the dog, Sager likely didn't anticipate this since he was no doubt anxious himself and thinking of dozens of other things and lacked the judgment of an experienced drover.

The problem with such situations, according to Ford, is that oxen learn faster than humans, creating an imbalance of power that can result in team and drover being at loggerheads. The training of an ox by a skilled drover takes about forty hours. On the other hand, it can take a person two hundred to three hundred hours to learn how to work a team of oxen. The result is that the ox may be fully capable of following its basic driving commands, willing and watchful of the drover's body movements and whip signals, only to be baffled by the nervousness—and frustrated aggressiveness—of the inexperienced drover. As soon as Sager guided the team from the water, probably already thinking of the need to direct them to grazing and also of the need to make camp with Naomi, the animals—their nerves further jangled by the yipping dog—sensed their chance and, spurred by their hunger, reversed direction and plunged back into the river. "The cattle were recently taken off of the familiar winter range over the river, and at the first opportunity, went back to where the feeding was good and no people were working them," Ford said.

That evening, Naomi and the six children set up camp by the edge of the river after John had sought the help of some men with a team to haul the wagon away from the busy ferry landing.

The animals, once they reached the Missouri side, walked all the way—five miles—back to their winter feeding ground. Sager was gone all that night and the whole of the following day, only to gather the oxen successfully to the Missouri bank late on the third day. Once Sager recovered the team, swimming them back across again with the use of a rowboat, he sought the assistance the next day of William Shaw, who suggested pelting the animals with stones to get them to move in the right direction. This had the intended effect. According to Ford, this was a common method of breaking a stubborn team by beginners. The reasoning, he said, was simple: spur the animals through pain without letting them think that their drover is responsible, since the stones are thrown from some distance away by others. "It's cruel," Ford said, "but it works."

Ford also mentioned another breaking method: After dropping the stubborn ox to the ground, lash each leg tightly with ropes and stretch the legs apart so the animal cannot struggle. Place a metal bucket over its head and then beat on it with wooden sticks—for two hours or until the animal is fully subdued. The ox becomes "traumatized into a trance that will last several days," Ford said. "By then, they are much better behaved."

4

KOYAANISQATSI

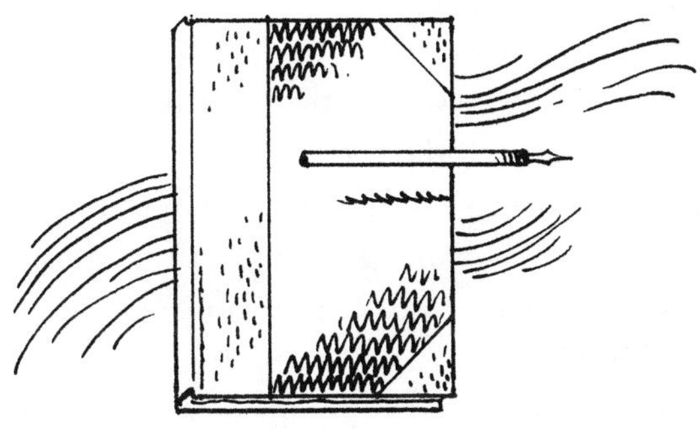

ST. JOSEPH, MISSOURI, today bears little relation to its distant self of the 1840s, with the exception that the river, narrower and deeper as a result of the Army Corps of Engineers retention, still flows along the town's bluffs. The downtown, which may once have been a solid, redbrick assemblage of buildings engaged in bustling commerce, is now full of vacant storefronts and crisscrossed with railroad tracks, flanked on all sides by roaring interstates with overpasses that scar the waterfront, and mile after mile of chain stores arranged in classic American four-lane sprawl. I had arranged to meet with Jackie Lewin, the town's historian and past president of the Oregon California Trails Association, and had hoped at the same time to discover a charming little riverfront town where evidence of the Oregon Trail would still be suggested by landmarks and buildings. This was not the case.

Our campground guidebook had given us two options: one was an in-town RV park and had sounded promising—"Free wireless Internet! Close to downtown!"—but turned out to be a one-acre parking lot crammed with decrepit motor homes and fifth-wheel trailers on blocks, squares of Astroturf laid at the fold-down front steps; and the other, although a few miles outside of town, at least sounded peaceful: "Campfire rings! Pool! Fishing pond!"

We had grown suspicious of these sales pitches. What passed as amenities that could be bragged about in the campground guide appeared, on personal inspection, to be marginally true, formerly true, or misleading to the point of outright dishonesty. This occurred to us halfway across the country when we stopped for a night in St. Louis and, directed by the guidebook to the campground closest to the Arch, discovered the charms of St. Louis's twin city, directly across the Mississippi River: Cahokia, Illinois. We arrived in Cahokia after driving all day from Kentucky, where we'd spent the previous five days at Mammoth Cave National Park as a sort of shakedown camping experience: to test our gear, to acquaint ourselves with living in a tent, and to adjust to cooking all meals on a two-burner stove set on a picnic table.

Mammoth Cave had provided the perfect introduction to our adventure: four days of peaceful camping in a green forest thick with hickory and beech trees and twittering birds, along with venturing underground on tours of the park's miles of caverns. We had checked in with the cheerful ranger, immediately set up the tent at our designated site; the kids delighted in rolling out their sleeping bags and foam pads, jostling for favorable positions in the tent's individual "rooms." That evening, after a meal of vegetarian chili ("Leah forgot the cumin!" I noted spitefully in my journal), we fell asleep to the joyful sounds of our neighbors' spirited singing of "The Lion Sleeps Tonight" around their campfire. They were born-again Christians from Indiana with three kids, we had learned earlier when Oakley kept wandering over to shake hands and see what they had to eat that he might enjoy. Accompanied by the trilling of crickets—the family's faces could be seen flickering orange in the firelight—the voices of the father and teenage sons echoed in the trees: "A weem o wep! A weem o wep!" as the mother and daughter crooned in soothing soprano, "Sleep my darlin', don't weep my darlin', the lion sleeps tonight."

"There's no irony there," Leah said as we lay in the dark listening. "They really mean it; they're happy." We envied the purity of their good cheer.

Over the course of a few days, we sank into campground life. Jonah captured numerous insects (Describing a click beetle: "He clicks by bending his neck and . . . Yow! He pinched me."); Ranger Dave, a pudgy, bearded Kentuckian with a hillbilly accent and a jaunty Smoky Bear hat, educated us on the geology of the caves ("After the underground river dried up, the *lairs* and *lairs* of rock continued to fall down for *millions* of *yairs* and pile up in great *jumbilations*."); and Leah and I took turns reading on the car's "back porch," a wide plank of wood that I had lashed behind our luggage box on the roof that enabled the reader, after pulling up the portable wooden ladder behind, to escape the fray—kids circling below like alligators—with, depending on the time of day, a cup of coffee or a can of beer. (I was reading Bill Bryson's *The Lost Continent*, in which he describes his epic childhood vacations, his manic father organizing weeks-long adventures in the family wagon. Bryson, his father now gone, was reporting on a tour of the country, alone, in a Chevy Chevette borrowed from his mom to rediscover the land of his youth after having lived abroad for twenty years.) All told, our time at Mammoth Cave was a few days of blissful, if somewhat suburban feeling, camping in a peaceful place.

When we arrived at Cahokia, however, an alternate reality emerged. We realized, or perhaps already knew but felt that we had no choice, given our commitment to retrace the Oregon Trail, that you can't really camp, in the traditional sense, anywhere near a city. (Steinbeck: "American cities are like badger holes, ringed with trash, all of them, surrounded by piles of wrecked and rusting automobiles, and almost smothered with rubbish.") Civilization, and all its attendant horrors, has moved on from the simplicity of the 1840s. And here in Cahokia there was a subtle danger in the abject ugliness, something that suggested the disturbing message of life out of balance from the 1980s movie *Koyaanisqatsi*.

As I pulled the car off Interstate 255, Leah giving directions from the *Woodall's* guide ("It has a pool!" she said, reading the editors' notes on the campground. "And a duck pond!"), we started to pass numerous rail yards and road houses, truck repair facilities, and sprawling gray warehouses. I was reminded, in what would turn out to be not for the first time on this trip, of *The Lorax* and imagined that the Once-ler, long ago left alone by the Lorax himself because of the hopelessness of the situation in Cahokia, was probably at this moment at the top of one of these grim steel buildings, breathing his raspy breath in derisive pleasure at the vastness of industry here. I was faced, as I saw the sign for the Cahokia rv Parque (the French spelling was an especially cruel joke, I thought), poking skyward amidst the heaviest industry in town, with the first glimmers of a family mutiny.

"What?" Finn said as I pulled to a stop next to the office, which was set close to the busy road and surrounded by fifth-wheel trailers and mobile homes that had obviously not been mobile for some time. "We are *not* staying here. This is worse than Myrtle Beach!" Little snob, I thought (or maybe I said it); a little ugliness would enhance his privileged little *Weltanshauung*. I stepped outside, shocked by the heat of the day, and walked past the pool where an enormous bald man—he was easily six foot five and must have weighed well over three hundred pounds—was at that moment preparing to throw with what looked like his full strength a Nerf football, gripped tightly in his bearlike hand, at a small child happily playing by himself in the pool. A group of heavily tattooed people in sagging bathing suits and cutoffs were sucking on cigarettes and drinking beer from cans by the pool; a radio was blaring the 1980s Whitesnake hit, "Still of the Night." The next moment the ball whizzed through the air in a blur and bounced violently off the boy's crew-cut head, driving his face forward into the water with a vicious smack. The big man grinned, glanced at me as I walked quickly past, and then chuckled heartily. The group at the pool's edge stopped talking for a second, saw the boy resurface, and then resumed their idle chat. Inside the office I was greeted by a very cheerful host, a chubby young man about eighteen years old.

"Kind of a rough crowd out there," I said.

"Yeah," he said, smiling pleasantly, "they're from the carnival." And then when I didn't register an immediate response, he added, "They're *carnies*. But they're nice folks. We've had them here a few years and never had any trouble." I signed us up for the night, paying the $20 fee happily as I was reminded of a scene in Philip Roth's *The Human Stain* in which the writer-protagonist delights in difficult experiences because of their potential for later use. ("Feeding that great opportunistic maw, the novelist's mind. Whatever catastrophe turns up, he transforms into writing. Catastrophe is cannon fodder to him.")

This was not catastrophe, of course, but neither was my opportunistic maw disappointed. The "duck pond" turned out to be a filthy, muddy hole—no water, let alone ducks—with a pile of trash and brush and railroad ties piled in the center. Our tent site was a patch of gravel adjacent to a vacant lot full of poison ivy and strewn with trash: McDonald's wrappers and Styrofoam cups caught in the brambles. At the site next to us sat a small dome tent covered crazily with a green plastic tarp, bunched up at the corners to fit the odd shape of the tent, and pulled taut with string. A few crumpled Marlboro packs had been tossed into our campfire pit, as had a small ashtray, its fabric-covered bottom, a little bag of sand, featuring a leopard-print pattern. Across the road, in front of an RV on blocks, a long-haired Persian cat was tied to a stake with clothesline in the shade of a picnic table. Its eyes were closed.

I'm not proud to report that both Finn and Jonah were in tears by the time I returned to the car and told them we were staying. Their idea of a camping trip somehow hadn't anticipated these kinds of places, and, to be fair, I hadn't warned them. I had a little talk with each of them, though, and promised them that they could have a "wild card" to be redeemed at a future time on the trip: ice cream (inadequate compensation, they said), or visiting an amusement park (better), perhaps.

As we set up the tent, our stakes bending and snapping as we drove them into the hard ground with a rubber mallet, Oakley bolted from our site and ducked between two motor homes across the drive. I followed him at a slow trot and saw him run up to a group of people sitting on lawn chairs in front of a motor home and then leap straight into the arms of a young woman as if he'd known her his whole life, jabbering excitedly and smiling up into her face. When I approached I explained his inability to heed, but she seemed delighted by his friendliness and gave him a loving squeeze. Sitting next to her was a very sunburned man, eyes bulging and bleary, clutching a beer can in a foam koozie, who said that if Oakley had grown up in *his*—this man's—family he would have learned to listen. "A little ass-whoopin' never hurt nobody," he slurred. I smiled and led Oakley away by the hand.

Back at the site a few of the campground kids had gathered and joined our kids in kicking a soccer ball around. Later we ordered a pizza and joined the carnies by the pool for a swim. A shirtless man with three brown stumps as teeth told me that the name of the big guy I had seen earlier and who was now, fortunately for our kids, gone, was "Big John."

"That's his name," he said. "Big John. It's not just what we call him or nothing or because he's big. His name is just Big John. Big"—he paused—"John." He also added, apparently as evidence of the truth of his name, that he'd once seen Big John lift one of the carnival's "tea cups," that part of the common carnival ride in which four people can sit and twirl around and around, up over his head and toss it onto the back of a truck. "He weighs four hundred pounds," the man said, raising his eyebrows and giving me an intent look, "but he can lift a thousand pounds over his head." I said I didn't doubt it.

When the pizza arrived, I opened the box and found myself looking at what looked like a large Mexican tortilla covered in a wan, reddish sauce and a few shavings of what must have been cheese but looked like grayish "oobleck" (from another Dr. Seuss book). It was "St. Louis pizza," I was told, which had a distinctively thin, unleavened crust. The pizza was cold and tough, and the kids, sitting in the shade, chewed it in quiet misery, not looking in my direction. Leah smiled at me and shrugged her shoulders as if to say, *You fucked up—not me!*

We fell asleep that evening to the roar of traffic, jake-braking trucks, and the buzz and whine of passing airplanes, train whistles, and police sirens. In the morning I was greeted with a friendly grunt by Big John in the bathroom, and we were on the road—the tent and car packed up in record time—by eight o'clock in search of breakfast. On the bridge over the Mississippi, in plain view of the Arch, we became stuck in rush hour traffic, with the stench of the river, sewage or whatever it was, wafting up through the car in a vaporous haze. We eventually found an oasis at LaClede's Landing, a little breakfast shop with ample coffee, juice, and bagels, and then, feeling restored, walked over to the Arch. A fountain inside the large underground lobby was spewing what looked like blue Kool-Aid, and Oakley, escaping from my grasp, managed to wade through it before I caught up to him and lashed him, howling, into the stroller. We took the five-seat shuttle to the top, which in size and shape reminded me of Woody Allen's Orgasmatron, from the film *Sleeper* (except that the kids were with us). From the top, our hands sweating from the height as we gazed out the small windows overhanging the ground far below, we joined a group of several dozen teenagers, the Free Spirit Singers from the First Baptist Church in Duluth, Georgia, looking outward, east and west, which apparently was the point: seeing the old world on one side and the opportunities to the west through the other. (Oakley was unimpressed. "Tractor!" he said, pointing at someone mowing the grass six hundred feet below.) I asked one of the attendants, a bright-faced young man who looked to be about fifteen but was probably working between college semesters, if anyone ever asked about the significance of the Arch or St. Louis as representing the "Gateway" to the West.

"Not really," he said. "They want to know if the Arch has ever fallen over." When I asked a National Park Service ranger at the base, she answered similarly: "They want to know where the bathrooms are." Gateway Arch, which is operated by the National Park Service, bills itself as the "Monument to the Dream." The literature, in an essay by the Pulitzer Prize–winning architecture critic Allen Temko, likens the Arch to the world's other transcendent architecture, the great pyramids and domes and obelisks that suggest "permanent architectural truths," and as such provides a venue for "democratic purpose." The hyperbole is typical of any number of places we would stop on our journey, which would attempt to define themselves as "*The Gateway*" to the West or "*The Key*" to the success of the overland pioneers—the elemental or pivotal feature without which the westward expansion couldn't have happened. We would visit dozens of such places and grow weary of the *we're the most important tiger in the jungle* rhetoric. St. Louis, even in 1844 when the overland migration started in earnest, was several hundred miles *east* of the edge of the wilderness. It was the most cosmopolitan city in the West, to be sure, but it wasn't anywhere near the gateway towns of Independence and St. Joseph, which could be reached by steamer from the St. Louis waterfront. And the Arch's designer, a Finnish-American named Eero Saarinen, hadn't been interested in the ultimate significance of the Arch as a "gateway" until he'd actually realized his design had been selected by the 1947 national design contest that sought to celebrate President Thomas Jefferson's Louisiana Purchase (and a local plan to revitalize the dingy St. Louis waterfront). Domes, obelisks, and pyramids had been immediately ruled out as being too modest; even the largest of domes, rivaling the Jefferson Memorial (completed in 1937) or the impressive dome at the adjacent St. Louis courthouse, would be swallowed, architecturally speaking, by the surrounding buildings. But an arch—an arch could be tall! "Only then," the Arch brochure reads, "did Saarinen realize that it could also be seen as a colossal 'Gateway to the West.'"

Back on the ground we wandered through the Jefferson National Expansion Museum beneath the Arch, literally underground, and learned that in 1844 Samuel Morse sent the first telegraph message ("What hath God wrought?"), from the U.S. Supreme Court in Washington, D.C., to Baltimore, Maryland; that Mormon founder Joseph Smith was murdered by an angry mob with his brother in Carthage, Illinois (apparently his 1843 edict encouraging polygamy hadn't been well received by the Gentiles); and that Edgar Allen Poe had perpetrated a hoax in the *New York Sun* that described a transatlantic hot air balloon that was supposedly flying between Europe and America (that old jokester). There were the usual wagon displays and grim photos of haggard-looking emigrants staring vacantly into the camera. Captions described the dust and unending misery.

Back outside, the kids rolled down the lush grass toward the river, and we were back on the road, headed west on Interstate 70, Leah driving, through the rolling countryside that soon gave way to flat prairie. As the odometer flipped one thousand miles, I was keeping busy by noticing billboards: TESTICLE FESTIVAL! (no explanation); and then a few miles later, a long sequence of signs all related to the same establishment: PORN LIQUIDATION!, XXX!, ADULT SHOWS!, COUPLES WELCOME! ("Couples welcome?" I said aloud to Leah. "Welcome to do what?"), and TRUCK PARKING! And as we passed this house of fun, which turned out to be a rusted double-wide set on a dirt lot, at seventy-five miles per hour a few minutes later, I noticed that not only was there indeed adequate truck parking, there was also a truck repair shop next door—a little entrepreneurial symbiosis, Missouri style. The next billboard was a bit more sobering and made me knock off taking notes: MISSOURI DEATHS LAST YEAR: SUICIDE: 631 HOMICIDE: 333 AIDS: 124.

As we sped along, I was also critiquing Leah's driving (which she loves), jotting down little notes on her habits: "She's driving at 77 MPH—not concerned with tearing roof rack plus stroller and baby carrier off roof. She mashes the pedal, building speed until, well past 85 MPH as the car begins to quiver, I holler, 'Slow down!' and then she settles back grudgingly to just under 80. 'You're just an old ninny; you drive like an old geezer,' she says by way of defense. [This is what, as I had recently learned in law school, is called the "*You're bad*" defense.] She also barrels up behind other cars and then when she's right on their bumper slams on the brakes and slows to whatever speed they're going, whether it's 45 or 65." I'm pleased, of course, that *she's* not keeping a journal.

And now here we were in St. Joseph in the northwest corner of Missouri looking for a place to stay that might be a step up from Cahokia. But the tourist guidebooks, thorough as they are, are not intended for traveling families looking for pastoral beauty on the cheap. They're published for the millions of retirees who roam the country in RVs and whose idea of a decent "campground" is one that has free sewage pump-out; "pull-through" sites, which allow the driver, typically a tiny old man, with hairy, oversize ears like Yoda visible above the machine's vast dashboard, who can barely see his mirrors, to pull in and out without having to back his behemoth (wife standing on the grass waving useless, frantic directions) into position; and, lately, wireless Internet so the couple can post photos of themselves on a family blog to brag to friends back in Iowa or New Jersey about the exotic places they're visiting.

But we were out of options. I needed to visit with St. Joe's historian Jackie Lewin the following morning at nine o'clock and so we needed to stay the night close to town. Accordingly, with the kids in full revolt against the Cahokia Redux place right on St. Joseph's strip, we chose the one just outside of town, AOK Kampground, the spelling of which should have been our first indication of trouble afoot. But, having been on the road since mid-morning and it was now late afternoon, we were desperate.

Leah, resigned, defeated, simply expressed a modest hope for tranquility. On the way down the dirt road toward the campground, we passed a rusting trailer park and then the campground came into view. A cinderblock building overlooked a green hillside with campsites below, next to what looked like a nice pond. On the hill a fifteen-foot-high slide—the kind outlawed in the 1970s by most municipalities and every American insurance company—stood next to a rusting swing set. There were only two other guests, at least, there were two trailers, but the place was deserted. As we got out of the car we realized why we were the only ones here: the interstate was just over the fence, and the roar of traffic was inescapable. There was a hill on the highway, the downhill closest to us, so that each passing truck jake-braked its way to the bottom with a shattering roar. A lone billboard rose above the pond, advertising to the highway traffic (and, mockingly, to us): Super 8 Motel $39.99.

We paid the $15 fee, though, and the kids were so happy. They burst from the car, bolting for the slide and swings. They swam and splashed in the pool; they devoured their mac and cheese (made with vanilla soy milk because we were out of regular milk). Balloo, our little dachshund, ran happily around the pond chasing frogs. Leah and I sat by the poolside with our backs against the chain-link fence, a view of the trailer park to one side and the interstate to the other, drinking Evan Williams sour mash bourbon out of our tin cups. Below us on the hill-side, the proprietor was cutting the grass with his vintage Farmall tractor, which pleased Oakley. By sunset an hour later, inured by bour-bon to the rush of trucks, we could enjoy the smell of fresh-cut grass and watch the sky turn deep blue and the clouds take on a cheerful roseate glow. Even the cell towers, their silent winking visible above the highway, seemed comforting.

We awoke the next morning to the dog vomiting in the tent, his retching noises accompanied by the scream of morning traffic. (I didn't notice any bird sounds.) By the look of things he must have found some fish parts at the pond. We cleaned out and packed up the tent as quickly as possible and got the hell out of AOK Kampground, Leah and I actively exchanging in heated quarrel about the folly of the trip—the words *dumbshit jackass* still ring in my ears—while pressing on to St. Joseph, where I hoped Leah could find something to divert the kids while I met with Jackie Lewin at her office. I thought darkly of the famous travel writers who had taken to the American road—Bill Bryson, Hunter Thompson, Paul Theroux, William Least Heat-Moon, Jonathan Raban, Tony Horwitz, John Steinbeck, John McPhee, Jack Kerouac, and Henry Miller—and cursed them all as frauds. They'd traveled alone, pontificating idly on the nature of wilderness and geology or the unique lure of exotic cities, offering up clever insights as they occurred to them, perhaps jotting notes in leather-bound moleskin journals at peaceful out-of-the-way cafes. (Only Robert Pirsig deserves my respect here: he traveled across the country on a motorcycle with his mentally ill teenage son.) I imagined Kerouac or Hunter Thompson on the road with Oakley. Or Henry Miller. What would he have to say in defense to his wife's scoldings about having forgotten to buy the milk? Would John Steinbeck have still loved Charley if he'd vomited rotten fish in the back of his vintage camper?

Jackie Lewin's office is in the St. Joseph Museum in downtown St. Joseph on the third floor of a former insane asylum, closed in the 1970s, a building that now serves double duty as a historical society and a museum for antique psychiatric-treatment devices. The incongruous setting is typical of Oregon Trail museums, which often have to compete vigorously for local dollars to fund an attraction that may or may not pay for itself with tourist dollars. Some sites, like the federally funded Gateway Arch and a gaudy carnivalesque trail museum that we would encounter by the highway in Nebraska, have obviously benefited from a very successful capital campaign, while others, even if they, like St. Joseph, are a significant place on the Trail, are reduced to operating on the backs of passionate volunteers or barely paid historians in borrowed space. The Trail attention in St. Joseph competes with the town's real celebrity, the outlaw Jesse James, who was living in St. Joseph when he was gunned down by fellow gang member, Bob Ford, in 1882. Jesse James–themed attractions dominate the town's identity. There's evidently little room for two major attractions.

Lewin has the serious air of a reference librarian, along with the oversize glasses, and she delightedly showed me some of the more unusual displays on our walk to her office, offering wry explanations of the exhibits. She pointed out devices for taming or handling the insane, chairs and dollies with straps and contraptions that made us both wince at the thought of what they were used for. There were also displays of works of art produced by past patients. Some very nice paintings hung on the walls. But the more interesting displays were the works created for reasons other than art. She pointed out an enormous crate built of lumber and chicken wire full of crushed cigarette packs. A sign explained that there were more than one hundred thousand of them inside, carefully collected and bound together with string by a patient who mistakenly thought that if he collected the packs, the cigarette company would offer the hospital some recreation equipment. There was no such offer, Lewin said. Next to the crate sat a television on a low table, its screen filled from the inside with thousands of handwritten notes. According to Lewin, this patient believed that since a television *sent* messages from people far away it should also receive them, so he had stuffed his letters into it for many months, until the staff observed him and put a stop to it before he caused a fire.

We sat in her office, surrounded by stacks of books and historic folios, flipping through pages of old photos and news clippings. Lewin's book, *The St. Joe Road*, documents how emigrants in the 1840s and '50s departed St. Joseph and met up with others coming up from Independence at the Vermillion River and other rendezvous points in eastern Kansas. She has devoted her scholarly life to documenting the material, finding old river crossings, emigrant cemeteries, and landmarks and leading tours of the area, both in Missouri and across the river in Kansas and even up into Nebraska. She generously gave me personal notes on where to find each of these places and urged us to start our search along the waterfront, where one can walk a footpath along the water's edge. She described St. Joseph in the 1840s as one of several dozen emigrant crossings up and down the Missouri River. The emigrants surged across haphazardly, not following a designated trail (at least not in 1844) and not forming a single caravan until they reached the rendezvous points, some sixty miles from the Missouri (a journey of several days), where they would typically organize into companies or "colonies," electing a captain, several officers, and judges, who would serve to enforce discipline as the need arose. Lewin directed me to the various points in her book, and showed me where the "first person to die" in the Independent Oregon Colony of 1844 was buried (William Bishop, at a cemetery near the Wolf River), and where the first people, a young couple inspired by the tranquility of the Kansas grasslands, were married (Cedar Creek Crossing: Martin Gilliam to Elizabeth Asabill by the Reverend E. E. Parrish). Just about every square mile of the map's grid, crisscrossed with hand-drawn trails and covered with notes about river crossings and existing landmarks, represented some significant event or unusual story that Lewin could recite from memory. Her scholarly dedication to the subject of the Oregon and California Trails, all accomplished with a minuscule budget from her command post in a tiny corner of a creepy building, is what makes our knowledge of trail history so thorough.

Riverfront Park begins its mile-long meander beneath one of St. Joseph's many highway overpasses and follows the water north along Wyeth Hill, one of the area's many steep bluffs that is part of the Black Snake Hills, that are said to be the combined result of glacial deposits, a grayish-yellow mud called loess, and eons' worth of topsoil blowing eastward in the winds and piling up along the banks of the river valley. As a result, the bluffs and river bottom are thick and rich with biomass. Tremendous cottonwoods grow along the banks, their trunks three and four feet across. As we walked northward along the river, white fluff from these trees danced in the morning zephyrs, piling up in drifts in the grass at our feet. The path is marked with historical signs: notes on the French fur trappers who founded the town, then called *Le Poste du Serpent Noir*, and later changed by Joseph Robideaux for his patron saint as Robideaux's influence increased; carefully sensitive tributes to the area's displaced Indian populations, predominantly the Kansa, Ioway, and Kickapoo; and descriptions of the explorations of John James Audubon.

A sign said that when Audubon came through by steamer in 1843, he was impressed by the diminished number of Carolina parakeets in comparison with his travels in the area fifteen years before. He estimated their numbers had been halved. He noted their suicidal tendency of flying to the apparent aid of an injured bird, the end result being that shooting one bird meant being able to exterminate an entire flock. In addition to killing more than fifty different species of birds, including hawks, falcons, swans, eagles, woodpeckers, whippoorwills, hummingbirds, and numerous varieties of warblers and finches, Audubon himself shot seventeen parakeets near here in May 1843. By 1920, the sign said, the Carolina parakeet was extinct.

But Audubon didn't get everything. The descendents of those that survived were in evidence everywhere that morning. Cardinals, red-headed woodpeckers, Baltimore orioles, kingbirds, flycatchers, and warblers were everywhere, all trilling, singing, eating, and mating, in a passionate spring bacchanal. Oakley joined the celebration by wandering the grass in the sunshine gobbling mulberries that had dropped to the ground. Even the insects, those not being eaten by the birds, anyway, were inspired: Raven noted that she saw "two dragonflies loving each other."

Back on the road we drove over the river into Kansas and began our search, as we progressed westward on U.S. Highway 36, for the various landmarks that Jackie Lewin had directed us to. (We passed a junkyard with a sign on the gate: OWNER WILL SHOOT THIEVES. KEEP OUT.) As we turned off the highway and began an aimless meander—the trail ruts (called "swales" by enthusiasts) themselves have long since disappeared or been incorporated into the road system in this part of Kansas—the only hope we had of finding anything was at the river crossings. Sure enough, as we were hunting for Cedar Creek, where the young couple was married a few days after leaving St. Joseph, we drove over a little rise and down the other side, at the bottom of which was a creek carving its way through the prairie, its banks shaded by cottonwoods. We pulled to the side of the road and got out. The silence was absolute. For the first time since leaving Charleston more than ten days before, there was no traffic noise, only the soothing rush of wind through the grass. We walked slowly through the tall grass, which came to the middle of our thighs, and set up a picnic in the shade by the creek. We sat down and passed around a bottle of cold lemonade.

"I could get married here," Leah said, wiping her mouth with her sleeve.

5

THE INDEPENDENT OREGON COLONY

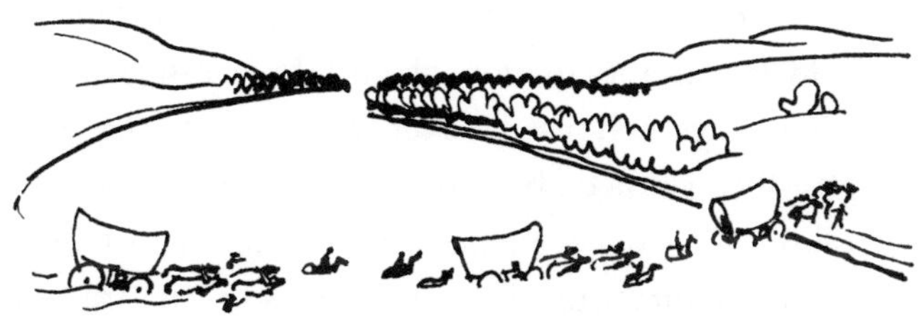

By the time Henry Sager returned his oxen across the Missouri River and rejoined his family on the western bank, the entire company had moved on, leaving the family alone on the edge of the Kansas prairie. Still feeling the pangs of leaving her home behind, Naomi supposedly declared: "The oxen were the only ones who had any sense." The family got underway immediately that morning, the older children running alongside the wagon in what must have been one of the few dust-free days of the trip because of the accidental solitude and the fact that the prairie was especially wet that year as a result of considerable rainfall. They drove all that day and well into the night before camping—setting up their canvas tent in the road in the interests of saving time. The river crossings in the first sixty-odd miles were generally fairly simple on this part of the trail. While tricky for an inexperienced drover like Sager, they were relatively shallow, the banks firm and not too steep; yet Sager would have been forced to manage these crossings alone: Cedar Creek, where two days before the young couple had been married by the Reverend E. E. Parrish (and where we stopped for our bucolic picnic lunch), and the Wolf River. Both streams were higher than normal, however, because of the rains, the currents swift and dangerous.

They were moving again with the first daylight and kept up this pace, some fifteen miles a day, for several days until they arrived at the rendezvous point, where all the trails, those from Independence, St. Joseph, Amazonia, Caple's Landing, and elsewhere on the river, joined together for the first real leg of the trip: north to the Platte River Valley. The rendezvous, called "Oregon Camp," on the Kansas prairie in May 1844 was a scene of busy preparation: men brandishing their firearms, mostly percussion-cap hunting rifles and a handful of old-fashioned flintlocks, in anticipation of buffalo hunting (and imagined bouts with Indians); women fussing over the fires with the new portable cookware and still concerned about the decorum of their clothes. While the women of the Oregon Trail period would learn of the practical benefits of wearing pants after days and weeks on the trail—dropping their Midwestern modesty and fashion sense by sporting their bloomers as trousers—they were no doubt still wearing the long dresses common to the Midwestern farmer of that era at the encampment. (Although, according to Frank McLynn, in *Wagons West*, this "deviant" trend, bucking their innate "bourgeois" sensibilities, was mostly a "post-1849 gold rush phenomenon.") One of the major reasons women would quickly realize how impractical long dresses were on the trail was the tendency for the hems of their dresses to brush the coals of the campfires and burst into flames.

The train had all the requisite equipment packed in their wagons, according to McLynn, the supply list resembling that which might well be packed aboard a ship for a similarly extended voyage to a distant shore: "knives, axes, hammers, hatchets, whetstones, spades, saws, gimlets, scissors, needles, lasts, awls, nails, tacks, pins, thread, wax, twine, shoe leather, pegs, ropes, cotton cloth, beeswax, tallow, soap, candles, lanterns, spyglasses, drinking cups, washbowls, camp stools, herbs, medicine and linament." And for food supplies: "It became almost a cliché that an overlander should have in his wagon two hundred pounds of flour, 150 pounds of bacon, ten pounds of coffee, twenty pounds of sugar and ten pounds of salt."

It was here, during the third week of May, that they organized their companies. (Six companies, more than one thousand people and the largest migration so far, would ultimately go to Oregon in 1844, organizing variously at Independence, Missouri; Council Bluffs, Iowa; and at this rendezvous point near present-day Seneca, Kansas.) The people gathered chose Cornelius Gilliam as "General" of a group that soon labeled itself the Independent Oregon Colony. The men chose a general in the military tradition because that is likely all they knew, since many of them were veterans of Indian skirmishes that occurred throughout the Southeast in the 1820s and '30s. The fact that this journey was fundamentally different from a military engagement would have serious repercussions later on, but for now the company members allowed themselves to be swept along in the excitement of beginning the greatest adventure of their lives. The Independent Oregon Colony, according to a letter written at "Oregon Camp" on May 15, 1844, by Gilliam to Nathaniel Ford, whose company was traveling in concert, included 48 families: 108 men, 48 women, and 167 children for a total of 323 people. "There were 73 wagons, 713 cattle and oxen, 54 horses, and 11 mules. The group included a minister of religion, a lawyer, a millwright, a tailor, a ship's carpenter, a cooper, a tailoress [likely referring to Naomi Sager], a wheelwright, a weaver, a gunsmith [the young John Minto], a wagonmaker and a merchant, plus three millers, two cabinetmakers, three blacksmiths [of which Sager was one], five carpenters and two shoemakers. Most of the rest were middling farmers."

Gilliam, described as good-natured if a braggart and prone to self-promotion, had had command experience in the Black Hawk and Seminole Indian Wars, and he was not shy about discussing his exploits. A native of Pisgah, Florida, who moved to Tennessee as a young man, Gilliam got his start as a "nigger catcher"—someone who tracked and captured runaway slaves, a skill he had cultivated from success in his teens as an animal tracker. This freelance career soon gave way to another role he relished: "[W]hen he ran for sheriff," his daughter, Martha Elizabeth, would later quip, "the people said, 'He is so successful catching runaway niggers, he will be good at catching criminals,' so he was voted in as sheriff." Soon after, Gilliam courted the young Mary

Crawford, and the two were married while she was still an adolescent. Gilliam also became interested in religion and politics and was soon serving alternately as a fire-and-brimstone preacher and as an official elected to the fledgling Missouri legislature—cultivating a character for himself as a tough, divinely inspired leader who would help clear the land of savages. "He was one of the Old Testament style of preachers," Martha Elizabeth explained. "He wasn't very strong on turning the other cheek." Gilliam also directed his wrath against the Mormons, who in the 1830s were still based in Missouri. (In response to repeated abuse and increased tension, the Mormons would eventually move en masse to Utah in 1847, establishing a unique twist to overland travel with the use of handcarts instead of ox carts.) It's not clear whether Gilliam had a hand in the most notorious of the Mormon massacres, at Haun's Mill, Missouri, in 1838, in which eighteen men (and a ten-year-old boy executed at point-blank range) were cornered in a mill building and slaughtered, but he likely would have enjoyed the event if he'd had the chance. "Father believed the Bible, particularly where it said smite the Philistines, and he figured the Philistines was a misprint for the Mormons and he believed it was his religious duty to smite them," Martha Elizabeth said. "He was a great hand to practice what he preached so he helped exterminate quite a considerable few of them." Michael Simmons, a "quiet, determined man" whose gentle manner would be overshadowed by Gilliam's bombast, would serve as second in command to the Colony.

The Independent Oregon Colony also included, as captains of smaller companies, William Shaw, who would soon be referred to as "Uncle Billy" (and who was married to the well-loved Daisy, whom everyone referred to as "Aunt Sally"), and Robert Wilson Morrison (who was married to the equally well respected Nancy), both Missouri farmers and respected family men.

At almost fifty years old, Shaw had none of the youthful vigor and excitability of Henry Sager; nor was he brash like Gilliam. According to accounts of the journey by his companions, Shaw was decent and kind, gentle yet firm when necessary, and his judgment under duress would prove an invaluable skill to all. A "wise, sober man, perhaps the best of those elected to command that year," Shaw also had experience as an

Indian war veteran, but unlike Gilliam he had not had actual command. He was originally from North Carolina and had enlisted in the War of 1812 at eighteen, helping to force the British away from Florida; he had served under Andrew Jackson at the Battle of New Orleans. Shaw was impressed, he recalled some seventy years later, with Andrew Jackson's sense of fairness—and firmness—in New Orleans; he had forbidden his troops from plundering the town in the wake of the British occupation, notwithstanding the city's vulnerability. "They supposed we were going to rob them, and fought for their property well, but when they found what we were after"—securing the town from the British—"they grounded their arms immediately. Jackson would not let any man touch anything in the town without paying them for it." Jackson's behavior around the time of the Battle of New Orleans would later be perceived as tyrannical—his imprisonment of judges who issued writs of habeas corpus, his declaration of martial law, and his iron-fisted rule of the town—but likely interpreted by Shaw as a show of necessary strength in turbulent and uncertain circumstances, where respect for the law, however lofty and laudable, was only possible if there was some measure of peace and stability. Shaw was a compassionate man, yet these observations would inform Shaw's leadership on the westward journey.

Following the war, Shaw settled in Tennessee, only to find that most of the land had been snatched up. He moved west to Missouri, where he met Daisy Gilliam—Cornelius Gilliam's sister—and the two were married in a Methodist ceremony. The Shaws raised their family—five sons and a daughter—in Missouri on what grew to be a successful farm. Shaw would recall that he cleared the land of its timber—hickory, walnut, hackberry, and acres of brush—by hand and sawed up "thousands of feet of lumber by hand for myself and other people." Sawmills would not arrive until the late 1830s, so every structure—houses, barns, and businesses—was therefore built of cut logs, and not sawn lumber, chinked with mortar at the seams. But by 1844 the boys, the youngest of whom was now an adolescent, were growing up, so the Shaws had seen the free land in Oregon as a chance to offer their sons the kind of success they had achieved as farmers in Missouri yet which, as a result of ever-rising land prices and the inequitable advantage that slaveholders had over nonslaveholders, was no longer possible there. In his later reminiscences Shaw specifically mentioned Senator Linn's proposed bill and the speeches of several missionaries, most notably Philip Edwards (who, ironically, would go on to oppose American expansion in the West and publish letters to that effect) who were urging people to go west and settle.

Shaw was especially inspired by the recent publication of the memoirs of Capt. Benjamin Bonneville. Washington Irving's best-selling *The Adventures of Captain Bonneville: Scenes, Incidents, and Adventures in the Far West* had been published in 1837 to great acclaim, and, while it lacked the surveyor's precision of John Charles Frémont's *Reports* whose thoroughness would ultimately benefit overland travelers who relied on it, *Adventures* was a perfectly timed masterpiece of derring-do. The buzz it created stirred something in the collective consciousness, even in the mellow-mannered William Shaw.

Benjamin Louis Eulalie de Bonneville, who, like Frémont, was a dashing Frenchman-turned-American soldier, had marched off into the Rockies in 1832 and spent three years in the West, enjoying a rollicking time at annual fur trapper and Indian gatherings, hunting big game, and ostensibly exploring on behalf of John Jacob Astor's American Fur Company. Everyone back East, meanwhile, after years passed and no word surfaced, began to believe he was dead, swallowed by the Western wilderness. When he resurfaced in 1835, however, he immediately befriended Irving, by then a world-famous author, and presented his journals and maps (in exchange for $1,000), which Irving promptly churned into a popular page-turner replete with high adventure and debauchery. Where Frémont tended toward personal aggrandizement and exaggeration in his journals, Bonneville displayed modesty and restraint, which is why he likely needed Irving to spin his tale in an engaging way and why someone like Shaw, who respected deeds over words, would have been impressed. (The book also helped Bonneville regain his military post, which had been revoked in absentia.) In Irving's words, Bonneville, although a respectable graduate of West Point, "had something of his father's *bonhommie*" in his character and went west on his "rambling kind of enterprise" among the fur trappers and Indians in the Rockies as a way to satisfy a personal longing and an "excitable imagination." Shaw, similarly modest, was thrilled by the book, in his tempered and measured way, and its promises of adventure in an unclaimed land.

After selling the family farm and showing up with his family at Caple's Landing, just north of St. Joseph, Shaw had crossed the Missouri a few days after most of the other wagons, and so was taking up the rear on the first leg of the journey across eastern Kansas to the rendezvous point. As a result, he was called on to bury a fellow traveler who had died in the night, some twenty miles west (ahead) of Shaw's family. William Bishop, a well-liked gentleman of some means, had hoped the dryness of the Western climate could temper his tuberculosis, but he succumbed on May 12, just before crossing the Wolf River—perhaps a result of the continued dampness of the weather. When Shaw arrived and gathered the man's belongings, he inspected the body and, before loading it in the man's wagon, told the bystanders to be sure there was no money in the man's pockets so he wouldn't be accused later—if the man's pockets were then found to be empty—of having stolen from a dead man. "I have always been a man that wanted to live with my character unspotted," Shaw said later. "They found no money on him; if he had money it was in the wagon," which he did not investigate. Shaw drove both his and Bishop's team as far as the Wolf River, where he was forced to stop as a result of the swollen condition of the river. He soon realized he would not be able to manage the crossing of his own wagon and Bishop's and so, apparently shouting to others on the far bank, asked that the agent of an Indian mission west of the river relieve him of the duty. The Indian mission, one of the many such outposts operated on Indian land for the purpose of integrating the Indians into a market and agrarian economy, was just to the west of the river. Increasingly, station agents would find themselves serving the needs of transient emigrants at the same time as those of the full-time Indian population, which would, because of the handouts, establish prairie slums in the immediate neighborhood of the station.

Once Bishop was buried, the agent could help get Bishop's wagon and team across the Wolf River so the belongings could be donated to the mission. "And I thought it was time he was put in the ground," Shaw noted wryly. The agent arrived and buried Bishop on the eastern bank and then willingly took possession of his belongings and wagon team. This incident was vintage Shaw: happy to help, careful to maintain propriety, and prudent, yet decisive, in the face of risks that might exceed his personal capacity. As a result, both teams were able to cross the deep, swiftly flowing river without incident. Shaw joined the rendezvous in time to be put in charge of a company of some forty-five wagons. The Sager family was assigned to Shaw's company.

Robert Wilson Morrison, the other man elected captain of a company under Gilliam, was as well liked as Shaw. A Missouri farmer who had achieved relative wealth, Morrison was headed west because he saw in Oregon a chance to level the playing field in the farming business. When asked by a family friend the night before they departed for the rendezvous point why he was headed to Oregon, Morrison, "who was naturally slow of speech," reportedly replied: "Well, I allow the United States has the best right to that country, and I am going to help make that right good . . . I am not satisfied here. There is little we raise that pays shipment to market; a little hemp and a little tobacco. Unless a man keeps niggers (and I won't) he has no even chance; he cannot compete with the man that does." Morrison then described his neighbor, Dick Owens, who kept a few slaves and as a result could weather a slump in the local economy. "If markets are good, Dick will sell; if not, he can hold over, while I am compelled to sell all I can make every year in order to make ends meet. I'm going to Oregon, where there'll be no slaves, and we'll all start even."

This speech—and "a very long speech for Mr. Morrison"—was noted by a young immigrant named John Minto, whom Morrison hired to help him manage his three wagons and considerable herd of cattle. Minto, cheerful, an expert hunter who was skilled with firearms and known for always breaking into song, was from a coal-mining family in Newcastle, England, having just arrived in the United States a year before. His family settled in Pittsburgh, where they had encountered continuous labor struggles, for which Minto had little patience. He was just twenty years old when he grabbed his favorite rifle, jumped on a steamer on the Pittsburgh waterfront, and made his way to St. Louis, working as a deckhand to pay his passage. "There I met men, with guns and beaver traps, who could talk of nothing but Oregon," Minto recalled. He also heard about the "rising republic" of Texas but was warned against it by a fellow shipmate who knew Minto's propensity to speak his mind: "'No, stranger; don't you go to Texas. They have slaves there, and you could not hold your tongue on that subject, and that is dangerous there.'" Minto decided to head for Oregon when he heard that young men were being hired to help families across in exchange for being fed and sheltered. He had discovered the Morrison family—there were three daughters—within a day of arriving at Weston, Missouri. After being told of a man who needed two hands, Minto had walked the three miles with his new friend, Willard H. Rees, whom he had met on the steamer from St. Louis, to the Morrison farm where he met Wilson and Nancy Morrison just finishing their breakfast. Morrison said: "I can furnish you bed and board, and have your washing and mending done; and you shall give me your help, as I require, to get my family and effects to Oregon." Minto and Rees were hired "in less time than I can write it" and were soon put to work. Morrison ordered Rees, after pressing some money into his hands within seconds of hiring the two young men, to head off to the mill on one of the Morrisons' horses and buy three hundred pounds of cornmeal for the journey. After Rees had left, Nancy asked her husband: "Wilson, you will feel mighty queer if that man serves you a Yankee trick and goes off with your horse and money."

"Well, if he does," Morrison replied, "he'd better not let me overtake him; that's all I've got to say." When Nancy laughed, Minto noted, to his joy, that his new owners not only had a sense of humor but were, in his estimation, "Trusting, and therefore trusty." He agreed to serve the family until they arrived safely in the Willamette Valley, Oregon. He would keep his word.

By May 20, the Colony was fully formed and ready to begin. It was the most exciting morning of these emigrants' lives, although the persistent rain had turned the prairie spongy and the road to mud. Everyone in the makeshift camp on the Kansas grasslands was up by 4:30, long before the sun, preparing a quick meal and harnessing the oxen teams. By the time the sun actually did rise, at about 6:00 that morning through a damp and chilling fog, the teams were yoked and hitched to the tongues, and the wagons were already underway, steadily rolling northward. (I have often envisioned this scene as set to music, an epic spectacle that would suggest all the power and portent of the first strains of Carl Orff's *Carmina Burana*: woodwinds and piano begin in a hushed, steady rhythm as the three hundred oxen strain at their yokes and begin to roll the seventy-three wagons forward, the men on horseback whooping, children running, ultimately giving way to the chorus chants—*O, Fortuna, velut luna!*—that would build to a crescendo—cymbals, tympani, trumpets, trombones—by the time all wagons were rolling in a line stretching more than a mile across the prairie.)

And then, once again, the rain began to fall.

The rain continued for more than a week during the last part of May 1844. Naomi Sager, now hugely pregnant and due any day, could no longer walk and was confined to the suffocating, moldy interior of the family wagon with the four girls, Catherine, Elizabeth, Matilda, and Louise, the cover flaps tied closed against the rain but effectively restricting ventilation. Each time someone touched the canvas a shower of water would come pouring in. The smell of their bodies in the confined space from the days on the trail must have surely added to the rankness. Not surprisingly, soon each person was nauseous—seasick—from the jarring and swaying and putrid smell of the wet canvas. First Catherine became green and pale, bolted for the flaps, and vomited out into the mud. Within minutes they were all vomiting, their heads hanging over the sides of the rolling wagon as waves of nausea washed over them—the excitement of the departure day long ago lost to their new reality. It was the same in every wagon with young children. Everyone's belongings had become soaked through. Each evening tents were virtually useless, bedding was wet, clothing was wet, and the prairie became a muddy, spongy mess.

Mountain man James Clyman, who was serving as guide in Nathaniel Ford's company, which was rolling just ahead of Gilliam's, wrote in his journal: "[A] tremendous shower came on before we fairly got saddeld and in 10 minuits we ware completed drenched with rain . . . it continued to rain all the way to the camp . . . wet as water could make me." Oxen and horses alike bogged down in ravines, the wagon wheels and hooves sucking at the mud.

The rivers, which most often could be navigated with ease except during the worst spring showers, soon began to rise.

6

AND THE RAINS CAME DOWN

The Sublime Awful

THE RAINS AND SUBSEQUENT FLOODING in the American Midwest, particularly in the central Missouri and Mississippi river basins, in May and June of 1844, were later considered to have set an astounding record: the worst flooding disaster of the nineteenth and twentieth centuries. Homes and businesses in Independence and St. Joseph were washed away, waterfront docks were stripped from their pilings, and whole towns, which at the time were constructed on river bottom, were swept clean and their inhabitants, those not swept away themselves, forced to rebuild on higher ground as the Missouri and Mississippi overflowed their already indeterminate banks and spread for miles in both directions. The flooding would surpass even the "incredible" flood of 1795, the river eventually rising thirty-nine feet above normal.

The 1844 flood would inspire President Harry Truman, a native of the Missouri River Valley (Independence), and therefore no stranger to the effects of heavy rainfall on the river communities, to commission an investigation by the Army Corps of Engineers to determine how best to prepare for another such event. The Corps report cited the 1844 flood as a worst-case scenario, precipitating a massive federal project following

World War II to narrow the Missouri and Mississippi Rivers; direct their flow; install dikes, levees, and dams; and contain the waters in controllable-level holding basins. Truman's fears were realized in 1951 by a flood that overwhelmed even these considerable efforts, inundating Kansas City neighborhoods and destroying its thousands of acres of stockyards. "Drowned livestock from the Kansas City Stockyards [between the Kansas and Missouri Rivers] and from farms upstream mingled with oil, sewage, sediment, and flotsam from thousands of destroyed homes," reads a subsequent United States Geological Survey (USGS) report on the 1951 flood. Such was the case in communities throughout the Midwest.

The next such flood occurred in the summer of 1993, which caused more than $10 billion in property damage, washing away entire sections of highway, again submerging thousands of homes and businesses, and covering millions of acres of farmlands for weeks during the height of the growing season. The USGS investigation considered the 1993 flood the most damaging, in terms of dollars and lives lost, of any Midwestern flood in American history. "The floods of 1993 were of historic magnitude as water in the Mississippi and Missouri Rivers reached levels that exceeded many of the previous observed maximums," the report reads. But both federal reports paid homage to the "Great Flood of 1844" and cautioned that its damage was only minimized by the fact that relatively few permanent settlements existed along the banks of the Missouri and Mississippi Rivers at the time. Some 1.3 million cubic feet per second flowed through the Mississippi at St. Louis in the flood of 1844, more than the 1951 and 1993 floods by a full one-third.

There may have been relatively few permanent settlements in the Missouri River Valley in 1844, but there were more than fifteen hundred emigrants attempting to make their way across the open Kansas plains to the Platte River Valley that spring. The crossing of prairie streams had, in years past, been matters of easy routine. A team of saddled riders would ride ahead of the train, carve a ramp in the banks with shovels, and then the wagons would roll across, up to their hubs in water but not needing to be floated across. The process could be easily managed by a determined, even inexperienced drover. But when the Independent Oregon Colony pressed northwest in late May 1844, the crossings of the swollen streams had become life threatening. Time and again, ox drovers were forced to disconnect their teams from the wagons and swim their teams across, the drovers clinging to their tails or lead ropes just to keep from drowning themselves. Wagons had to be floated across on makeshift rafts of cottonwood logs lashed together with rope.

When the company approached the swollen banks of the Vermillion River, still in Kansas, an incident occurred that seemed innocuous at the time but that would begin to set a pattern of frivolous delays that would have dire consequences for the company in the coming weeks. One of the Gilliams' married daughters, Ms. Gage, was suffering from some mysterious sickness—perhaps seasickness from spending days in the stifling wagon, perhaps dysentery—and Neal Gilliam chose to halt the entire company so that she could recover. The company camped for a day and a half on the southeast side of the river, Gilliam choosing to delay the crossing until he was sure his daughter felt well enough to continue. Meanwhile, Nathaniel Ford's company, which had famed mountain man James Clyman serving as "treasurer" and the equally famous Moses "Black" Harris serving as guide, started a few days after Gilliam's, overtook them, crossed the Vermillion, and continued northward into what is now Nebraska for the final stretch to the Platte.

The company was starting to grumble. John Minto, chafing to keep moving, would later note that the delays had a tendency to break the momentum of the group. "Our men all did everything better when traveling every day," he said. "Even one day's idleness made them slack in starting the next morning." And then, in an offhanded dig at Gilliam's leadership style, said, "Neither would it be possible for any man, whatever his title, to retain long control over free men, if it is suspected that he cares first for his own."

One night in late May progress was also hampered by the theft of six cows, "all first class," by a small band of Indians who, after slaughtering them and eating as much as they could, realized the danger they were in from this gun-toting, red-blooded gang of emigrants and fled to the Indian station for protection. Morrison, with John Minto for company, returned to the station on horseback and appealed to the station agent for repayment. Minto, on arriving at the station, observed the sad condition of the Indians and would comment later: "The poor hungry wretches had seemingly stolen that they might live." Nonetheless, the agent promised delivery later that day of the "choicest oxen" that the station had received from a recent resupply. True to his word, he arrived at the sodden camp several hours later with six oxen and in the company of the local chief, "a man of great natural power," according to Minto. The chief had also brought "the freaks of his grown-up children," so described because of their tremendous size, who, as a respite from the rain, assembled in one of the emigrant's tents in silent council around a fire. Here, one of the young Indians produced a young raccoon and proceeded to roast it over the fire, first burning the fur off so that the already close and dank tent was filled with the choking stench of burnt hair, and then, while the meat was "still rare," passed it around to his brothers for their lunch. "Their faces"—observed Minto as the ragged group sat in the tent devouring the raccoon—"showed little concern over any danger they might be in; though in an adjoining tent some of our boys—not the bravest, I think—were expressing eagerness for the general's permission to 'kill the Injuns.'" Why Gilliam didn't allow violent retribution, as he no doubt would have liked, is unclear, but his judgment was probably reinforced by the calming presence of the white station agent—and Morrison's and Shaw's level-headedness.

But the incident had made the company nervous, and from then on Gilliam required that they carefully execute their military drills every day and have "night guards" stand sentry to protect the cattle and horses from thieves. One night, while most of the camp was asleep, two shots crackled, and the men came tumbling out of their tents, clutching their guns and shouting "Indians!" at each other as they rushed off into the darkness in the direction of the shots. As it turned out, there were no Indians this time. Two young lovers had wandered out into the prairie to enjoy a quiet reverie under the stars and, on return to the camp, were mistaken for Indians. The sentry had shot—he missed—before they could identify themselves.

On the morning of May 31, Naomi Sager gave birth to a daughter in a tent while the party was camped alongside the muddy trail. Gilliam announced that they would stop the wagon train for three days to allow her a measure of rest, such as it was. Later that morning, the rain let up briefly, and the sun came out. The prairie wildflowers were in full bloom, and the green grass sparkled in the morning sun. The damp moods of the group began to lift. As Naomi went into hard labor, Sally Shaw had shooed the Sager children away to the Shaw tent, where the Shaws' daughter, Mary, prepared meals for them during the delivery.

A sense of prudishness prevailed over the birth, which was reported to have been long and painful for Naomi, perhaps exacerbated by her diminished health due to the dampness and discomfort of the wagon ride. From the record it seems clear that the women presided over the delivery, but it's likely that Sager himself was involved, especially considering his experience as a lay doctor and his frequent use of Dr. Gunn's *Domestic Medicine*.

Gunn devoted several chapters to pregnancy, under a general banner called, "Diseases of Pregnancy," which pretty much sums up how he felt about the health needs of women in general and pregnancy specifically. He mentions cramps, swelled legs, the "constant desire to make water," and "want of sleep." A short chapter devoted to labor details the progress of contractions, dilation of the uterus, and the various pains and discomforts women feel as the actual delivery arrives. When the height of contractions and dilation occurs, Gunn recommended allowing nature to take its course and, uncharacteristically, not intervening with some drastic measure. "This is the precise point of time in which so many injuries are done, by ignorance and officiousness, in attempting to force nature into premature exertions." He further recommended allowing "the dictates of DIVINE WISDOM" the freedom to relax the womb and produce a healthy baby. He continues to describe in a methodical way how to deliver the baby, cut the cord, and, all while ensuring the mother's comfort, deliver the afterbirth. But the above methods were for an easy birth. A difficult birth required opening the bowels with enemas and the administration of frequent bleedings with the lancet—for "relieving tedious or difficult labour."

The girls were not told what was about to happen; indeed, they thought their mother was dying from a mystery illness that they hadn't realized she was suffering from. A group of women in the company stood outside the Sager tent, nervously chattering in low voices while the men in the company, Sager included, went off hunting for small animals. Naomi named the baby Roseanna, after Henry Sager's aunt, and he wrote the name along with the date in the family Bible.

The Reverend Edward Evans Parrish wrote in his journal: "A frolic in Mr. Sager's family to-day. Cleared off and had a fine afternoon. Camped on a round hill. Much lightning, wind, and rain is noted . . . camped for two days out of respect and care for motherhood."

Later that afternoon the children filed into the maternity ward, such as it was, and were allowed to visit briefly with their mother and the new baby. When the next youngest Sager, Louise, only three years old, saw the baby, she had a jealous fit and tried to attack the newborn. "When she saw the baby in Mama's arms, she began to scream and kick. If Catherine had not held her hands, she would have struck at the tiny red face," Neta Lohnes Fraser wrote in *Stout-Hearted Seven.*

But that evening the rain returned, coming down again in torrents, so that the camp was barely able to build fires and cook supper. Exactly how the company built fires, with the prairie so wet, is a bit of a mystery, but they must have collected wood in the river bottoms and stashed it in the wagons to keep it moderately dry. Mountain man James Clyman referenced one woman's attempt to build a fire in the rain one evening in June: "[T]here was one young lady which showed herself worthy of the bravest undaunted poieneer of [the] west for after having kneaded her dough she watched and nursed the fire and held and umbrella over the fire and her skillit with the greatest composure for near 2 hours and baked bread enough to give us a verry plentifull supper and to her I offer my thanks of gratitude for our last nights repast." Another emigrant attempted to fry bacon in a skillet, only to have the weak fire continue to be doused by water. The group, too hungry to care or wait further, passed around the tepid meat and devoured it half raw.

The evening after the baby was born the four Sager girls slept by themselves in the family tent, their father and mother and new baby sleeping in the larger tent that had served as maternity ward. Frank and John Sager had agreed to sleep under the wagon. The girls clung together that cold evening, but Louise remained inconsolable and, not surprisingly, since it was the first night of her life without her mother close, cried fitfully for her mother all night. She "sobbed and cried and tried to break away from Catherine"—who was nine years old at the time—"until she could fight no longer. She subsided in a small heap of misery just inside the tent flap. Too tired to try to move her, Catherine tucked a blanket over her and went to sleep herself," Fraser wrote. But some time later, either sleepwalking or aroused by restlessness, Louise wandered out of the tent and called into the night for her mother: "Mama, Mama!" In the process, she stepped across a smoldering campfire.

Catherine, who was asleep until this point, awoke to the sounds of screaming and jumped from her bed. Sager heard the shouts and charged from his tent, as did the two boys, who tumbled from beneath the wagon and came running. Louise's dress was in flames. Terrified, she had run screaming back into the tent amongst the other sleeping children, the hem of her dress and a blanket she had been dragging ablaze. Sager and the boys doused the flames immediately. She wasn't injured, but Sager slept the rest of the night across the opening of the girls' tent.

This was the first of many incidents that would cause some in the company to question the parenting style of the Sagers. Why hadn't they anticipated the needs of their three-year-old? How had she been able to wander, unnoticed, from her tent in the middle of the night? Had she not stumbled into the campfire, she could have wandered the open prairie and died of hypothermia. Historian Frank McLynn interpreted Parrish's comment about a "frolic" in the tent as an indication that Sager had opened a bottle of liquor to spread good cheer, but there's no further comment in the diaries to corroborate this suggestion. This is a plausible explanation, though, considering Sager's penchant for letting his emotions get the better of him, even to the detriment of his otherwise good sense. It certainly wouldn't be the first time he celebrated while his wife quietly suffered.

In the days before the birth of Rosanna Sager, two more people in Shaw's company died, apparently of the combined effects of typhoid and pneumonia. The record is silent on who they were. The whole train stopped as graves were dug and the bodies were interred in the ground, probably placed in coffins hewn from logs of cottonwood, which was soft and easy to carve.

On Sunday, June 2, the last day the company respected motherhood, another minister in the group, a Mr. Cave, admonished everyone, according to Reverend Parrish, who apparently administered very little in the way of religious services on the journey, to "Fight the fight of faith and lay hold on eternal life," a quote from I Timothy (6:12). The remainder of the Epistle, which Parrish did not record, continues, "whereunto thou art also called, and hast professed a good profession before many witnesses." The emigrants had just buried two more of their members, and seen the birth of another in a squalid, muddy tent hundreds of miles from any real civilization, so the Reverend Cave was likely attempting to provide a measure of comfort, assuring his new friends that wherever they were headed they had chosen a noble path and could take comfort in their good company. They just needed to keep faith. The next morning, Monday, June 3, Parrish was back to his obsession with the weather and noted in his journal: "Very cool this morning. Health of the camp improving. At six o'clock all hands engaged in making an early start."

Over the course of the next few days the company enjoyed a brief spell of mild weather as the rains relented; the only incident recorded seems to have been a quarrel between a young Clark Eads and a member of another family. Parrish noted: "Last night had a 'court' trial. Young Eads was charged with attempting to shoot a man in a quarrel. The court ordered him bound over for good behavior." The court's "judges" sentenced Eads to be tied to a stake driven into the ground for a night and guarded by the hapless John Minto, who, because of his youth and lack of family commitments, would often find himself assigned to these unenviable tasks. He later wrote of the incident: "[T]he duty devolved upon me as junior officer. This was in itself very disagreeable,"—sitting all night in the company of a violent man tied to a stake—"but rendered doubly so by the young fellow trying to quarrel with me, while I acted as guard."

"He remained tied all day," recalled B. F. Nichols, nephew of Benjamin Nichols, who was a teenager at the time and delighted in observing the boy's punishment, "and the rain came down in torrents. Eads got the benefit of the cleansing and cooling flood and it cooled his ire to a very great extent. Yet there was lurking beneath the surface an amount of unadulterated cussed-ness seldom found in a boy of his age."

Nichols recounted that the punishment had only a temporary effect, however, and he gleefully recorded the results in his reminiscences. A few days later, the boy was in trouble again, this time with his mother. She attempted to discipline him for "some obstreperous conduct," the young Nichols said, "but the boy did not purpose to be controlled in any such manner, so he let fly with his right and landed on her under jaw. It staggered the old gal but she was grit to the backbone, red headed, muscular as an ordinary athlete."

The mother shook off the blow and, in a flash, responded.

"The blow received from the boy brought her to the front in full fighting trim," Nichols said. "She squared away and shot out her right straight from the shoulder in the most approved pugilistic manner, catching her son just below the eye. The place on his cheek first turned white, then red, a little blood oozed through the skin. Then they side stepped, feinted, parried, exchanged in rapid succession."

Nichols duly recorded the ensuing exchange of blows: "The mother, by a dexterous swing with her left, caught the lad on the jaw near the base of the ear and I thought he was going down and out but he rallied quickly, ducked his head and made a rush like going to butt, doubtless intending to take her about the midships. She quickly side stepped and caught him around the neck with head under her arm. They tug, they strain, they writhe and twist like a toad on a red ant hill until at last they both go down, the boy above and the mother below."

Only then did the boy's father, Moses Eads, intervene, Nichols dutifully recording the dialogue as he remembered it. The father "caught his cub by the back of the neck, jerked him to his feet, shook him soundly with the remark, 'Clark, what are you a doin' fiten yer marm?' 'I don't keer, she hit me first,' replied the boy. 'Look out now, none of yer sass. It won't be marm if I git holten yer.'"

To which the mother added: "Well, I did hit 'im and I'll do it agin and give him the allfiredest beaten that ever he got if he don't mine me."

Moses Eads sighed and said, "Ole woman, you better let that job out. He is gittin too big to whup. I'm afered you'll bite off moern yer can chaw." The boy must have minded his mother after that, because there is no further mention of his activities in the journals.

But the company pressed on, arriving at the banks of the Vermillion River, which was swollen yet passable, since Ford's company had made it across in the previous few days, on about June 7. Gilliam again chose to halt the company, hoping the weather would clear the following day, and again calling attention to the poor health of his daughter, who had apparently not recovered. Minto, who was among the first to arrive at the Vermillion and observe its condition, wrote: "The first wagon arrived at 1 o'clock p.m., and some of the wagons might have gone over then, though the stream was rising rapidly." Whether Minto meant that only some of the wagons could cross, or whether he thought they could have all crossed but the first ones without difficulty, isn't clear from the record. Reverend Parrish was similarly frustrated, however, which suggests that most of the emigrants thought the whole company could have crossed safely that day, noting in his log: "This causes some dissatisfaction in camp, as they think they might have gone over yesterday."

Gilliam's hesitation, whether from fatigue or indecision, proved ill timed, and the company's already grim outlook was soon further dampened.

Shaw recalled: "Such a rain fell that night as I have never seen since or before."

By the next morning, the Vermillion was a raging torrent, flooding the bottoms so that much of the company was forced to retreat, eastward, to find higher ground just to keep from being swept away. Crossing the river was now impossible. "Had we moved as we should on the sixth, we should have crossed the Big Blue [just to the north in Nebraska] with or before Ford's company," Minto recalled. "Our delay was a grave misfortune."

They remained on the wrong side of the Vermillion for seventeen days.

During the first three weeks of June, rain fell in sheets—unabated—and the camp was forced to keep moving backward away from the flooded bottoms. The men had hoped to build boats to cross the river, only to be foiled when the trees themselves were soon covered by rising water.

Minto wrote: "It rained every day from the seventh to the seventeenth, inclusive, and sometimes very heavy." He noted that the only bright side was the relative warmth of the spring rains. "The rains, although almost incessant, were warm, and youngsters, like the writer, were out with their guns nearly all the time we were water-stayed at Black Vermillion."

Minto, ever cheerful, wandered the prairie with his "fowling gun" and hunted wild turkeys, marveling at flocks of passenger pigeons, which he noted were "flying in flocks southward." While Minto was an avid hunter, he admitted to being overcome by the picturesque beauty of the countryside to the point that he could not bring himself to kill anything. "I found that my destructiveness was very much lowered by the effect of the surroundings—the joy of freedom in the rich and beautiful country making me indifferent about killing things." He took half-hearted shots at turkeys, relieved when he missed. When they entered hedges, he allowed them to hide and didn't beat the thickets to flush them out.

There is conflicting evidence in the record about whether the entire Ford expedition was across the Vermillion River sooner than Gilliam's. James Clyman had Ford's company several days behind Gilliam's. Minto has Gilliam's two days behind Ford's. Notwithstanding Minto's reference to Ford's company being ahead (which is where the confusion exists in the record), it seems to make the most sense that Ford and Clyman were indeed behind Gilliam's company and that Minto was merely mistaken as to *whose* company had successfully crossed the Vermillion River the day before Gilliam's company arrived, only to be held back by Gilliam and then stranded by the rising river. This is likely because Clyman makes reference to finding the "canoes" at the Vermillion crossing, which he believed were left by Gilliam's company. Which means that, judging from the dates in his journal, they effectively crossed four days behind Gilliam's company. The confusion in the record is exacerbated by the fact that the companies were so spread out, often over thirty miles or more, and groups of each company mingled with groups of the other. Either way, Clyman and Ford were getting just as wet as those in Gilliam's company. Clyman wrote, in his typical expressive way (replete with reckless spelling), of the frequent thundershowers that passed through day and night those first three weeks of June, which must have been terrifying in the thin and leaky shelter of the canvas tents and wagon covers: "[A] Splendid natural meteorick Exhibition the electrick Stupendous rocks & deep chasms & dark raviens illuminated with dazzeling brileancy too bright & glancing for the eye to dwel on & might truly be called the Sublime awful."

Parrish's journal was filled with notes on the dreary weather—June 12: "Still rains and water still rising," and June 13: "Still raining, waters still rising." On June 14: "This morning it still rains . . . At noon it still rains." This observation was coupled with pleas to God that the weather would break: "O, that it might please the Lord to cause it soon to cease."

Driven crazy by the delays, the men of Gilliam's company eventually waded into the stream and cut down large cottonwoods, fashioning crude "canoes" by hollowing out a channel in the logs and rolling the wagons, one by one, in place, the wheels in the grooves—so that the craft resembled precarious catamarans. They lashed the axles to the logs, and the wagons were then floated across, one by one, probably guided by ropes spanning the river and moving diagonally across the stream using the force of the current for propulsion. "This was expeditiously accomplished," Minto recalled, "and the wagons were loaded on easily by the men of the company applying their own arms and broad shoulders; but as the stream fell rapidly, the bank of the further side became exposed, and in order to bring the loaded wagons to firm land beyond it was necessary to use oxen and log chains up the bank."

Gilliam's son, Washington, recalled: "This little stream that at low water could be stepped over detained us seventeen days in one camp."

On June 17—finally—the families of Gilliam's company were safely across, and then the whole company charged off, as swiftly as the spongy earth would allow, toward Nebraska. Of the time on the banks of the Vermillion, Shaw wrote, "Our cattle got fat, but it did not do them much good, the men drove them so fast afterwards that it killed them off."

7

FLOWERS IN THE GRASS

AFTER THE CRUSHING TRAFFIC AND VISUAL POLLUTION of Cahokia, Illinois, and St. Joseph, Missouri, the rolling wheat fields of Nebraska—absolutely silent but for the gentle rush of wind and an occasional *chack!* from a red-winged blackbird sitting on a wooden fencepost—offered the welcome reprieve of an idyllic, open-air sanitarium. I thought of William Shaw's observation, which he made decades after arriving in Oregon: "Even if they made me governor, I would never go back to Missouri." At Alexandria Lake State Recreation Area, we spilled from the car like depraved war veterans, accompanied by a cascade of trash and road debris that had nestled around our bodies in the car on the drive through northeastern Kansas: crumpled scraps of paper, plastic juice bottles, coffee cups, books, pens, pencils, crayons, and filthy, balled-up clothing.

The peacefulness was startling. We stood in the grass by the lake, stunned, the car engine ticking in the heat, and let the hot, dry wind on our faces whisk away the stress and cramps of the road. We breathed deep, the sight of the undulating waves of grass causing us to wobble at the knees in sensory ecstasy.

"I *love* Nebraska!" Leah sighed, closing her eyes.

"Me too," I said. "Funny, you never hear anything about Nebraska—except for that Bruce Springsteen album."

And then we heard the train's whistle blast, a shrill screech coming from the west, which was soon followed by the pulsing roar of a diesel engine and the pounding tumult of steel on steel. A second later the train whooshed upon us—not one hundred yards away—in a dizzying display of power. Oakley's jaw dropped open, his long blond hair swept back in the accompanying breeze, and his blue eyes opened so wide as to provide the most vivid expression of awe I had ever seen. Dozens of cars, heavily laden with coal, rumbled swiftly by—*clackety-clackety-clackety*—for a full minute, our chests buzzing with the vibration, until with a rush and a swirl of dust the train was gone, in its place the same idyllic silence. A lone fisherman at the water's edge hadn't flinched.

"Holy shit!" I said.

"I hope that doesn't happen too often," Leah added, eyeing our tent site and its close proximity to the tracks.

"Pop," Finn said, "you owe me a quarter." (For every foul word, he received 25 cents.)

This part of Nebraska, near the town of Fairbury, population 4,262, would be our stopover for the next several days. It was where my Oregon Trails guide, *Maps of the Oregon Trail*, a collection of hundreds of annotated maps, said we would have the best chance of seeing the vestiges of trail ruts—swales—in the eastern portion of the Oregon Trail, still carved into the landscape like faint ribbons. We hadn't seen any, since in Kansas they'd long ago been plowed under or incorporated into paved roadways. But here, perhaps because of a concerted effort in 1900 by the state of Nebraska to preserve the trail's fading heritage, you can still, supposedly, catch glimpses of its path. The guide's creator, Gregory Franzwa, had hit the road in the late 1960s with his wife and kids and documented every mile of the trail, tromping over public and private land with a compass and survey tools, assiduously taking notes on the location of every landmark mentioned in diaries and logging every visible swale. (Inexplicably, he'd done it again a few years later, publishing *The Oregon Trail Revisited*, a copy of which I also had, jammed on the dashboard with the dozens of other Trail books I had been accumulating at various bookstores and museums along the way.) When I called Franzwa, now in his eighties and still self-publishing books on American history, for his observations about the families that had gone west in the 1840s, he'd said, "Hell, that was almost forty years ago. I can't remember what I did last week." But he did say he'd felt the Trail came to life in Nebraska, that he'd felt the "power of place" begin to emerge. I hoped the same would be true for us, since our first efforts—pulling off onto some unnamed, numbered country roads shortly after crossing the state line—had failed. Franzwa's map told us where to stop and in which direction to look. And, after hopping out of the car and squinting at a hilly field, I had pointed at a curve in the land and thought I saw the faint suggestion of an old roadway.

"Swales?" Leah had snorted. "All I see is grass and dirt." She then did her best impression of Chevy Chase (as Clark Griswold) during a scene in *National Lampoon's Vacation* when he was standing at the edge of the Grand Canyon beholding the panorama in a forced expression of wonder: she pushed out her lips and bobbed her head forward and back like a chicken—for about three seconds—before jumping back into the car. I had to agree. I had demanded that we pull off the road dozens of times on the drive through Kansas and southeastern Nebraska when the map said swales would appear, and we still hadn't seen anything. Our kids, long ago bored with the abstraction of looking for signs in the land of people who had passed through more than 160 years ago, hadn't even bothered to get out of the car this time. The power of place would have to exert a little more in the way of physical evidence.

Here in Alexandria we were indeed camped alongside the railway, and we would soon discover, some fifteen minutes after our first experience, that this was the main rail corridor across Nebraska. The ranger had told us that the trains usher coal from the mines at Gillette, Wyoming, to the rail hub in St. Joseph, Missouri, where it fuels a power company and is also dispersed on other trains for an untold number of Midwestern and Eastern power stations. Trains would pass every ten to twenty minutes, round the clock, each hauling more than one hundred laden hopper cars. (Trains headed in the other direction ran light.) A little cursory research suggested that each laden coal car weighed over one hundred tons (more than 200,000 pounds), which meant that each train was hauling, by conservative estimate, 100,000 tons or 20 million pounds of coal. I simply couldn't fathom a hole in the earth that size.

Once recovered, we split up in teams and got to work setting up our site. Our chores were becoming routine: One or the other of us would prepare the evening meal, which involved unloading from the back end of the car our two large plastic tote boxes of food, the two-burner propane stove, and the large plastic ice chest that served as our refrigerator, and then setting it all out on the grass or picnic table. The other would unlash the wooden ladder from the roof rack, lean it against the car, then climb aloft and unlock the roof box, and start emptying its contents: sleeping bags, pads, backpacks, and, finally, the tent.

This was my favorite job. I would climb onto the top of the car and, like Zeus throwing thunderbolts, stand on the back porch and fire the sleeping bags and rolled foam sleeping pads at the kids, trying to knock them down as they attempted to dodge my rapid fire. When caught unaware—and this was the whole point—they would go sprawling in the grass or let out a surprised grunt. We would make a big mess, gear, clothes, and sleeping bags scattered for fifty feet in all directions, which, once the tent was set up, could then be tossed—another opportunity for horseplay—into the tent. The kids' job was to set up the sleeping bags and pads.

Cooking was far less entertaining, but it was more peaceful. One reason was that the cook had unfettered access to the beer, which had been sloshing around in ice all day, and when I was cooking I could usually work through two cans, sucking joyfully and noisily at the cold brew to slake the dryness in my throat, in the course of an evening's meal preparation. It was bliss, the red sun setting over the golden fields or through the trees, and the dinner invariably tasted better for it. At the end of a day's drive or other adventure, Oakley would usually demand a "cozy bottle"—a baby bottle of milk warmed over the stove—so that he, too, if the cook was lucky, would enter a hypnotic state during meal preparation, splayed out on a sleeping bag or pillow in the shade with his baby blanket clutched in his free hand. If timed well, this break could last fifteen minutes.

We had determined before we left that instead of having to decide what to eat each day we would establish a set menu of five dinners: macaroni and cheese, vegetarian chili, bean burritos, spaghetti, and veggie burgers. (We don't eat meat.) The entrees would be supplemented by green vegetables, either broccoli, peas, or salad. This cycle meant we would resupply every three to five days, depending on availability of fresh vegetables, milk, and ice for the cooler.

That first evening in Nebraska we fell asleep to the chattering of crickets and the noise of the breeze in the trees, punctuated by the occasional roar of trains.

The following morning I left the family to go on a scouting expedition to find traces of the trail, this time in earnest. With a bottle of water, an apple, and my bird book, I drove off in a cloud of dust, the car skittering on the loose stones in the road. It felt like I was driving on marbles. If I went too fast, the car started to slip sideways toward the ditch. These sorts of solo frolics would be purposefully brief, few, and far between. This was a family trip and, while I needed to do certain research on my own, such as pore over archives, I was really hoping that most of the trip could involve the entire family. Both Leah and I had been wilderness trip leaders (before kids) and maintained an active interest in wandering the wilderness, sans vehicle, which set up an odd dynamic: we each wanted to continue feeling as though we were rugged outdoor types, yet we also wanted to include our children in the process. As a result, we agreed on this trip to pursue as many full-family excursions—hikes, bicycle rides, and museum visits—as possible yet punctuate them with solo experiences to maintain our levels of sanity. Because, as we had discovered only minutes into this cross-country trip, driving down the highway for hours at a time with a bunch of kids is simply no fun. While driving time was inevitable, we were determined to spend more than one night at most campsites, preferably three or four, so that we could sink into a place and the kids could enjoy a full cycle of several days of exploring to enjoy the rhythm of the outdoors without the accompanying hassle of nonstop driving. When I left they had unlashed their fishing rods from the roof and had sallied forth on their bicycles to get worms at the park's Snak Shak, which we learned the night before served homemade pie every night of the week to a bunch of friendly locals.

A few miles away, I pulled to a stop at the crest of a hill to consult the map, just opposite an abandoned stockyard. Its cattle chute was still intact. I turned the car off. It was silent except for crickets in the grass next to the road, the somnolent rush of wind, and occasional twittering of birds. A red-winged blackbird was perched in a tree shading the barn. Looking at the map I realized that behind me, only one mile away, was a spot where the swales were supposedly clearly visible. I restarted the car and turned around, cornered left a mile back, and drove slowly to where, just before the road crossed the railroad tracks, the map said the trail should appear, at a slight angle, over my left shoulder, to the east as I drove south.

I stopped several times and got out, looking to both sides and climbing up on the berms, sometimes thinking I saw something and then changing my mind. I rolled farther downhill and saw a break in the fence to the left. I stopped the car and got out, walking to the shoulder and looking eastward, into the rising sun, and then I saw the ruts—unmistakably leading away from me and into a stand of trees. I returned to the car, shut it off, and grabbed my binoculars. The ruts were clear because the grass, waist high all around, was shorter, maybe only ankle high, and often nothing at all grew so that the ruts themselves were just hard-packed earth. I paced the distance between the two ruts with my feet: six of my feet. About the same as a car. But the ruts themselves were far narrower than a car's or truck's, only about four or five inches wide. The wide tires of a modern vehicle leave ruts that are at least a foot wide. I had seen this same phenomenon in vintage photos of trail ruts, looking surprisingly narrow in comparison with modern dirt roads. I followed the trail for a few minutes, reveling in the beauty of the grassy landscape and the silence of the morning, until it ended at a barbed wire fence. Beyond, the ruts disappeared in a thick tangle of undergrowth. So, for the first time, at 9:45 a.m., June 14, I could honestly say I was standing in the exact spot where the Morrisons, Shaws, Sagers, Parrishes, Nicholses, Gilliams, John Minto, and the others, passed 162 years before.

It would have been about the same time of year, and the weather must have been similar, at least once they left behind the protracted rains and flooding they'd experienced in Kansas. The temperature on the car's thermometer told me it was a pleasant seventy-seven degrees; a gentle breeze was blowing from the southwest. The group must have been at its most buoyant right now, fully enjoying the firm grasslands that made for speedy travel. The good spirits of the Nebraska grasslands in early summer were infectious. I sat in the grass between the ruts in the sunshine and ate an apple.

Rock Creek Station, just to the south of Fairbury, Nebraska, has had a storied involvement with the settlement of the West, first as a challenging creek crossing—because of its steep banks and frustratingly rocky streambed—that provoked the emigrants to set up elaborate systems of tow-and-easing chains to lower and raise their wagons through the ravine, and then later, when the flush times of the Gold Rush hit, as a toll bridge and supply station (it also served briefly as a rendezvous for the Pony Express). It was also where James Butler Hickok would earn his notoriety as a gunslinger and become emboldened to call himself "Wild Bill" in an effort to cultivate his emerging interest in controversial celebrity. The station is now a museum devoted to telling the story of the station's service, featuring saddle displays, vintage photographs, maps, interpretive signs, and a model of the gun Hickok used to murder David McCanless, who was unarmed at the time, and two other station agents who had attempted to come to McCanless's aid.

I was the sole visitor to the museum. The other person present, the park's only full-time employee, whose name I learned was Judy Weers, had the sort of effusive enthusiasm I had come to expect from these visits. Most historical sites we would visit, even in the height of summer, were often empty, their lone employees no doubt bored to the brink of madness. Weers gushed about the station's history, in particular the cowardliness of Hickok and the bravery of the young boy, McCanless's twelve-year-old son, who was a witness to the murders but who was not allowed to testify at Hickok's trial. (Hickok was acquitted.) She insisted I watch the movie in the museum's little playhouse, a melodramatic rendering that described the "fateful events" of July 12, 1861, illustrating how Hickok engineered the murders and subsequently got away with it. It also gleefully reported the circumstances of Hickok's own murder in Deadwood, South Dakota, in 1876: he was shot through the head while holding what would come to be known as the "dead man's hand"—a pair of aces and a pair of eights—apparently as revenge by someone he may have wronged over the years.

Weers then shooed me out the door so I could explore the station's miles of trails and take in the full essence of spring on the Nebraska prairie. She stood outside the little museum building and pointed to a deep ravine flanked by blooming wildflowers and waving grasses. The ravine, deeply rutted and leading down to Rock Creek proper, was where the trail had come through. It cut such an obvious swath through the prairie that it was not hard to visualize the passage of many thousands of oxen and wagons charging up this grassy hillside even through the distance of 160 years. It's been determined that an estimated 500,000 emigrants made the crossing by covered wagon between 1840 and 1869, when the transcontinental railroad was finally connected. They all would have come up this hill.

Weers said the state of Nebraska had nurtured the land to recover its natural, pre-white-settlement environment so that it now features only native plants: buffalo grass, Indian grass, purple poppy mallow, switchgrass, yellow evening primrose, prairie wild rose (purple), hairy vetch, yellow coneflower, black-eyed Susan, and common mullein with velvety leaves and the beginnings of yellow blossoms. Unlike the taller Kansas grasses, Weers told me, which are less nutritious to grazing stock, the buffalo grass of Nebraska was "God's own oxen feed," and had strengthened the emigrants' animals to their full potential for the trek across the Platte River Valley. This must have been especially true in the 1840s, before the Gold Rush period when the endless teams of oxen would eventually strip the land alongside the Trail like swarms of locusts.

Whenever out on a solo hike I was acutely cognizant of the fact that my time was limited. Leah, left alone with four young children at a campsite, could happily manage them for about three or four hours without her spirits suffering. As a result, I developed a method of absorbing as much as I could in the allotted time. I would take careful note of everything I saw, including the presence of flowers and birds, the essence of people's conversations and mannerisms, consciously burning these images and sounds into my mind (and memorializing them in my notebook). I also moved quickly, attempting to emulate Larry McMurtry's character, the Kickapoo Indian named Famous Shoes, from *Lonesome Dove.* Famous Shoes, an expert tracker, had a loping gait and could cover many miles without food or water, often moving faster than people on horseback. I'm not sure if McMurtry based Famous Shoes on a real person as he did several of the other characters in the book, but he was a particular inspiration to me on my time-pressed sojourns. I would lace up my boots tightly, snug the straps on my backpack, pull my cap lower on my head, and then trot off at a good clip to explore, stopping only to make notes, take a swig of water, or grab a handful of nuts and raisins. Like Famous Shoes, I could cover three times as much distance than if I were walking.

At the bottom of the hill I trotted past three covered wagons set up on display adjacent to several replica buildings, which Weers told me had been built as exact models of the original station buildings. I stopped long enough to measure the distance between the wagon wheels: six of my feet, the same as the distance between the ruts I had seen earlier in the morning.

I kept running and passed over the little wooden bridge spanning Rock Creek, which hadn't, of course, been there in the 1840s, but was built by David McCanless in the 1850s as it became clear that profits could be had from building bridges over rough crossings and charging an exorbitant toll. John Charles Frémont had written in his diary about a crossing he made on June 22, 1842: "Our midday halt was at Wyatt's Creek [Rock Creek] in the bed of which were numerous boulders of dark ferruginous sandstones mingled with other of the red sandstone." Frémont had also noted the existence of a forgotten deck of playing cards, "lying loose on the grass, [which] marked the existence of our Oregon emigrants."

Another sign quoted emigrant Joseph Ware on the crossing of Nebraska's prairie and, specifically, on the frustrations of crossings such as Rock Creek: "You cannot, on the average, make more than 15 miles per day [because of the creek crossings]," Ware had written. Another emigrant, Thomas Eastin, complained that the guidebooks failed to mention the ordeal of fording prairie streams. This was no doubt because the people who had made the guides were traveling on horseback or on foot and weren't considering what it would take to bring a fully loaded wagon across the continent.

Looking down into the ravine I saw the same steep sides and large, reddish boulders—still there—in the middle of a slow-moving stream. I made a loop around the property, noting the trilling presence of an eastern kingbird in the top of a cottonwood and a meadowlark in the grass, and decided it would be a good place to bring the whole family for a hike the following day. It seemed suitably authentic, with the covered wagons, the "native prairie," and clearly visible trail ruts. I wanted the kids to get a glimpse of what the prairie was like then and at the same time get a feel for what it would be like for a large family to move through the landscape at a walking pace.

On the drive back to the campground, I wanted to make a detour: a grave site in my *Maps* guide that was supposedly still visible if one followed the Trail for a while away from the public road. On the way through town I passed a McDonald's on the main street with a sign out front that read, ACCEPTING APPLICATIONS. SERIOUS APPLICANTS ONLY, and then stopped for a newspaper (headline in the *Lincoln Journal Star*: MANY IRAQIS VIEW BUSH VISIT AS A STUNT), and some lunch at Ray's Apple Market ("Hometown Proud"). I picked up some fried chicken—I occasionally eat meat when not in range of my family—and some ice and more beer, and then took off in the direction of the grave.

A few minutes later, I pulled to the side of the road where the Oregon Trail clearly crossed the road at an oblique, northwest angle, and, toting my lunch and a can of beer, did my best Famous Shoes impersonation and trotted off, following the trail ruts up a grassy hillside. A minute later I heard what sounded like electronic chatter, like the sort of noises R2-D2 made when he was excited, and, looking in the direction of the noise, saw a pair of bobolinks diving at and scolding each other. One would alight on a single stem of grass and call, and the other would settle about fifty feet away and respond. They followed me up the hill, always staying about the same distance away from me and persisting in their warbling calls. At the top of the hill, the full force of the breeze hit me square and at the same time I caught sight of a granite marker, which appeared to be about one hundred yards off the Oregon Trail route. A bronze plaque fastened to the stone read:

> On April 16, 1849, the twenty-five members of the Boston Newton Joint Stock Assoc. left Boston, Mass., to travel overland to the goldfields of California.
>
> On May 29 at Soldier Creek, near present-day Topeka, Kansas, one of the founders of the association, 25-year-old George Winslow, a machinist from Newton Upper Falls, was suddenly taken violently ill with cholera.
>
> The company remained in camp for three days, and Winslow appeared to be recovering. Late in the afternoon of June 6 the company reached the point where the Oregon–California Trail crosses the present Neb–Kansas state line. There, David J. Staples, Winslow's brother-in-law, described a 'terrific thunder shower, lightning flashed sometimes dazzling to the eyes. Rain falling in torrents.' George Winslow's death probably resulted from exposure to this storm. At 9 am on June 8, 'painlessly as though going to sleep, he died.' 'He was borne to the grave by eight bearers. The last chapter of Ecclesiastes was read.' As a token of their respect each member of the company placed a green sprig on the grave.

I plunked myself down in the grass and as a token of respect to George Winslow, opened a can of beer and poured some over his grave before taking a slug myself and tucking into my lunch.

As I ate I thought idly of the preconceptions I had had about taking this trip. I had thought—hoped—that the trip would involve long hours of ponderous reading in the shade of cottonwoods, languorous naps in the prairie grasses on sunny afternoons while the kids played in the grass like the children in the opening scenes of the TV version of *Little House on the Prairie*. I'm not sure what I was thinking, but books were now piling up unread, and our days were absolutely filled with the acts of caring for the children, especially, although not exclusively, Oakley, who needed constant attention. Preparing meals, washing dishes, setting up and taking down the tent, and packing up the car. I pulled out my notebook and wrote: "And our life is so much easier than the emigrants'. They trudged next to their wagons for 12 to 20 miles each day, hustling the children along. At night the women set up camp and cooked supper over an open fire while the men drove the stock off to find good grazing. (Last night, as an attempt to bond with my historical subjects, it took me 15 minutes to light a fire using flint and steel and char cloth, cursing when I nicked my knuckles with the steel. Another quarter to Finn.) And once firewood became scarce, as the emigrants entered what is now western Nebraska and started up into the Wyoming high country, they began using buffalo chips to cook over. They must have been exhausted, as we are each night—but in comparison have no right to be."

When I returned to the campground, Leah said that the kids had had a perfect day: fishing for bass in the lake, catching turtles, and reading their books in the shade. She didn't have the shell-shocked stare I sometimes recognize in her face after she's been alone with them for too long. During her training for her master's degree in social work, she said she recalled a study of stay-at-home mothers of young children that likened the effects of their stress with the stress of combat soldiers, accompanied by the kind of deep fatigue of always having your senses cued to hyperalert.

The peacefulness of Nebraska's grasslands was having an effect on everyone. That evening, in the long prairie dusk—the sun wouldn't set until long after 9:00 p.m.—we rode our bicycles over to the Snak Shak and sat at the counter, each ordering a slice of pie: coconut cream, apple, and cherry. A handful of locals were just finishing their dinner, and we lingered over coffee and dessert chatting with them about our trip. They were pleased we were enjoying their town, and the restaurant hostess delighted in our love of her pie. We found ourselves ordering more pie and more coffee, and before we knew it we'd spent more than an hour happily talking about nothing in particular. (Despite our interest in the simplicity of the grass, the dry breeze, and the silence, they seemed especially interested in having us visit all the area's attractions, but about all they could come up with was a former skunk farm, which they said still carried the stink.) After promising to return the following night, we rolled back to the tent slowly as the stars came out, enjoying the warm night breeze, sated with happiness.

The following morning we had an early breakfast so that we could enjoy a hike at Rock Creek before the heat of the day set in. We'd loaded lunch of fruit, crackers, cheese, and water bottles in two backpacks and lashed the three-wheel yuppie stroller to the roof. Once arrived, the kids wandered the museum briefly, asking questions about the Pony Express, which only ran for a little over a year, between 1861 and 1862, before being made redundant by the telegraph, and the replica of the gun that Hickok used to kill McCanless and the others. They also delighted in the displays of the covered wagons set outside right next to the Oregon Trail ruts since, unlike at all the other museums we'd visited until this point, they were allowed to climb up inside. In fact, it soon became clear how dangerous these contraptions were as, while the boys were attempting to roll the wagon, Raven was scrambling on top of the wheel. Only by stopping the wheel did I prevent a likely leg-crushing.

Tumping our backpacks, we crossed the little bridge at Rock Creek and then followed a three-mile path that wound its way along the original Trail. With Oakley in the stroller, which was creaking and sloshing under its fifty-pound load of child and water bottles, the five of us were walking about the same pace as oxen. The kids were going shirtless now, and while we hadn't bathed in days, no one felt especially dirty since the air was so dry. My hair felt like dusty straw. We must have made an unlikely sight, but everyone was happy as we sauntered along in the morning sunshine.

We drank more than a gallon of water in two hours. We saw prairie clover, prairie coneflower, and, as we crested a hill, noticed that the ruts on the hilltop were especially visible because of lines of white daisies growing exclusively in the path. The two white lines arced down the hill, curved right, and then disappeared in a stand of trees below. It was an arresting sight, these ruts turned to flowers, the most tender memorial to the passing of these families that one could imagine. We could see for miles in all directions, the only sound an occasional fluty trill from a western meadowlark (Nebraska's state bird!), the frantic buzzing of a dickcissel in the top of a cottonwood, or the *dee-dee-dee!* of a killdeer protecting its nest from some unseen foe. It would have been a view similar to that of the emigrants except for a solitary grain silo about five miles away and patches of wheat fields, already brown because of a drought that was affecting much of the West this summer. We decided to stop for lunch—crackers, PB&J sandwiches, apples, and raisins—and plunked ourselves down between the flowered ruts on this singularly beautiful prairie hilltop.

We departed Alexandria State Recreational Area at about nine-thirty the next morning after a breakfast of eggs fried together with a can of refried beans. It was another beautiful day that promised to be just as dry and hot as the previous week. The day before Leah had picked up a compact disc she'd found lying in the dirt road at the campground. Some fisherman had probably dropped it from his car and not noticed. Curious, she'd brushed it off and read the handwriting in black marker that said, "Mix—my songs." She put it on the dashboard in anticipation of our long drive the next day, hoping for some local flavor.

Now, after having struck the tent, loaded the roof carrier, packed the back end with our kitchen supplies, and hoisted the bicycle rack in place, we were tooling along State Highway 81 at seventy-five miles per hour, and she slipped it into the player. We were not disappointed. It proved to be a collection of popular country and hip-hop tunes (not our usual fare, but we try to have open minds), many with lurid lyrics that, while not overtly profane were shockingly pornographic. The first song, which I later learned was 50 Cents' "Candy Shop" (a sample: "You be a nympho, I'll be a nympho" and "I melt in your mouth, girl, not in your hands"), caused Leah and me to lunge for the controls to turn it off. Something made us stop, though, and we didn't actually turn it off, since it occurred to us that the kids probably wouldn't get it. One of the benefits of raising children without television and other mainstream media is that they retain an innocent naïveté that makes them oblivious to even 50 Cents' hard-core provocations. We left it on, cautiously listening to the words, and then, when we were satisfied there was nothing too obviously damaging, cranked it back up again. The song had a thumping beat, and the kids were soon waving their hands, slapping their thighs, and singing along to the catchy chorus, "Take me to the candy shop! I'll let you lick the lollipop!" as the car sped north across the plains to the Platte River Valley.

The next song, "Save a Horse (Ride a Cowboy)" (by the country duo Big & Rich), was similarly sexual ("I'm a thoroughbred, that's what she said, in the back of my truck bed, as I was gettin' buzzed on suds"), but it too had a catchy jingle and its lyrics were vague enough to be appropriate for the young ears in the car. (This song proved to be Leah's favorite.) Another song on the disc, my favorite, was the theme to *The Dukes of Hazzard* ("Just two good old boys, never meanin' no harm"), replete with breezy banjo and guitar strumming.

The song that was most popular with the kids, though, was an old C. W. McCall tune called "Convoy," in which the male singer (McCall himself) croons in a throaty bass about a cross-country, high-speed rampage by semi—friends in loaded rigs falling in behind along the way—and they all dodge "bears" and blast through tollbooths without paying. Finn and Jonah, especially, were positively giddy when McCall boomed the final line: "So we crashed the gate doin' ninety-eight, I says, 'Let them truckers roll—ten-four!" They demanded that we play the disc again and again, which we were more than happy to do, since we had five hours in the car until we reached our next stop, Ogallala, Nebraska.

If Henry Sager had been in the car with us, I know he would have been singing along, and probably swinging a bottle of hooch out the window at the same time and throwing empties at passing trucks. And William Shaw? While less likely to let himself get too carried away, I think I could see a smile tugging at the corners of his broad mouth, nodding his head to the beat, and quietly singing in his gravelly whisper: "Save a horse, ride a cowboy!"

8

AN INCH DEEP AND A MILE WIDE

THE REST OF THE MONTH OF JUNE continued as it began, with constant rain. In fact, John Minto would note that of the first six weeks of the trip the group experienced only eight days of clear weather. The last major river to be crossed, the Big Blue in southern Nebraska, would have been an easy wade most years, barely rising to the wagon wheel hubs. But it too was a raging torrent in late June 1844, and once again, Minto was asked to chip in with extra service, this time by guiding the Morrisons' horses across the Big Blue. The group arrived at the river's swollen banks early in the morning of June 22. "Here I had an adventure," Minto recalled.

Whether to show off his horsemanship or from genuine necessity, Minto chose to ride a four-year-old filly into the river bareback, with only a bridle, and no bit or reins, around the horse's nose. The young horse leapt straight into the river, off a bank five feet high, and promptly disappeared underwater beneath her rider. "She went in out of sight, carrying me down by my hold on her mane," Minto said. Rather than staying with the animal as a horseman familiar with river crossings would, Minto panicked and did the one thing he shouldn't have: he released his hold on the mane.

"I let go instinctively and came up before her," Minto said, "but as she rose, as the nearest object in sight, she came directly toward me, striking with her forefeet on the water." The animal pawed frantically at the water between her and Minto, whose quick reactions saved his life.

"I instantly threw myself over on my back to save my head and face, but for several strokes she pawed the water away from my breast," he said. "It was a close call."

Minto was not the only one in the company to have a close call with crossing the Big Blue. A few days before, James Owens had nearly drowned while maneuvering a set of canoe-rafts in the swift current. The Reverend Parrish wrote: "He cramped while swimming. Thank God for his escape."

After the Morrisons' horses and wagons were across, Minto recrossed the river and turned to the task of guiding the Morrisons' herd of cattle across, hoping to find a smoother entry into and out of the river. Three miles downstream he found a favorable bank, but the current was flowing deep and swift. "The water was here ten feet below the bank, but the current was very strong," Minto said, "and the point we were to leave projected sharply into the stream, causing a large and strong eddy below, along the course of which were formed funnel-shaped whirls as large as a barrel head upon the surface."

Undeterred, Minto crafted a plan to have each of the four "guides," all single men like himself, direct the more powerful animals across first, thereby inspiring the rest of the herd to follow. The men would swim, positioning themselves downstream of the oxen and grabbing hold of the animals' withers. To deter the oxen from deciding their own route, the guides would swat at the oxen's cheeks to direct them to the desired exit on the far shore. It seemed a simple enough plan.

"But this proved hazardous," Minto said. "Without thinking of the string of suck holes,"—and not remembering the lesson he'd ostensibly learned just hours before—"I went in with the lead ox, but before I had time to get to his head, he was taken right down by one of the whirlpools. Thinking I could save myself and not hinder the beast, I took my hand from him. Then the water clutched and pulled me under."

As quickly as the eddy sucked him under, it shot him back to the surface, for a split second, where he caught a fleeting glimpse of the men standing on the bank watching him, no doubt reevaluating the wisdom of the plan and at the same time thinking Minto was lost. In that moment, Minto saw one of the boys break from the group and start to run for camp. And then—he did not even have a chance to take another breath—he was dragged under again, into another whirlpool.

Minto realized he was drowning and began to struggle against the swirling current. Ever pragmatic, he did not review the transgressions of his life, however, but began to reason his way out: "No, I did not pass in review of my sins, as I have read of; I did not seem to see my mother weeping for me." Instead, he realized he would need to take another breath if he was shot to the surface again or he would go down for the last time. He resolved to break free from the swirls, while underwater, and kick for the main current.

"As this passed like a flash, I felt something touch my right side, and put out my hand—finding the object to be the back of an ox, which by superior strength had overtaken and was passing me," Minto said. He leveraged himself upward and shot to the surface, gasping, and collapsed over the tall shoulders of the swimming ox. "How restful it was just to keep my hold," he said. "He was aiming for the proper point, and after resting a little further, I swam back, below the eddy, thinking I would trust the courage and strength of an ox in the future."

He added wryly: "I was twice reported drowned that day."

It took three days to get the entire company across the Big Blue, and almost immediately the weather began to improve, but not before one last squall, on the night of June 22, terrorized the camp. "Here a small cyclone struck us in the night," Minto said. "It blew the most of the tents loose and cast water down upon us in sheets rather than drops. Its roaring through the trees, and casting down branches from them, was fearful for a few minutes, and after it was over the fact that neither man nor beast was hurt, though thoroughly drenched, was truly wonderful."

The following morning, the group made a grim discovery: a human skeleton was lying in a thicket, a broken arrow "indicating its mortal wound" lodged in the breast. The emigrants often made similarly startling discoveries. In Kansas they had seen a corpse up in a tree, an Indian wrapped in blankets in ceremonial burial. And as the 1840s wore on, the Trail would eventually be littered with graves, both Indians and emigrants, hurriedly buried in shallow graves, often without a coffin, so that their remains would be exposed by animals or scavenged by Indians. (Between 1840 and 1869, when the transcontinental railroad was completed and the overland crossing by wagon ended, an estimated one-tenth of all who left Missouri—and an untold number of Indians—would succumb to accidents, disease, and, especially later, violent death.)

But the weather had lost its grip on the group, and the squalls became exceptions to the fair weather of the prairie summer. "The sun rose clear and it continues clear and windy, the water and mud fast disappearing," wrote Parrish on June 27. And then the next day: "Camp all a bustle to get off. The road is now better, the land more rolling. The most of the way from the Big Blue River runs through a beautiful level country."

Gilliam's son Washington had a similar memory of the days after the last of the river crossings: "After we crossed the Blue we were not troubled with high water to any extent worth mentioning. Our worst obstacle was miry roads, but with every day's travel the road improved in this respect."

On the evening of July 1, after the group had circled the wagons, grazed the animals, had their supper, and staggered off to bed, the night watchman thought he saw a band of Indians creeping stealthily toward him. In a blind panic, he fired his gun in the general direction, and immediately the whole camp was in disarray, men pulling on their trousers and grabbing rifles, spilling out of their tents, half-dressed, in a blind testosterone-fueled charge.

As Minto passed the Morrisons' tent he overheard an exchange that initially puzzled him: Nancy was asking where her gun was.

"Oh, you will not need a gun," Morrison replied.

"Well, Wilson, I hope not, I am sure, but I want to be ready in case there is need."

He responded that her gun, a flintlock, was hanging from the bows in the wagon cover, its powder horn and pouch with it. He departed for the guard tent.

What Minto overheard next, as he was passing the Shaws' tent, explained the reason Morrison knew his wife wouldn't need the gun. Wash Shaw, William Shaw's second son, burst from the tent with only one leg in his pants, a gun in his hand. But William Shaw explained: "The boys are getting very careless, John; somebody has fired a gun outside the cattle." Shaw knew it was another spooked guard, but while there was no danger this time, he also knew of the real danger posed by having young, untrained, and unseasoned men "guard" a large group of cattle and sleeping emigrants. Apparently, the guard had seen nothing but shadows.

"It makes my flesh creep, even now,"—some fifty years later—"to think of the undrilled condition we were in. This Captain Shaw, whose wife was the sister of General Gilliam," Minto said, "was by nature much more capable of leadership than her brave, impulsive brother, who from the day we voted him his title had never got his head down to the importance of drill, or even a plan of defense in case of a sudden attack; and we were now just entering the great game range," and therefore the hunting ground of the Plains Indians, "and liable to such an attack any day or night. I saw the funny side of the false alarm then, but now I do not wonder at the unrest Mr. Parrish's journal betrays."

Parrish's journal had betrayed the stirrings of dissatisfaction in Gilliam's leadership a few days before this latest incident, apparently as a result of the avoidable delays and the lack of military drills to prepare for Indian attacks. Parrish's journal merely observes that the General "will not resign," an apparent indication that Gilliam was considering stepping down, although this is the first reference in any diary to that effect.

General Gilliam proclaimed July 4 a rest day: "A rest for the cattle, wash day for the women, and a day to hunt for the men." It was a dry day, clear and warm, and the break was a welcome respite from the rigors of the trail.

"After the usual breakfast of sowbelly, slam-johns, and hot biscuits, the women began the task of drying out the bedding, boxes and barrels," reads a passage in *Shallow Grave at Waiilatpu: The Sagers' West*, by Erwin N. Thompson, an account of the Sager family's ill fortune published by the Oregon Historical Society. Thompson's book was written in reaction to the fictional accounts of the Sagers, most notably Honoré Morrow's 1926 bestseller, *On to Oregon*. Thompson, who served as an historian at Waiilatpu, the Whitman Mission National Park operated by the National Park Service in Walla Walla, Washington, had gathered the facts to produce the most ambitious account of the lives of the Sagers that exists. Most significantly, he had the generous assistance of three surviving granddaughters of the Sager girls (the book was written in the 1960s), who granted interviews and access to their personal files despite their advanced age, and gleaned numerous details of the lives of the Sagers that don't survive in diaries. (The last of the granddaughters died in the early 1980s.)

That afternoon, Independence Day, the Sager family collapsed in the grass—the girls helping their mother down from the wagon to rest. She had not recovered from giving birth and both she and the baby remained dangerously weak. Riding in the damp wagon had not helped. Naomi must have been able to nurse the infant—there's no mention otherwise in the record—but the two were reduced to malnourished waifs, Naomi barely able to walk and the infant listless and skinny.

Both Naomi and Henry Sager were sick with something else, too, having likely contracted typhoid in the squalor of the Kansas plains. The typhoid bug, like cholera, is transmitted by fecal-oral contact. Unlike cholera, which can kill a person in just a few hours by causing violent dehydration, typhoid is a lingering illness that people can carry for weeks or even months, sometimes recovering fully and sometimes relapsing. But it tends to be most debilitating on those whose constitutions are already compromised, whether by stress, malnutrition, lack of sleep—or the ravages of childbirth in a muddy tent followed by a month of wallowing in the back of a rumbling wagon.

The group proceeded northwestward, following the trace of the Big Blue and then the Republican Rivers for several days until they reached the point where a small, virtually waterless plateau about thirty miles across gradually descended to the Platte River. So that on July 5, they began a virtual sprint northward for the Platte River Valley. They camped on the open prairie, without benefit of a river and its attendant firewood, for one night, reveling in the expanse of the sky.

"Not a tree or a bush was in sight, but a boundless view of grass-covered country," Minto wrote. And it was here that Nancy Morrison played her first trick on Minto. Gathering a bunch of an unusual plant in her hands, she approached Minto and a group of young men as the group rested at noon on the sixth to let the cattle graze in the lush grasses.

She told them, "If any of you have left girls behind you, you should have treated better, just touch this weed and it will tell on you by wilting. John, you try it first."

"I stepped toward her and did as she required," Minto recalled. "The plant wilted, and figuratively speaking, I wilted, too. It was my first sight of the sensitive plant, and the experiment with it afforded great fun for those present."

Minto may have had another reason to feel exposed—and embarrassed—in the presence of Mrs. Morrison. He'd had a premonition, when he first approached the Morrison family on their Missouri River camp, that their thirteen-year-old daughter, Martha Ann, would one day be his wife. "If my thought had been given voice it would have been, 'There, Johnny Minto; there goes your wife that is to be.'" Minto's next reaction, after flushing privately, was to break into song. "I felt something akin to shame at my prompt thought, but the reader must understand that my mind had been nurtured on a diet of Scotch and English ballads, the lines of which moved it now: 'The farmer's lad grew up a man, and the good old farmer died, And left the lad the farm he had, with the daughter for his bride.' " Martha Ann Morrison was thirteen years old at the time. She and John Minto would indeed marry, in 1847, when she was barely sixteen and he was twenty-three. Perhaps Mrs. Morrison had a premonition herself and was testing its effects on Minto.

The significance of the Platte River in the Westward Migration cannot be overstated. It was a veritable highway with all the necessary attributes for swift overland travel (that is to say, three or four miles per hour or fifteen to twenty miles per day): clean water, abundant nourishment for stock, firm and relatively flat landscape, plentiful game, and an efficient east-west orientation allowed emigrants to move in the exact direction they needed. The Platte River was the original Interstate 80, more than one hundred years before it was given that name. In fact, I-80 today follows the Platte River, and the adjacent Oregon Trail, for more than two hundred miles, across almost the entire state of Nebraska, between the towns of Grand Island and Ogallala. National Park Service historian Merrill J. Mattes, who dedicated his life to the study of the Oregon Trail, wrote that the Platte and North Platte Valleys were "one immense transcontinental route of transcendent importance in American history, the grand corridor of westward expansion." Consequently, he would call the westward route of the 1840s, '50s, and '60s "The Great Platte River Road" and go on to write a book under the same name, published in 1969, which is still considered the definitive volume on the history of that part of the Oregon Trail.

In the book Mattes referred to the river also as "Nebraska's Seacoast" and said that before Nebraska was a state or a territory the region was known merely for its river. Nebraska, in fact, means "flat water" in Omaha Indian. The word *platte*, French for flat, was given by eighteenth-century French fur trappers.

"The Platte River dominates Nebraska geography, and its dominant characteristic is its flatness," Mattes wrote in *The Great Platte River Road*. And since the surrounding terrain, the aptly named Sand Hills, resemble the gently rolling dunes of the Atlantic seashore, frequented by wading birds, even today, such as whooping and sandhill cranes, it was an obvious comparison to call it Nebraska's seacoast.

The Platte River does not carve a deep swath in the landscape; instead, the river is broad and shallow and has therefore been described often as being "an inch deep and a mile wide." (Another well-known quip about the Platte, attributed to overland '49ers, is that it is "too thick to drink and too thin to plow.")

The Platte's source is, of course, the snows of the Rocky Mountains. The South Platte begins in the high peaks southwest of where Denver now sits, and the North Platte, which the emigrants would follow against the current as far as Independence Rock, flows northward from the peaks just northwest of Denver into Wyoming and along a curved arc that skirts the Laramie Range before spilling out onto the Nebraska Sand Hills. The two branches join at what is now the city of North Platte, Nebraska.

Two years before, John Charles Frémont also referred to the Platte as Nebraska's "coast," and commented on viewing it from afar that it appeared to be surrounded by a "range of high and broken hills; but on nearer approach were found to be elevations of forty to sixty feet, into which the wind had worked the sand."

Frémont, who had also traveled up through Kansas, noted the change in flora, commenting on the appearance of *cacti* and *amorpha*—sage—that he noted to his delight was in full bloom and "was remarkable for its large and luxuriant purple clusters."

By the time the emigrants reached the Platte Valley, with the pungent smell of sage, which is not unlike the herbal aroma of rosemary, in the air, they had truly arrived in the West—and their spirits soared. For the first time in their lives, the air was absolutely dry, the sun an orange globe that set cleanly over sandy hills, and the light on everything around them a tawny gold.

Once they arrived at the Platte River, the Independent Colony saw their first buffalo, which caused a ripple of excitement in the traveling community. "It is difficult to form an estimate of the numbers to be seen at a look," Parrish wrote. "Mr. Simmons says they are thicker than he ever saw stars in the firmament." The herds, which were estimated to include more than one million animals, tripped a visceral urge in the group's men, which would result in a cultural divide that would finally bring about the collapse of Gilliam's fragile leadership.

Despite his sickness, Henry Sager was among the first to grab his rifle, give a lustful whoop, and charge off on horseback in pursuit of a stampeding herd, leaving the boys to drive the team and ditching the ailing Naomi no doubt grumbling about her husband's folly. Or perhaps she was too far gone to notice.

"Father was a perfect Nimrod in his love of the chase," Catherine said of Sager, "and here he found ample scope for his favorite pastime. Leaving the team in care of one of the boys, he would take his fun and sally forth; and not only would the mighty buffalo fall before his unerring shot, but also the timid antelope was bourn into camp upon his shoulders."

On July 11, a group of similarly inspired men—Gilliam in the lead—charged off in pursuit of a herd of buffalo. Parrish described the thrill it brought: "Buffalo racing is a business of much diversion, indeed. A horse of common speed will run up on them immediately. The hunter then dismounts and fires, then loads and mounts again, and soon comes within shot once more. The process is continued in this way until he has taken all he wants." But Gilliam had a left a void in leadership, appointing no one to lead the group to the next camp. Morrison and Shaw had departed early in the morning on horseback to scout the next camp. It fell to John Minto, who was positioned ahead with the Morrisons' teams, to lead the group. He noted: "[Gilliam] did not speak to any particular officer, and in the ardor of the hunter seemed to have forgotten the responsibility of the general . . . I stood with my whip in the middle of the roadway, seeing a few young hunters gallop after their leader as they mounted, feeling I had as much right to be in that chase as the general himself; but seeing the need of attending to the selection of camp, and finding fairly good one close at hand, drove to the riverbank and unyoked."

The men killed fourteen buffalo that day, but by the time they were finished with the killing, soon realized that the sun was setting and they were many miles away from the camp and would therefore require sending to the camp for pack animals. But it was too late in the day, and the thrill of the chase had evaporated, so that by the time the men returned to camp no one was inspired, apparently, to return to the meat. It lay out on the open prairie, getting doused by a rainsquall and then warmed by the sun, so that by the following day the meat had all spoiled. The incident fractured the camp, and Gilliam was once again the focus of the frustration—for holding up the progress of the group in pursuit of buffalo meat and then allowing it to spoil.

"That night, angry meetings were held as the men drifted back into camp," reads a passage in *Shallow Grave* on the incident. "By nightfall the protest had reached a crescendo . . . morale and discipline were shattered."

Parrish was exasperated. The following morning, July 12, he noted: "The camp is a scene of confusion. Part of the company want to be off, and the other part want to stay and save the meat. . . . Forty thousand pounds of the best beef spoiled in one night. The animals were run through the hot sun the greater part of the day and then shot down and left to lie in the hot sun during the afternoon until near sunset before they were gutted, and then left through the night with the hide on. . . . God forgive us for such waste and save us from such ignorance."

Minto was furious: "There was much confusion as the result of this chase, and there was a growing dread of the consequences of being under such a man's orders, as Mr. Gilliam had shown himself to be—a headlong leader of unreflecting and wasteful slaughter."

Michael Simmons, the company's second in command, promptly resigned as a leader. Minto said: "Colonel Simmons, whom I had never seen with a gun in his hand, was right in refusing to share longer the responsibility with a man who at rest would stop the train at the convenience of his own child, but did literally nothing to help along, or prepare the men and boys from whom he should have expected obedience in how to carry into effect his orders." In response to Simmons's resignation, Gilliam knew he would have to hold an election but also felt compelled to make a fiery speech about the need for discipline in his ranks.

"He made a threatening declaration as to the punishment he would inflict on any one who presumed to leave camp without his permission," Minto said, "and his hand was raised to emphasize his declaration that he would 'hang upon the nearest tree the man who dared to leave the company.'"

Even before Gilliam had lowered his hand and taken a breath, a well-liked young man, Daniel Clark, called his bluff by jumping on his horse and shouting, "If any of you men or boys intend going to Oregon, come on; I'm going."

Incensed, but powerless to stop him—he would have to shoot one of the camp's most well-respected individuals from his horse—Gilliam only blustered: "That's all the sense he has." And stalked off to his tent. The following day, just before breakfast, as Gilliam was leaving his tent, he noticed a man on a horse with a rifle across his saddle—loping off for a morning hunt. Gilliam roared: "Who are you? Going hunting without leave? I'll . . ."

But his wife cut him off: "Neal, be careful."

Gilliam resigned his command in a huff, "They may all get to Oregon as they can, without me. I'll have nothing more to do with them." The lone hunter was another of Gilliam's brothers-in-law, Louis Crawford, who had apparently thought the mandate applied to everyone but family.

Parrish said, "The General seemed quite 'cantankerous'. . . . The colony was called together by the General, who, after a short, abusive speech, tendered his resignation."

The resignation was complete, and the group hastily assembled elections for new leaders, greatly relieved to be free of the bombastic and unpredictable Neal Gilliam and, at the same time, to have a chance to put two leaders in place who had proven their abilities. William Shaw and Wilson Morrison were unanimously voted to the positions of leaders of two companies.

The only words Shaw recorded of the events with were: "They fell out; some got mad and left. Morrison and I stayed behind." In Shaw's mind, that's all there was to it. The two companies would travel together.

9

BOREDOM AND DISEASE

THE FRACTURING of the Independent Oregon Colony's leadership could not have come at a more opportune time. The weather was fine and dry—the Reverend Parrish's journal fairly bursts with notes in praise of the sun and clear, blue sky—and the group was surrounded by plentiful game, large herds of buffalo, and numerous antelope, whose fatal flaw was a burning curiosity that would bring them within rifle range of the emigrants' camps. Most emigrants were awed by the spectacle of the free-roving game and the vastness of the Platte and the surrounding Sand Hills. Parrish noted: "An attempt at description would appear in the character of a romance." He restrained himself.

The Ford company had by this time caught up with the Independent Colony. Mountain man James Clyman's prolific journal entries veered unabashedly into the territory Parrish avoided. He wrote of "a deep vally amid the bare clay Bluffs which realized allmost all the fabled scent of the much Fabled Spice groves [of] arabia or India for more than 2 miles the odours of the wild rose & many other oderiferous herbs scented the whole atmosphere." But the poetical waxings of Clyman, perhaps jotted during a spectacular sunset that stirred a certain longing, soon gave way to boredom when the emigrants realized that the endless views and rolling hills were indeed vast, and the trail led along this unchanging route for many hundreds of miles, culminating in more trackless wilderness in the Wyoming high country. Only when the company approached western Nebraska, some 250 miles later, would any landmarks appear: the tall bluffs of Courthouse and Jailhouse Rocks, the jutting spire of Chimney Rock, and the imposing cliffs of Scotts Bluff. Meanwhile, trundling along at two or three miles per hour on the back of a horse through the Platte Valley, Clyman wrote on July 13, "[N]o place in the world looks more lonesome and discourageing than the wide Prairies of this region neither tree bush shrub rock not water to cherish or shelter him and such a perfect sameness with a alusive ridge all around you meeting the Horizon in all directions." Hour after hour and day after day: Clyman, Shaw, Minto, and Morrison, and the other guides and leaders in the saddle, the rest of the men trudging alongside their lead team of oxen, while Naomi Sager, Sally Shaw, Nancy Morrison, and the other women and children rode the wagons or walked along beside the trail to avoid breathing the wagon dust.

On July 14, Clyman wrote, "[Y]ou Suppose your course to lie over some one of those horizontal ridges when after several hours anxious fatigue you suppose you are about to assend the highest pinnacle and some Known Landmark—what is your disapointmint to find ridge rise beyond ridge to the utmost extant of human vision."

By the middle of July, many in the company were also laid low with the creeping effects of typhoid. Henry and Naomi Sager, E. E. Parrish, George Saunders, who was one of the company guides, and many of the children were by now suffering the debilitating effects of this intestinal bug.

The journals provide few details to describe what it felt like to be suffering the effects of typhoid, not to mention while walking or riding in a bouncing wagon. Parrish's journal is the most thorough, with notes that consistently refer to the sickness—what he called "cramp cholera"—each day he and others suffered: July 21: "My health is very poor." July 22: "My health is about the same." July 23: "My health is still very poor." July 24: "We remain in camp to-day to rest the cattle, wash clothes and doctor the sick. I am some better to-day." July 25: "My health is a little improved." But exactly *how* poorly he felt, can only be guessed at.

When we were traveling along this part of the trail in central Nebraska—where the Colony began to suffer from typhoid—I began to wonder and decided to look into the disease so that I could conjure its effects while surrounded by the same environment that the emigrants experienced. I called my brother, Trevor, who is a resident in family practice medicine at Maine Medical Center in Portland. I would typically catch him during one of his rare quiet moments of an "on-call" rotation, which meant he was suffering from lack of sleep and was very much in a medical frame of mind, probably lying in a bunk in the doctors dayroom or at home collapsed on the couch following a two-day rotation. It was my favorite time to speak with him, since the words poured out unchecked, and I would be offered an uncensored vision of a given medical condition. I would be sitting alongside the trail somewhere, perhaps beneath a sage or juniper bush, doing my best to conjure the "power of place" by imagining the disease affecting someone in this spot. Placing a call on my cell phone on an afternoon in July, I asked him about typhoid.

"It's is not very pleasant," he said, his speech slurred from lack of sleep. "Fever and headaches are the first symptoms, and in kids it can lead to seizures and a coma. The way to treat it is by maintaining the patient's hydration, and of course today by antibiotics, but it's incredibly contagious by fecal-oral contact. You wipe your ass and then touch some food, or drinking water gets contaminated, and before you know it everyone who's eaten the food or come in some contact with it has caught it. That's what happened with Typhoid Mary."

Mary Mallon, an Irish immigrant living in New York in the late nineteenth and early twentieth centuries, was a domestic servant and food worker who was able to carry the disease without feeling its effects and therefore subsequently became known as a "healthy carrier," the first such person to have the designation. Between 1900 and 1907 Mallon infected some twenty-two people with typhoid (one of whom, a young girl, died), while moving from job to job, before a health inspector tracked her down at her house of employment and had her forcibly isolated on North Brother Island in the East River.

Salmonella typhi, typhoid's technical name, is a bacteria, but it doesn't result immediately in the "bloody flux," the vicious and violent diarrhea commonly associated with its more aggressive bacterial cousin, cholera, which wouldn't strike the westward emigrants until 1849. Typhoid spreads when sanitation is poor, such as conditions on the Kansas plains that summer, and today is easily treatable with antibiotics and rehydration through an IV tube. But it is a killer, if a slow one, and continues today to infect some sixteen million people each year, of which six hundred thousand die annually, mostly in Third World countries of Asia, Africa, and Central and South America where basic hygiene and sanitation are poor. It can only be carried by humans, but because of its slow stealth and because of its broad range of effect on people, it's a tricky disease to manage, which is one reason why the emigrants were helpless to contain it.

Typhoid's slow incubation period, a week to twenty days, is why the colony didn't begin to be affected by the disease until they'd reached the Platte Valley, assuming they were infected during the rains in Kansas. And this explanation makes sense, since none of the journals mention the disease's symptoms until mid-July, and the deaths that occurred previously were the result of other preexisting causes, such as tuberculosis. It must have been an especially cruel realization: now that they were free of the Kansas rains and boggy prairie, and the sun had emerged to dry out the bedraggled travelers, to be knocked weak, nauseous, and feverish by an insidious illness.

The first phase of the disease involves the infection descending into the digestive system and bowel, where it begins to slowly disintegrate the intestinal *mucosa*, the lining. A low-grade fever begins to build over the course of a few days, and the patient begins to sweat, suffer from lack of appetite, bouts of coughing, and prolonged headaches. As the bowels cramp and lose their effectiveness in processing food, the victim becomes constipated and, as a result, the skin becomes blotchy.

Henry Sager and E. E. Parrish—and a few others, including Naomi Sager, who likely confused her symptoms with the difficult childbirth—were probably at this first stage when the colony first encountered the buffalo herds on the Platte River plains. Sager would be criticized not only for leaving his sick wife behind on these hunts but also for ignoring his own sickness, and his eventual deterioration has been blamed by several historians on his decision to spend a couple of days hunting buffalo instead of resting. I asked Trevor about whether charging off after a herd of buffalo for an extended hunt could worsen one's response to typhoid.

"Not necessarily," he said. "It could go either way, depending on how bad a case it was. But since he was already immuno-compromised, it would have further weakened and dehydrated him, that's for sure. And that's the last thing a patient suffering from typhoid needs." Trevor had treated such patients in clinics in Central America and described their listlessness, their blotchy skin, and high fevers.

If left untreated, or if the immune system fails to check the infection's advance, the infection will progress to the second stage—by eating away at the stomach and intestines themselves. This is when the high fever starts. If the immune system cannot stop the infection at this point—if the immune system is already compromised by fatigue, lack of sleep, stress, poor nutrition, or, say, childbirth—then the infection spreads to the bloodstream. Constipation then gives way—with frightful violence—to pea-soup diarrhea, which turns bloody in the more advanced stages.

The disease eventually spreads to the bone marrow, liver, and bile ducts, passing all the while through the body and into the stool, a potential source of further contamination, particularly to those administering to the sick. The last phase of the disease is the most horrific for the patient, who by this time would be running a high fever and have been passing diarrhea for some time. The small intestine, wracked thin and nearly useless by the disease, begins to spasm, a function called *shigella*.

"It's when your sphincter and lower colon spasm continually and you have the urge to shit, but you can't," my brother explained. "It's pretty debilitating and you end up anemic, losing proteins, especially if you're stressed anyway, as the Sagers were. Shigella doesn't necessarily kill you—we've all experienced it in mild forms when we have diarrhea—but it wears you down. The Sagers certainly didn't have many reserves at that point."

In its advanced stages, typhoid can also cause hemorrhages—internal bleeding—because of the toxic effects on blood vessels, and that is one of the real dangers of the disease. As a result, the body goes into shock and one begins to suffer "disseminated intravascular coagularopathy:" because of the trauma, the body uses up its clotting factors, and you get hyperclotting. Your body constantly bursts blood vessels and then heals up again. This internal trauma leads to a condition called *purpura*, a purplish rash on the skin that is the result of the constant internal bleeding and clotting.

Such was the condition of the Sagers, Henry worse off than Naomi, during the second two weeks of July 1844.

I hung up the phone feeling shaken—and walked off in search of a place to wash my hands.

Henry Sager's trusted medical book, Dr. Gunn's *Domestic Medicine*, doesn't refer specifically to typhoid, at least not by that name. In mid-July Henry Sager, in attempting to treat the illness, would have had to guess at the cause and attempt to treat the symptoms: the high fever, vomiting, weakness, intestinal distress, and almost constant pain in the bowels. This search for a cause—and cure—would have led him to a chapter in Gunn's book dedicated to an affliction called "Bilious Fever" and, consequently, a violent treatment for his and Naomi's sickness.

To differentiate bilious fever from other fevers, such as ague, and to effectively diagnose the disease, Sager would have followed Gunn's advice to look for his and Naomi's pulse to be "tense and full" and for the persistence of "great pain in the head; the tongue changes from white to brown, as the fever increases," and "as the fever increases; the eyes acquire a fiery color and expression, and the whites have a yellow tinge . . . and his bowels are very costive, and his urine highly colored." One can imagine Sager reading these words as the wagons were circled one evening on the Nebraska prairie, accepting Gunn's conclusion: "[B]y these symptoms, any man of common sense may be enabled to distinguish BILIOUS FEVER."

Bilious fever, which is nothing more than a nineteenth-century name for a fever accompanied by gastrointestinal distress, was to be treated boldly, according to Gunn. "This formidable and dangerous disease, may in most instances be easily subdued, if you will divest yourself of irresolution and timidity in the commencement of the attack," he wrote. What he meant, not surprisingly, considering his predilection for the procedure, was that the person treating the victim should make full use of the lancet and bleed the disease out of the patient's bloodstream. But first, he wrote, "give a good puke of tartar of emetic, so as to cleanse well the stomach—taking care to make its operation fully effective, by giving warm chamomile tea. When the fever comes on, *bleed freely*, and regulate the quantity of blood drawn, by the symptoms and the severity of the attack." Gunn also recommended doses of castor oil, calomel, and jalap.

"All diarrheal diseases, including cholera, were treated in the same way," wrote Dr. Peter Olch in the *Overland Journal*, the Oregon-California Trails Association quarterly, in an article called, "Treading the Elephant's Tail: Medical Problems on the Overland Trails." Because of its convenience and its immediate soporific effects, the administration of laudanum—opium—would have likely been the most popular medication of patients afflicted with gastrointestinal illness accompanied by fever since it would have been the one treatment that would have, at least, made the patient more comfortable. "An opiate such as laudanum or morphine was administered to alleviate the griping, colicky pain, quiet the bowel, and diminish the frequency of passages," he wrote.

Dr. Gunn was passionate in his fondness for opium as a cure-all: "Without this valuable and essential medicine, it would be next to impossible for a Physician to practice his profession, with any degree of success," he wrote. (Next to impossible, no doubt, so as to dull the pain of his other barbaric treatments.) Gunn called opium the "monarch of medical powers, the soothing angel of moral and physical pain." He then dashed off a burst of doggerel in its praise:

Charmed with this potent drug, the exalted mind,
All sense of woe delivers to the wind:
It clears the cloudy front of wrinkled care,
And soothes the wounded bosom of despair.

Olch, writing in the *Overland Journal*, also mentioned the frequent use of calomel as a purgative— "to the point of salivation and accompanied by capsicum"—hot pepper—"or cayenne pepper as well as camphor." Then the patient was rubbed all over with mustard plaster "to counteract the muscular spasms."

Dr. Gunn's second favorite remedy, next to the lancet, was the use of "glysters" or "clysters"—enemas—to cleanse the patient's bowels from gastrointestinal illnesses like bilious fever, colic, and cholera. Throughout the book, Gunn repeatedly pours forth, so to speak, on the healthful benefits of enemas: "Language almost fails to express the great value of this innocent and powerful remedy, in very many diseases to which mankind are daily and even hourly subject; and I most sincerely regret to say, that it is a remedy not only too little known, but too seldom used in the western country, both by Physicians and in families," Gunn wrote. "This disregard for the great virtues of clystering, must either arise from the supposition that the operation is too troublesome, or from a false and foolish delicacy, which forbids the use of an instrument, by which thousands have been preserved in extremely critical circumstances and with which every mistress of a family should be perfectly acquainted, so as to be able to administer a clyster when required in sickness."

To treat an "obstinate, severe and tedious case [of bilious fever]; in which you will find that the most active purgatives will not answer your wishes and expectations," he recommended a warm bath followed by "injections of glysters, made of warm soap-suds; or molasses and water, pleasantly warm but not hot, to which may be added a little vinegar." Gunn predicted that "these injections will cool the bowels, and remove from the larger intestines any offensive matter."

Sager could have also found guidance in Gunn's book in chapters dedicated to the treatment of "Inflammation of the Stomach" and "Inflammation of the Intestines," but Gunn's recommended treatment didn't vary much from that suggested for bilious fever: judicious use of the lancet and repeated clysters. "This being a very dangerous disease, and the life of the patient depending on the bold and free use of the *lancet*, you are not to be deterred from its use, by any apparent feebleness of the pulse," Gunn wrote regarding treatment for stomach inflammation. Similarly, intestinal inflammation required immediate bleeding, "the object being to arrest the disease instantly, and before mortification can take place, which," Gunn added, in case the seriousness of the possibility of death was not fully understood the first time, "always when it occurs, terminates the matter fatally."

None of the treatments, of course, could have had any effect on typhoid, which slowly ate away at the innards of its hosts as the Colony worked its way west along the Platte River. Parrish, however, began to improve slowly as the company crossed the plateau between the South Branch and North Branch of the Platte, began gaining in elevation, and approached the landmarks of western Nebraska. The Sagers condition, meanwhile, gradually worsened, so that by the time they joined the North Platte, Naomi had been permanently assigned to the interior of the wagon and Sager took no more hunting trips. The group was now making a brisk pace, covering some twenty miles each day, which could only have further exhausted the couple.

"A lot of these illnesses were the culmination of a sequence of events rather than one specific disease," Trevor told me another time when I called him for his feedback on the disease. "Typhoid is bad, and it alone could have killed them—but they had so much going on and were so stressed. They didn't have much of a chance."

Needless to say, the bleeding, had they done it, would have had the effect of draining the good along with the bad. "Bleeding is obviously not helpful," Trevor told me. "It weakens you. When you bleed someone, you take out the red and white blood cells—which is your immunity—and you're taking out proteins and iron. If the idea was, 'There's something bad in your blood, so let's get rid of the blood . . .', you're not changing the concentration. You're left with fewer stores of health. The human body only has about three or four liters of blood, which holds about 20 percent of the body's water; the rest is stored in other places. And if you're losing blood from your gut, your blood will start to suck water out of the rest of your body. Eventually, you can get vascular collapse."

While Parrish improved as the Colony entered western Nebraska, the Sagers both began to deteriorate as the disease began to tear into their digestive systems and cause their fevers to slowly escalate. That the Sagers and others with typhoid even lived through the month of July, enduring their frequent clysters, lancets, mustard baths, and dips into the opium vial, was the real miracle.

10

MEN AND MASCULINITY

THE BOLT OF LIGHTNING and attendant thunderclap struck simultaneously and were so bright and loud that my body levitated for a split second, the noise reverberating in my chest like an electric shock. Balloo, who a moment before was sound asleep on one of the children's sleeping bags, shot into the air with a yelp, giving a shake that sent water spraying everywhere, and scuttered into Leah's sleeping bag in abject terror. Everyone was instantly awake and huddling closer to Leah and me.

I looked at my watch: 5:00 a.m.

It was the end of a very long night of intermittent thunder showers, during which Leah and I had attempted to keep the kids dry by positioning their sleeping bags away from the worst of the leaks. They were now marooned on the one dry patch in the absolute center of the tent. I was soaked myself, unable to find a spot where the water didn't shower down on my face or to escape the steady drips slowly making puddles inside the tent around my sleeping pad. We were now six foam islands, barely afloat, and the rain was coming down in sheets, the thunder and lightning upon us with a vengeance. (It didn't escape my notice that we were experiencing the exact sensation that the families of the Independent Oregon Trail Colony felt when they endured night after night of rain storms on the Kansas prairie.)

We were now in western Nebraska, camped on the shores of Lake McConnaghy, an enormous reservoir that captures the waters of the Platte in the middle of the Sand Hills near Ogallala, and we felt truly exposed to the elements as the rain slashed our tent and the wind whipped at the canvas in shrieking gusts.

Until this moment the kids had, by some miracle, slept through the night, but it was now getting light and we decided to get up and see what we could make of the day.

"Do you think there's a breakfast place open in Ogallala?" Leah croaked.

"It's Sunday morning," I said. "And this is church country. Anyone in his right mind is home in bed dreaming about the Lord."

I dashed from the tent to the car, parked about one hundred yards away in the sand dunes, and dropped the ladder so I could root through the roof box for our raingear. It was cold, and my hands were soon freezing, my knuckles turning bright red as I fiddled with the latch. I grabbed the bag with the rain jackets and ran back to the tent, my T-shirt already soaked through. We were soon fully dressed and clad in our matching Wenzel rain jackets. Our sponsor, Wenzel, "The Camping Company," based in St. Louis, had provided us with numerous items for which we'd be thankful throughout this trip, even though we occasionally looked like a sports team in our matching getups. At these moments we'd taken to calling ourselves "Team Wenzel."

Team Wenzel bolted for the car, and by 6:00 a.m. we were driving the lonely road that skirts the lake feeling cold, hungry, and depressed, wishing we'd had the sense to tow a camper behind our vehicle like every other family now camped on the shores of Lake McConnaghy. My stomach growled. The kids were silent, numb with misery. Leah, inexplicably, was cheerful, confident that we would find somewhere open that would feed us.

Within minutes, the lights of a restaurant appeared in the gloom ahead.

"I don't believe it," I said. "The sign says, OPEN."

Julie May's parking lot was nearly full. Behind the restaurant a middle-aged man in rubber boots and an apron was standing next to a large pit fire—sheltered from the rain by a corrugated tin roof—with a garden hose in his hand. He was spraying a fine mist onto a whole pig that was turning on a spit. He waved as we walked to the front door. Inside we were greeted by a rush of warmth and good cheer that caused our spirits to soar. Waitresses were shuttling large plates of pancakes ("slam johns," as the emigrants would have called them) and eggs; an attractive woman in her fifties with a big smile, obviously the boss, greeted us at the counter and directed us to the only unoccupied table. My heart sank a moment later, however, when I noticed a sign at the counter that said they didn't accept credit cards. I didn't have any cash, and the nearest ATM was probably miles away. I decided to leave Leah with the kids and go off in search of an ATM, when it occurred to me to ask for directions.

"Well, there's one in Ogallala"—as I thought, ten miles away—"but we take checks!" the woman said. For the second time in as many minutes, I was incredulous.

"But I'm from out of state," I stammered. "From South Carolina."

"That's okay, you look like a trustworthy guy." I could have kissed her.

Julie May's was our house of worship that morning. A sign on the table said that the restaurant subscribed to the SLOW FOOD MOVEMENT, which meant the dishes were prepared with organic ingredients from scratch and, as much as possible, from local sources. We should expect to wait for our food and the orders wouldn't necessarily come out at the same time. This was fine with us, happy as we were to dry out and absorb the warmth. As anachronistic as it seemed—in the middle of the Sand Hills—this was the Chez Panisse of Nebraska, and it was our good fortune to find it at the most needed time. Leah and I enjoyed cup after cup of dark roast coffee; the kids ate mountains of pancakes; and by the time we staggered out more than an hour later the clouds were breaking up, the sun beginning to poke through.

Back at the campsite I set up a clothesline between aspen trees and began to haul out our sodden sleeping bags, pillows, and clothing to dry in the breeze. The kids disappeared into a grove of aspens to play hide-and-seek or build forts and chase each other through the sand. Leah pedaled off on her bicycle to see about a shower. When I had finished, I heated up a cozy bottle for Oakley and prepared a little nest for him in the morning sunshine, taking the moment—as I was wont to do in my fleeting glimpses of peace—to reflect on my position in life.

One of the original reasons I was drawn to the story of the Independent Oregon Colony was an attraction to the men in the story. The fathers and husbands were badasses: hunters who could fell a buffalo from the back of a galloping horse, farmers who cleared and plowed vast tracts of land with muscle power alone, blacksmiths who forged all the metal fittings of the farm in their workshops by hand. Indeed, they were jacks-of-all trades—veritable Renaissance men who crossed the continent and then forged an entire culture in the Pacific Northwest. And at the same time they were family men, devoted to their wives and children in ways that would shame modern men. They spent a day at work that involved both their hands and their minds and then came home to women who were equally skilled, albeit in the skills of the hearth: sewing, cooking, gardening, and careful frugality. Reading their journals and reminiscences, it became clear: these men—those who survived, anyway—were profoundly satisfied with their lives.

One hundred-sixty years later, husbanding and fatherhood has changed a lot. The middle-class man is no longer a man of diverse skills, both physical and mental. His popular image is that of a couch potato jockeying a TV remote control; if he's lucky, he works five days a week in a Dilbert-esque cube farm so he can have health insurance and provide a steady paycheck for his family. (Just see Joshua Ferris's new novel, *Then We Came to the End*, a hell-on-earth description of corporate life in an enormous building he calls the Death Star: "How we hated our coffee mugs! our mouse pads, our desk clocks, our daily calendars, all the contents of our desk drawers. Even the photos of our loved ones taped to our computer monitors for uplift and support turned to cloying reminders of time served.") And he comes home—to a wife who has also spent the day at the office—and wonders why his life is so unsatisfactory. His obese children lie limply on the couch with an electronic game control in their hands and stare slack-jawed at the television screen. No wonder he, too, turns to the television and beer can for sustenance.

As a husband and father of four young children, I've attempted to resist embracing the vestigial shreds of middle-class manhood: Saturday lawn mowing and T-ball games; Sunday sports on television. Despite holding office jobs, having served almost a decade as a magazine editor, I've nonetheless always attempted, in a fruitless, aimless sort of way, to cultivate physical skills, as though by hanging onto these activities I can retain a connection to the attributes that used to define a man. I occasionally wield a chainsaw against the hapless shrubs in my backyard, although in Leah I have competition, and make fair use of hand tools, to fix a dining room chair or make some modest improvement to our home. I have maintained my professional captain's license and taught people how to handle sailing ships at sea and to use navigational tools. But unlike Billy Shaw and Wilson Morrison, I don't *need* to do these things to survive and be successful. My income is derived from sources that require me to sit on my butt and, increasingly, jockey a computer keyboard. Was there some unseen force, aside from these physical labors, that nonetheless made these men men? Some parts of their identities that I could, more than a century later, identify with? Here, in the journals of the Independent Oregon Colony, was a perfect parable that might offer life lessons in the timelessness of fatherhood and husbanding.

The undoing of Gilliam as leader of the expedition offered an explanation. Gilliam was a blowhard, quick to anger and insensitive to the needs of the group. His leadership was doomed to failure. That he listened to his wife when she cautioned not to hang the deserter was an admirable quality, though. Shaw and Morrison were cautious and compassionate, saw themselves as parts of a team with their families, and their leadership was embraced by everyone in the group. As a blacksmith and handyman, Sager had just as many hard skills as everyone else in the group yet he couldn't control his brood and was often at odds with his wife. As a result, he seemed always to be making bad choices that would have dire consequences. Which was I, a Sager or a Shaw? Just the day before, Leah and I were setting up camp; one setting up the tent while the other was making dinner. The kids were playing in a grove of aspen trees about one hundred yards away. We had thought Oakley was with them, and when we called them for dinner they said they'd thought he was with us.

It meant he must have been gone for almost an hour.

In a panic, I set off down the sand to the water's edge, forcing away images of the steep banks of the reservoir, the shifting sands that created deep holes that could swallow up a child instantly. When we first arrived we had all gone for a swim and I had been careful not to let Oakley wander too far out of reach. His fearlessness was such that he would wade in over his head, realize he couldn't breathe, and then turn back to the shallow water, spouting and choking. He would do this again and again, sometimes requiring me to fish him out before he drowned. And now I had let him wander away unattended altogether.

I found him playing in the water with a group of children. He was still wearing a diaper, which was so swollen with water it looked as though it weighed twenty pounds. He was shivering, his body wracked with spasms, but he was rolling and playing with a couple of children whose parents had the sense to supervise them. The mother said he had been there the whole time, and they were just beginning to wonder whose child he was. They had first thought he belonged to a group that had left a few minutes before. That group said they thought he'd belonged with them. I picked Oakley up in my arms and hugged him tight.

"You scared me, Oakley," I said. "You need to stay with me and Mama."

He smiled at me, his lips blue with cold. "What," he said. It wasn't a question, just an observation that I was saying something that didn't make sense to him and that he wasn't concerned. I repeated myself again and again, and so did he, getting frustrated with my persistence: "*What!*"

A Sager moment.

When I was in college I took a course called "Men & Masculinity." It was taught by a pair of sociology professors and was intended to be a sensitive response to feminist studies, which were a big deal at the school, largely because of its unusual gender-based anatomy. Hobart and William Smith Colleges, on the shores of Seneca Lake in Geneva,

New York, are officially two separate institutions: men live in one set of dorms on the main campus and women in another, perched on a hill above (no doubt so they can keep a wary eye on the shenanigans of their male counterparts). The schools have a single president but separate deans' offices, the women of which advocated an aggressive feminist identity that informed all facets of the women's lives there. In most other ways, however, Hobart and William Smith was a traditional Northeast "liberal arts" college, which is to say it had (and still has) fraternities, and the focus of one's life there was to minimize serious studies and maximize the number of hours spent around a beer keg with a plastic cup clutched in one's hand. Yet the two colleges shared a faculty and had the same dining hall and common areas, which meant that an appreciation for feminism had a way of making itself known to even the most assiduous devotees of the fraternity lifestyle. In addition, the gender split had an effect on the curriculum, and this "Men & Masculinity" was a direct result. If women had feminism as a serious discipline, couldn't men devote some serious thought to the study of their own gender? What did it "mean" to be a man or to be "manly" or to be a father in this day and age? These were questions we sought to answer for an hour and a half twice a week. (Today, Hobart and William Smith is the only college in the country that offers a minor in Men's Studies; no school offers a major. Women's Studies is so common that you can even get a BA in the subject at several online universities.)

The result of our examination, according to our professors, might lend itself to a more solid appreciation of one's manhood than that offered by modern American culture—the stoicism, bravado, and physical aggression. But when the traditional shell was all stripped away, what, actually, was left in its place?

My time at Hobart, the early 1990s, was about the same time that Robert Bly, with the publication of *Iron John*, that paean to modern manhood, was advocating that men reidentify with their traditionally masculine selves by, among other things, charging off into the woods (like the Grimm Brothers' Iron John from which Bly got the book's title) with other men on self-examination retreats and that they invoke rites of initiation for their sons as a celebration of coming of age. By relishing the stuff of manhood they could feel good about their identity as husbands and fathers. As if to remind us of the consequences of pursuing stereotypical male behavior in the modern age, we also read Thomas McGuane's *Something to Be Desired*, in which the main character, Lucien Taylor, mirroring his own father's behavior, drinks too much, abuses his wife, sleeps around, and generally serves as a bad role model to his young child. The book works toward fragile resolution by having Taylor humbled by the experience and attempting to patch up what's left of his family in a way that fathers and husbands of earlier generations may have thought unmanly: by being emotionally available.

I recall another one of the readings for the course compared the life spans of football players with those of cheerleaders. The irony, according to the essay, was that the cheerleaders, as representations of vulnerability in their scanty clothing, would outlive their counterparts on the field, the football players, who were well muscled and covered in pads. The analogy was intended to compare the way women process stress, by sharing it, with that of men, who repress it, thereby suffering greater casualties from stress-related diseases, and consequently dying younger.

Conversation in class led inevitably to certain men suggesting a role switch: they would embrace the traditional role of the mother by staying at home and rearing the children, "Mr. Mom" style, if the women accepted the role of breadwinner. A book on my shelf today is typical of that view: *How Tough Could It Be? The Trials and Errors of a Sportswriter Turned Stay-at-Home Dad*, by Austin Murphy, a writer for *Sports Illustrated* who took a few months off work to stay at home with the kids while his wife cultivated her own career. The cover photo shows a man wearing an apron that says "#1 Dad" while holding a mop in one hand and a frying pan, dripping soap suds, in the other. The story leads to an acceptance that women have traditionally carried the heavier burden than men and at the same time a realization that maybe a new male identity based on serving as the principal homebody didn't quite fit anyway. "With all this extra time in the bosom of my family," Murphy writes, "I was looking for a few more transcendent moments, was hoping to be awash in more bliss than this. . . . I am exasperated, snappish, tendering frequent apologies."

His wife—well aware of the job's challenges—responds: "'The job is inherently frustrating because so much of parenting is reaction.

Seconds before departing from our home in Charleston, South Carolina, our neighbor Josh snapped this picture. Finn and Jonah are wearing their piano recital attire. Note the wooden ladder for getting to the roof box and the "back porch," which was extra storage and, while in camp, a place to enjoy a measure of solitude.

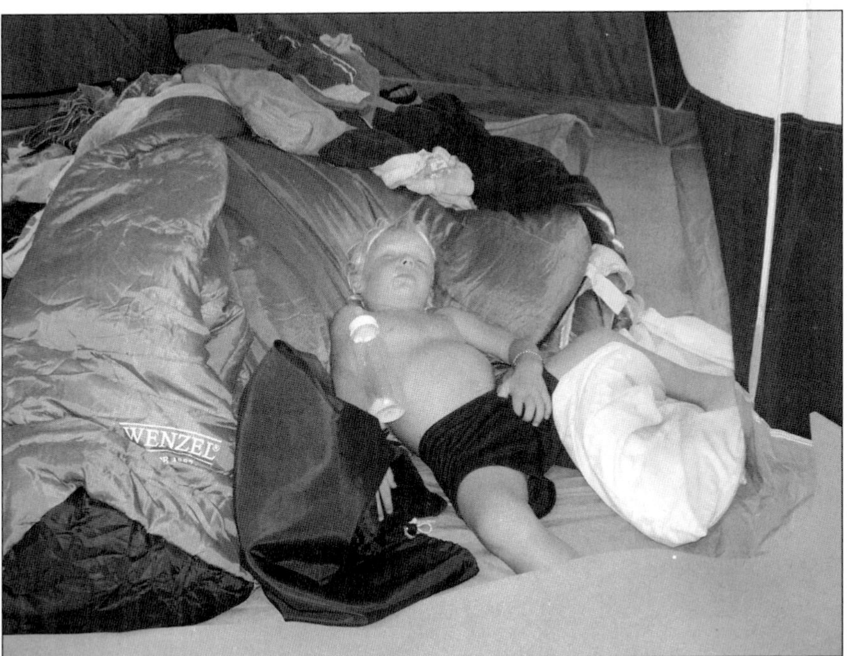

Like a Bowery drunk, Oakley lies asleep in the tent with an empty "cozy bottle" at his side. Independence Rock, Wyoming.

Finn scrubs his clothes on the washboard in Independence, Missouri.

Oakley tries out being a pioneer at Missouri Town 1855 near Independence, Missouri.

Leah stands on the Nebraska prairie at one of the numerous stone markers erected by the State of Nebraska along the original Oregon Trail.

Preparing to ascend Chimney Rock, western Nebraska.

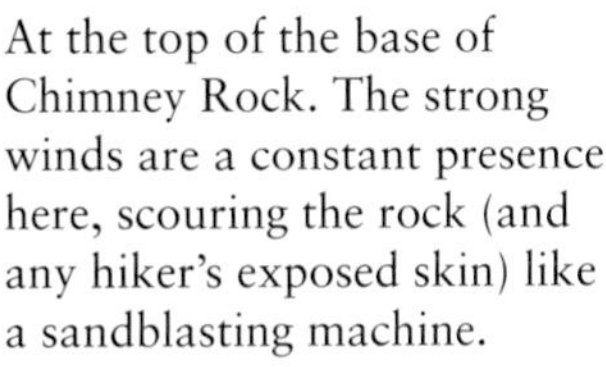

At the top of the base of Chimney Rock. The strong winds are a constant presence here, scouring the rock (and any hiker's exposed skin) like a sandblasting machine.

Setting up the tent along La Prele Creek at Ayres Natural Bridge, Wyoming. The natural stone bridge is visible in the background.

At the top of one of the Black Hills, just north of the Laramie Range. The Oregon Trail skirted along the north edge of these hills and climbed steadily in elevation until it was over a mile high in the center of what is now Wyoming. John Charles Frémont was the first to accurately map this portion of the Oregon Trail in 1842–43.

Jonah's pioneer nap, Independence Rock, Wyoming.

Oakley at the start of our excursion on the wagon train.

Sunset in Rattlesnake Pass along Sulphur Springs, just west of Bridger Pass on our wagon train adventure. It was here that we had our encounter with a five-foot prairie rattler.

The wagons circled at sunset in Rattlesnake Pass.

Team Wenzel at the Continental Divide in the Wind River Range, Wyoming.

The Snake River in Idaho runs through an increasingly steep canyon that the pioneers followed. This represented the roughest part of the journey and is where Naomi Sager died of typhoid.

We've arrived at our destination—Cape Falcon on the Oregon Coast near Manzanita.

You're not following through on plans so much as you are reacting to emergencies.'"

Murphy acknowledges in the book's epilogue, though, that during the course of the six months he spent at home he had stumbled over an emerging sense that modern male identity can gain sustenance from regular connection with the home and its routine duties. His connection to the routine, in fact, is what brought him into his children's consciousness. He quotes the feminist writer Anne Roiphe's book, *Fruitful*, for its suggested way to resolve male-female identity issues: "Bring men into the home."

"Who knew? While cutting the crusts off Willa's sandwiches, I've been on the cutting edge of social change, a foot soldier in the long slog toward happier families in which moms are allowed to use their college degrees, to use their brains, to make some money without it feeling like they're working a double shift every day," Murphy exalted.

Back at work as a traveling sportswriter, Murphy nonetheless continues with the routine chores he'd discovered while home full-time and finds sustainable happiness in the process: "When I'm home, I'm cooking a couple of nights a week. I'm grocery shopping, laundry folding, floor sweeping—you name it. . . ." His wife acknowledges his new role with joy: he was "more willing to take on the responsibilities of parenting, rather than just the fun part."

The fact remains that modern manhood, when compared with its historical self, is pretty boring, though. And it's more restrictive in its possibilities than modern womanhood. Women who marry and have children can effectively choose between being the primary caregiver or career maven, or some combination thereof. It's more complicated and more difficult to manage, to be sure, but both are acceptable and are equally encouraged. But there's still something ridiculous—from the man's perspective—about a stay-at-home dad. It takes a strong constitution to get away with it for very long and not feel as though you're leading an awfully lonely, personal crusade. (My neighbor, Joey, who stays home with his young daughter while his wife works full time, stands as a powerful example, and I enjoy our discussions on his life's challenges.)

Yet we're no longer allowed to take shelter in traditional notions of manhood, expecting our wives to care for the home while we toil away at the office. As a result, our available identities have shrunk while those for women have broadened. How true this is came home to me recently while reading Maureen Dowd's scathing book, *Are Men Necessary?* She grudgingly concedes they are—but just barely.

An article I found on *Psychology Today*'s Web site addressed this issue in an essay about modern fatherhood called, "Father's Time," by Paul Roberts and Bill Moseley.

"The modern mother, no matter how many nontraditional duties she assumes, is still seen as the family's primary nurturer and emotional guardian. It's in her genes. It's in her soul," the article reads. "But mainstream Western society accords no corresponding position to the modern father. Aside from chromosomes and feeling somewhat responsible for household income, there's no similarly celebrated deep link between father and child, no widely recognized 'paternal instinct.'" It then quoted Margaret Mead's quip that fathers are "a biological necessity but a social accident." The article maintained that fatherhood in the current age is "probably tougher, psychologically, than at any other time in recent history" because of the absence of role models. Yet this transitional time, according to the writers, "holds hidden promise." The article cited a Penn State study by a pair of research eggheads who mapped out the modern father-child bond in ways that offer some hope for modern fathers.

To put the study in context, the article pointed to the economic necessities that resulted in a gulf between fathers and their offspring. In the 1700s and early 1800s, American men worked close to home and were more likely to be involved in home life. Parenting books were written for fathers. (*Gunn's Domestic Medicine* is probably the best example, written as it was by a man and expressly for the male reader.) Children of failed marriages were typically put in the custody of their fathers, although this was likely an example of the courts' view that, upon marriage, women became "property" of the husband. By the Industrial Revolution, however, fathers were "removed from domestic life" and child-rearing manuals emerged that were written predominantly for women. (Numerous health books on our shelves at home testify to this.) By the twentieth century, this image—that fathers went to work and women cared for the children—had crystallized.

So what should modern fathers do? What role do they really play in their children's lives? The Penn State study concluded that fathers "parent" differently in that they play with their children more. And that's a good thing because children learn emotional self-control as a result, and through physical play they learn the rules of socialization. That's it. Apparently the tussling on the living room carpet, the games of gotcha-last, and clipping clothespins to my kids' earlobes are the secret to a successful fatherhood.

The hidden promise of modern fatherhood, according to the study's authors, was in its possibilities. In other words, we can cast off our old stereotypes and just do what seems most natural. "Culturally speaking," one of the study's authors was quoted, "there is so much more that fathers are 'allowed' to do."

I looked at Oakley dozing in the sunshine. He was just finishing his bottle and was beginning to stir, looking around woozily and blinking in the bright light.

"C'mon, Oaks," I said, flicking him on the forehead with my middle finger, "let's go find the kids."

Ash Hollow is a cut in the steep bluffs that form a rim along the southern edge of the North Platte River about twenty miles west of Ogallala. It was where the Oregon Trail joined the North Platte as emigrants left the South Platte and traversed the plateau between the two branches, and where a notoriously steep embankment scared the daylights out of those who handled the teams. The slope forced the emigrants to set up makeshift windlasses, tying ropes to their wagon axles and using people and oxen to slow the descent, to lower the wagons down the precipices, giving the site the name Windlass Hill. But the scramble was worth it: at the bottom of the hollow a natural spring bubbled up from the ground. And the steep canyon walls, tufted with junipers, scrub pines, and at the bottom a large stand of cottonwoods, provided ample shade so that the whole effect created an ideal oasis for the emigrants of the 1840s.

Today, Ash Hollow is an historic park operated by the State of Nebraska Parks Commission. As we stood on top of Windlass Hill, looking down the deeply rutted, and impossibly steep, swath where the wagons had passed more than a century before, we could see for miles in all directions: the North Platte surrounded by green and the Sand Hills, brown and scrubby, undulating away to the horizon. We were told by the owner of Julie May's that we shouldn't miss the historical pageant that was being offered today. The pageant was to commemorate reconciliation between white settlers and Indians, groups of which clashed near here in the mid-1800s. Our arrival at Ash Hollow would mark the second time (the first was in 2005) since the 1850s that groups of white Americans, mostly ranchers and farmers in their fifties and sixties, would assemble peaceably with a band of Native Americans, direct descendants of a series of bloody skirmishes that are described at the park's visitor center.

Not surprisingly, the incident started innocently enough. In August 1854, a cow wandered away from a Mormon camp near Fort Laramie, about one hundred miles west of Ash Hollow, and wandered into a Lakota camp. It was nabbed by a young Sioux named High Forehead, who slaughtered the animal and had a fine feast with his friends.

The next day, however, the army sent Lt. John L. Grattan, a twenty-one-year-old officer recently graduated from West Point, in command of twenty-nine soldiers to the Indian camp to apprehend High Forehead and bring him in for justice—on the business end of a noose. They brought along a light howitzer for intimidation purposes and confronted Chief Conquering Bear, demanding that he turn over the culprit. Grattan was hotheaded and was described by a later commander of Fort Laramie as itching for a fight. "There is no doubt that Lt. Grattan left this post with a desire to have a fight with the Indians, and that he had determined to take the man at all hazards," he said. To make matters worse, Grattan's interpreter, Augustus Lucian, was drunk.

Chief Conquering Bear, himself a Brulé, had represented the numerous Indian tribes, signing the 1851 Fort Laramie treaty that would allow Indians to collect annuity payments from the federal government, but his was a fragile leadership. While he was considered by the Americans to be in charge because of his position at the 1851 treaty talks, and therefore answerable for his people, he had no real authority over the numerous tribes at the camp, and he explained as much to Grattan that morning. He couldn't turn over High Forehead if High Forehead didn't want to go, he said. High Forehead, of course, refused as well. According to the

Indian version of events, Conquering Bear even offered several ponies as payment for the cow, but Grattan refused, insisting that High Forehead be turned over and arrested.

Within minutes, the talks deteriorated and Conquering Bear was lying facedown in a pool of blood, killed by a shot to the back of the head by one of Grattan's men. It was soon an outright firefight, Indians and soldiers blasting away at each other at close range. A few more Indians died, but Grattan and his men were drastically outnumbered and were soon surrounded and quickly cut down. All thirty of the American soldiers were killed.

The Indians, terrified of what they knew would happen, hastily decamped and fled into the wilderness.

The following summer, however, the army got its revenge. The War Department recalled Gen. William S. Harney from a post in Paris and ordered retribution. In Harney they couldn't have asked for a more determined officer. Known for a mean streak, Harney would eventually be court-martialed by the army four times during his career, once for beating a woman slave to death with his hands. During the Mexican-American War, Harney had earned a brutal reputation for executing thirty American deserters, including the hanging of a wounded man who had had his legs amputated the day before.

Harney departed Fort Kearney, Nebraska, in August 1855, with his band of dragoons and on September 3, surrounded a Sioux camp just west of Ash Hollow—and summarily killed some eighty-five men, women, and children. The survivors, seventy women and children, were gathered together and marched to Fort Kearney as prisoners of war.

At the base of Ash Hollow, we wandered the displays—chuck wagons, spinning wheels, and a blacksmith pounding horseshoes—and chatted with the reenactors. We learned from the blacksmith that one should never—ever!—strike the face of the anvil with the hammer while the hardy was resting in the hardy hole. (The hardy is a steel wedge inserted into the top of the anvil and used to shape steel. If left in place when striking the face of the anvil, it presents an upward-pointing knife edge to the fingers clutching the hammer. You can lose your fingers in a flash.) The most interesting of the reenactors, who seemed to live the part without effort, was a bandy-legged mountain man dressed all in furs and high leather boots. His scraggly beard was down to his chest, and his matted hair held in place by a sweat-stained cowboy hat. We had been told to look for him, since he had a reputation as an entertaining drunk who could throw a hatchet into an upright log from thirty yards. Finn and I wandered up to him and he thrust hatchets into our hands, and before we knew it we had all (except Oakley) joined in the fun, tossing hatchets at a tree stump with joyful abandon. It was all I could do to hit the stump, let alone make it stick (Leah, actually, proved to have the best aim), but time and again, by way of showing us the correct method, the man, reeling from the effects of whatever he had in the earthen crock at his feet, sent the hatchet singing through the air with a *whiz*, and it would strike the center of the log, its blade buried two inches into the wood, with a satisfying *clunk!*

Afterward, we gathered on the grass for the start of the pageant, which was to begin with a performance by the Indians, descendants of those murdered by Harney's men, who we were told had driven down from a reservation in South Dakota for the occasion, a distance of some four hundred miles. They were a bedraggled bunch, wearing Disney T-shirts and cheap sunglasses, and it was hard not to notice the awkwardness felt by the gathered whites.

The chief was impressively dressed, though, in a pair of fringed leather pants decorated with thousands of colorful beads. He wore a full headdress of eagle feathers and carried a long staff that was decorated with snake rattles and feathers. The only incongruity to his outfit was a pair of dazzling mirror shades.

The chief, raising his staff to focus our attention, introduced a group of young men and girls who he said would sing a few songs and play their ceremonial drum. But first we would sing the "Flag Song." Everyone stood up, all the ranchers taking off their cowboy hats and holding them to their hearts as a show of respect, the sun beating down mercilessly on their pale heads, while the chief wailed at the top of his lungs for a full five minutes. Meanwhile, the leader of the performers, a young man of about twenty-five with a long black braid and wearing a T-shirt that said, "Indians 1997 World Series Champions" on the front, was pounding away on a huge drum.

We had been told by Oakley's physical therapist that this sort of raw, yet controlled, stimulation was the best thing for him. She said he suffered from something called Sensory Integration Disorder, which meant that he was unable to effectively process the chaos of the outside world and exhibited "disorganized" behavior when certain situations became too much for him. When combined with his hyperactivity and what she described as his "oppositional defiance," he could be a chore to manage in all but the most controlled environments. He would freak out in supermarkets and other large stores, especially those with fluorescent lights. For some reason, the public library in Charleston made him particularly berserk. On numerous occasions, Leah had attempted to bring the kids there after school, only to suffer profound humiliation as Oakley cleared the shelves of books and ran screaming through the stacks. Needless to say, we minimized his exposure to these places and came to understand what he could tolerate and what he couldn't. We had actually been warned not to take him on this trip because of his condition, but, so far, perhaps because of our ability to watch over him and tend to his needs virtually all the time, he had thrived, enjoying living out of a cozy tent and playing outdoors every day.

I looked at Oakley and saw that he was transfixed. He was sitting quietly in his stroller, his whole attention focused on this group of performers as they sang and beat the drum in a steady rhythm that reverberated in the canyon walls. He sat through the entire performance absolutely silent—for forty-five minutes—as the Indians pounded their drums and wailed in feverish pitches.

When the performance was over, however, and the whites, dressed in vintage pioneer clothing and wearing beatific expressions on their faces, trooped on stage and began singing, "Let's Join the Wagons," swinging their fists in front of their chests in spirited chorus, Oakley lasted about two minutes before he let out his own pitched wail and started thrashing in the stroller. Their tuneless songs, while well intentioned, stood in marked contrast to the timeless spirituality of the Indians' opening act.

As Oakley worked himself into a state of fury, I whispered to Leah that maybe we'd had enough. As I led him away—encouraged by a saccharine duet about rolling with the wagons, sung by a man and woman in pioneer garb with looks of forced ecstasy on their faces—he screamed at the top of his lungs, "All done! All done!"

I agreed, and, after a brief picnic in the grass behind our car, we got the hell out of there.

11

INCIDENTS AND ACCIDENTS

WHEN JOHN CHARLES FREMONT passed through the last part of Nebraska in July 1842, he was traveling northward, crossing the triangle of barren, sandy plains sandwiched between the North and South Platte Rivers along the Front Range of the Rocky Mountains in what is now northeastern Colorado and southwestern Nebraska. The towering shapes of Chimney Rock and Scotts Bluff stood some thirty miles to the east, and the ragged, jutting peaks of the Black Hills, the snowcapped Laramie Peak rising the highest at more than ten thousand feet, about the same distance to the west.

Under the direction of his German assistant, Charles Preuss, Frémont had sent a party up the North Platte, where the Oregon Trail curved northward to skirt the range, and he had followed the South Platte upstream, perhaps hoping to find some previously unnoticed route that could provide a shorter road across the Rockies than South Pass, which required pressing some fifty miles farther north. But in this he was disappointed. Laramie Pass, virtually a straight line west through the front range and then across the Medicine Bow Mountains, was far too steep for wagons. South Pass, a low saddle just south of the Wind

River Range in western Wyoming, would remain the choicest route as long as people crossed the continent in wagons.

The mountains present such a steep, uniform face, running as an impenetrable north-south barrier, that it would be many decades before travel through this part of Colorado and Wyoming would be feasible. To make matters worse, the temperature on the ground in mid-July 1842 ranged from a daytime low of 102 degrees to a high, on July 8, of 108 degrees—calculated in early afternoon by Frémont in the shade of his horse. His barometer told him they were at an elevation of 5,440 feet above sea level, and they were climbing gradually higher every mile.

"Buffalo have entirely disappeared, and we live now upon the dried meat, which is exceedingly poor food," Frémont wrote on July 12, 1842, as he rode north. Despite the heat, he was able to maintain his careful celestial observations, which he would then pass on to Preuss, who would transpose it into his evolving maps, and take notes on the geology, which continued to amaze him: "The marl"—calcium-rich clay—"and earthy limestone, which constituted the formation for several days past, had changed during the day into compact white or grayish white limestone, sometimes containing hornstone; and at the place of our encampment this evening, some strata in the river hills cropped out to the height of 30 or 40 feet, consisting of a fine-grained granitic sandstone; one of the strata closely resembling gneiss." Frémont rejoined Preuss's party at Fort Laramie, at the junction of the Laramie and North Platte Rivers, on July 16.

To find a favorable crossing of the Platte, the Independent Oregon Colony also followed the South Platte, briefly, before cutting north and joining the North Platte for the journey through western Nebraska's clay bluffs that Frémont saw two years before from the west, striking, vertical cliffs and unusual formations rising more than six hundred feet high, that broke the monotony at long last.

The crossing of the South Platte was strategically challenging because of the shifting sands. In 1846, Francis Parkman, the Boston Brahmin whose *The California and Oregon Trail* would be published the following year, noted this was because the depth of the water varied greatly—and suddenly.

"First the heavy ox-wagons plunged down the bank," Parkman wrote of a group of emigrants he witnessed crossing the South Platte, "and dragged slowly over the sand-beds; sometimes the hoofs of the oxen were scarcely wetted by the thin sheet of water; and the next moment the river would be boiling against their sides, and eddying fiercely around the wheels. Inch by inch they receded from the shore, dwindling every moment, until at length they seemed to be floating far out in the very middle of the river."

It was while crossing the South Platte that another incident occurred involving the Sager family. The crossing was shallow—less than a foot deep if the wagons were kept moving at a good clip and not allowed to pause and therefore sink into the shifting sands—but wide, about a half mile, which meant the drover had to maintain his awareness of the fragility of the crossing for some time. Just to cross this distance, at a reduced pace because of the unsure footing, would have taken at least a half hour. And Sager must have allowed his attention to drift (not surprising, considering his debilitated health), because as the animals reached the far side and gained sure footing on the north bank, they sensed dry land and broke into a trot, the heavy wagon lurching dangerously.

Sager cursed and yelled—"Whoa! Whoa!"—striking the oxen repeatedly with his switch in a vain attempt to check their gathering speed. But, of course, this had the effect of exciting them further, and they charged uphill, taking the rise of the bank at full speed—and at an awkward angle. The top-heavy wagon teetered precariously on two wheels, looked as if it would regain its stability, and then dropped onto its side with a splintering crash, the oxen bellowing and pawing at the earth in fear.

Naomi, the baby, and the four older girls were trapped inside. Sager himself was almost crushed by the falling wagon—his face scraped open by a piece of hardware as the wagon went over—but he jumped clear just in time. He clawed at the canvas flaps and started pulling the girls free. Catherine crawled silently from the debris; her dress was torn off from the waist down so that her bloomers flapped in the breeze and her bare, white legs were exposed, but she was unhurt. He found Elizabeth and Louise pinned by supplies. But they too were unhurt, and scrambled out, huddling together by the wreckage of their wagon. Three-year-old Matilda was crying hysterically and complained that her arm hurt, but she too climbed free of the wreckage and ran to her sisters to be comforted. When Sager saw his wife, he was sure she was dead. She was lying motionless with her face down, her arms wrapped limply around the baby, which was screaming.

Sager took the baby from her arms and placed her with Catherine, who walked to the side of the trail and sat down on a mound of earth that the wagon wheels had made. "If Mama is dead," she recalled thinking, "I'll take care of you as long as I live."

Frank and John Sager dug the tent from the wreckage and set it up alongside the trail and Sager lifted Naomi from the wagon and placed her carefully inside. Louise began screaming when she saw her mother's limp body carried to the tent. John picked her up and swung her onto his shoulders and walked away, to give his father peace to tend to his mother.

"For a long time she lay insensible," said Catherine. Naomi finally lifted her head and responded weakly. She was not dead. But she was knocked senseless and did not revive for several hours.

Meanwhile, Shaw paced not far away. He had halted the train, and the men had righted the wagon, which wasn't seriously damaged, gathering the Sagers' belongings back into their wagon and locking the wheels. Another wagon had also tipped on the steep bank, but no one was injured.

But Shaw was anxious to keep moving if Naomi were well enough to travel. Sager said that she was, and he carried her to the wagon. The wagon train made a few more miles that night before camping on the open prairie.

I asked Dixon Ford for an explanation of the Sagers' wagon tipping over, and he said it was due entirely to "drover inexperience," that Sager should have anticipated the oxen charging up the far bank. He should have gotten ahead of the lead team and checked any excessive speed before the team could charge off of its own accord. (The Sagers' tipped wagon was an experience I would come to remember, with considerable anxiety, once we joined our own wagon train adventure in Wyoming.)

Once striking the North Platte, just west of Ash Hollow, the Colony rolled past Jailhouse and Courthouse Rocks on July 25; on July 27, they passed Chimney Rock, a narrow spire that emigrants in later years (no time for sightseeing by this bunch) would climb to enjoy the views of the Nebraska plains to the east and, barely visible on a clear day as a dark, jagged smudge on the horizon, the rising peaks of the Rockies to the west.

"We were traveling fast, and the road was good," John Minto recalled. "I am today hunting on horseback. I pass the morning going around the base of Chimney Rock. This, and the bluffs here, which at a distance look so like large city buildings, are all of soft stone formation, and are evidently wearing away fast." Minto also noted that some of the families were anticipating the fact that buffalo would be fast disappearing as they approached the high country of modern-day Wyoming. "Some of the families are drying buffalo meat by tacking the steaks together and hanging them over their wagon covers outside. Gritty? Yes, but not worse than Platte water."

On July 29, the company camped at the base of Scotts Bluff, where the trail briefly leaves the North Platte because the bluffs drop straight into the river in haphazard "badlands," short, jumbled bluffs and twisted canyons not suitable for wagon wheels. (Early groups of pioneers, such as the Independent Oregon Colony of 1844, generally veered well south, several miles away from the river and around the enormous cliffs of Scotts Bluff, but by 1850 a narrow cut through the bluffs themselves, only a few hundred yards across, was discovered and the Trail subsequently passed through it.) At Scotts Bluff the company was treated to the sights of numerous wild animals that would now become commonplace: grizzly bears, deer, antelope, and, hopping on the cliffs above the camp, bighorn sheep. (Interestingly, bighorn sheep will be reintroduced to the Wildcat Hills, just south of Scotts Bluff, in the coming years as an attempt to reestablish this species' easternmost habitat.)

The following morning, the company was treated to a phenomenal sight as they rounded the bluffs. Laid out before them was a valley that swept westward, the green, snaking swath of the Platte arcing northwest around a set of dark and jagged, snowcapped peaks: the Rocky Mountains. The dry westerly breeze would have hit them full force as they traversed into the valley and rejoined the North Platte, the elevation now rising rapidly with every mile. The valley provided sure footing, and the team made good progress that morning.

But the speed didn't last long.

Later that day, on July 30, after the company had paused briefly for lunch and to graze and rest the teams, the children were playing a game Frank had invented: As the wagon rolled along at two or three miles per hour, the children would climb the rising spokes of a turning wheel, and, after being lifted off the ground, they could then hop off the wheel and onto the seat of the wagon. From there they slid off the front of the wagon onto the tongue, where they balanced for a second with their hands on each of the rear oxen's hind quarters. And then, with one hand on the rump of one of the oxen, they would jump off the tongue and onto the ground, rolling in the dirt so that they were clear of the wagon's wheels. They had been playing the game for months as a way to stave off boredom.

The book *Stout-Hearted Seven* records the following conversation that took place that day:

"Don't you kids know that is dangerous?" one of the other emigrants in the company had warned.

"Pa let us do it," Frank responded.

And, when Naomi had registered her disapproval to Sager, he'd shrugged it off: "They don't have much fun, Naomi. Long as they are careful, I think it's all right."

No sooner were the words out of his mouth than Catherine, leaping to the ground with her left hand on the rump of the rear off-ox, caught the hem of her dress on an axe handle that was protruding from the wagon. Her leap was arrested, and she dropped to the ground, directly in front of the rolling wagon. Before Sager could stop the team, the front wheel—and then the back—rolled over her left leg, snapping the femur like a twig in two places. The team kept walking.

Sager picked his daughter up in his arms, and ran after the team to stop them, Catherine's leg dangling at a sickening angle. When the animals stopped, Sager looked at his daughter's mangled leg and broke into sobs.

"My dear child," he said, "your leg is broken all to pieces."

He had another reason to cry: his most able hand at tending campfires, cooking, and other domestic duties, was too injured to help and was now a liability herself.

Inexplicably, *Gunn's Domestic Medicine* wasn't much help for traumatic injuries. The only reference in the book that would have appeared to have been some help, a few paragraphs on "Bone Set," refers to an herb called boneset, which, ironically enough, was used by certain Native American tribes for the treatment of typhoid. It would have no application treating broken bones.

But from his years as a lay doctor, Sager was an expert at treating such injuries. He carefully set Catherine's leg and splinted the bone in a makeshift cast and placed her back in the wagon. A German doctor, Theophilos Dagen, was called, but he declared Sager's cast "as good as if I'd done it myself."

The company arrived at Fort Laramie, officially called Fort William at the time, later that evening. It was a welcome respite for everyone, as a cheerful relief from the vicissitudes and rigor of the trail and as a beacon of civilization, however crude and unsavory, in the endless wilderness. They were sick and exhausted, but they were still only one-third of the way to their destination. The fort, which was built by the trapper William Sublette in 1834, was operated by the remaining trappers of the American Fur Company, who had morphed their occupation into the cultivation of buffalo hides when beaver became scarce and fell out of fashion. "When the bulky buffalo robes took the place of the neat packs of beaver skins, the trader replaced the trapper, and the fixed trading-post displaced the shifting rendezvous," reads *Fort Laramie and the Pageant of the West*, a history of the fort by LeRoy R. Hafen and Francis Marion Young.

The lively fur trapper rendezvous, in which trappers and Indians would gather in seasonal orgies, at river junctions and other convenient geographical locations, were transient phenomena, and they disappeared with the beaver trade. The gatherings that ensued at the forts, while just as debauched and raucous, had the sanction and protection of the federal government.

Eight years before, in 1836, Marcus and Narcissa Whitman, in the company of their traveling companions Henry and Eliza Spalding, had stopped at Fort Laramie and been treated to the unique flavor of the mountain-man-and-Indian celebration. The soldiers and Indians were thrilled to be visited by two white women—the first to ever travel this far overland—and treated them to meals and rousing songs, the mixed-race children (white fathers, Indian mothers) bursting from the Indian camps and surrounding the approaching wagons.

A few weeks before, Narcissa Whitman and Eliza Spalding had treated men of the American Fur Company "to tea," setting out oilskin cloths on the bare ground next to the banks of the Platte River and serving tea in tin cups, and sugar with iron spoons. Now, the fur company men responded with similar kindness, hosting the women to a tea inside the fort that included tables and chairs. Narcissa delighted in the comfort of the chairs, made as they were of buffalo hide.

Such was the significance of the fort: the crudest of comforts provided what seemed like a restorative oasis in the wilderness. Eliza Spalding noted: "It is very pleasant to fix my eyes once more upon a few buildings, several weeks have passed since we have seen a building."

The same was true for the Independent Oregon Colony, when they crossed the valley between Scotts Bluff and the Laramie River on August 1. James Clyman couldn't help noting with derision the exorbitant price of flour at the fort, which back East would cost less than $10 per barrel: "Superfine at 40 dollars a barrel; Spannish at 30."

But he allowed that Fort Laramie was a welcome sight after months on the open trail: "[A]bout 4 o'clock in the afternoon we hove in sight of the white battlements of Fort Larrimie and Fort Platte whose white walls, surrounded by a few Sioux Indian lodges, shewed us that human life was not extinct."

That night, John Minto was walking through the camp, which was set up outside the fort adjacent to the Indians' camp, while most were asleep, when he noticed that two of the designated guards for the night were shirking their duty. Minto went to the tent of one of the men and was confronted by a young man's mother. "It is not John's turn to stand guard tonight," the woman said. She was resolute and wouldn't let Minto rouse him.

Minto turned to report his findings to Shaw, when he passed the tent of the other man designated for duty. He saw that the man's tent was lighted from within and that he was moving around inside.

"In disgust," Minto said, "I got to the guard tent just as Captain Shaw came from being around the cattle. I told him with some heat of both of these skulks, and he replied, 'Well, John, I expect they're afeared'"—of the proximity of the Indians—"'but let's not say anything about it; let's you and me take their places.'" Minto's anger left him as quickly as it came on, and he and Shaw together stood guard that night.

"Brave and true, patient, carefully watchful, Uncle Billy Shaw," Minto noted.

The following morning Minto wandered the Indian camp, taking note of the buildings and the customs of the Indians in awe, describing a bucolic scene that seemed otherworldly: "I started out after breakfast to look at the camp of the Sioux Indians," he recalled. "There were here some twenty lodges, or tepees. There were not many men in sight. One group of three or four, and two or three walking about singly, were all that appeared. I met one that looked as though he were on dress parade. I have never seen a man walk more proudly. He was well dressed, too. At the tepee which he had left, I noticed the spear or lance, and shield near the opening, which was the best of its kind I ever saw, being ornamented with nude figures of men and horses and buffalo. The skin was of buffalo skin, as I judged, though I did not touch it, or any of the other things I saw. At several of the tepees, groups of children were playing, tumbling about with the dogs; at some, old women were at work dressing skins."

When Minto returned to the camp, he saw Martha Morrison doubled over in laughter. When she saw him approach, she laughed even harder, and he realized she was laughing at him. "John, John, come here!" she said.

"I went," Minto said, "and she was holding her sides to repress laughing, and three Indian women were standing side by side on the opposite side of the fire."

"John, if I understand these women's signs," she said, "they think you belong to me, and want to buy you for a husband for that one in the middle. They offer six horses."

Minto walked away in embarrassment, but not before sizing up the young woman, who "did not look to be over twenty-two or twenty-four years of age."

12

UP THE ELK'S PENIS

A Family Ascent

IF NEBRASKA DIDN'T HAVE CHIMNEY ROCK it wouldn't have much in the way of dramatic physical features to brag about. The vast plains in the eastern part of the state gradually give way to the undulating sand hills that roll for more than two hundred miles westward until meeting the bluffs of western Nebraska that serve as modest foothills to the Wyoming high country. Lest visitors to Nebraska come away thinking the state is all about grass, sand, and windmills, however, the state has put a silhouette of the needlelike spire on its state quarter and on its license plate. Chimney Rock is Nebraska's El Capitan; its Statue of Liberty, its Space Needle, its Devil's Tower, and its Grand Canyon, all in one three-hundred-foot sandstone formation that stands in a lonely section of dusty prairie bluffs along the North Platte in the farthest reaches of the state.

There are so few rocks in Nebraska, John McPhee quipped in *Annals of the Former World*, that when one does break the surface, "it is such an event that it is likely to have been named a state park." Such is the case with Chimney Rock. (To be fair, there are a handful of other famous rocky outcrops nearby, including Jailhouse and Courthouse Rocks, but they tend to get less attention.)

And Nebraska likely won't have Chimney Rock in another hundred years or so when erosion finishes the job of reducing this lonely spire to nothing but a sand hill. The almost-constant winds, whipping up sand from the base and surrounding bluffs, are scouring away at the soft stone; and frequent storms, with violent intensity, reduce its height and girth at a rate of a few feet each year. Great chunks of the spire fall away during storms such that historical photos of the past 150 years show a remarkable thinning and overall diminishing of the tower's height that is easily visible to the naked eye. The rocky spire itself, jutting from a sandy mound about two hundred feet high, is now barely one hundred feet tall and resembles a modest drip castle.

But because it's the only distinct landmark for miles around, save the featureless cliffs of the surrounding bluffs, it cuts an impressive figure rising from the windswept prairie.

And it's great fun to climb.

We pulled into the remote—and empty—parking lot of the visitor center in the early morning, hoping to be up and down Chimney Rock before the heat of the day began to broil the surface of this parched landscape. We had taken to wearing broad-brimmed hats, secured to our heads with stampede strings pulled taut beneath our chins, yet our noses and lips were nonetheless cracked and peeling from weeks of following the Trail. We had bought our lids at a reenactor's store in Liberty, Missouri: felt crushers, a broad-brimmed farmer's hat, and a cute flower-patterned bonnet for Raven. Yet the combined effects of wind, sun, and sand were simply inescapable. I'd long since given up trying to apply Chapstick to my blistered lips. They had been chapped and bleeding for more than a week, and I was okay with it. Leah and I concentrated our sun-resistant energy in trying to keep the kids' faces and shoulders from getting too badly burned.

Inside the visitor center we learned that the fur trappers and emigrants who first traversed this landscape in the 1820s and '30s were reminded of home and hearth when they first saw Chimney Rock on their journeys west along the North Platte Valley. It so clearly resembled a chimney, and it was this image that they so longed to see so many hundreds of miles from their homes, that they gave it the sentimental name. That, and the Indian name made them blush. Native Americans called it what it clearly looked like to them: Elk's Penis (a very large elk's penis, to be sure).

One traveler, the scholar-cum-lawyer William Marshall Anderson, who traveled this way in 1834 in the company of fur trapper William Sublette, could bring himself only to refer to the spire's initials—but then couldn't resist the obvious resemblance to a phallus: "We are now in sight of E.P., or Chimney Rock, a solitary shaft . . . one of the most notorious objects on our mountain march."

Another traveler, the painter Alfred Jacob Miller, simply referred to it in the French: "*Puine du cerf*."

We wandered the exhibits briefly: a miniature covered wagon for the kids loaded with faux bags of dried fruit and sugar (filled with sand) and barrels of flour, antique housewares and hardware that had been jettisoned from wagons, and vintage photos of the rock. There were also numerous quotations from travelers who had begun to "see the elephant" at this point in the journey. Seeing the elephant was a common expression of overland travelers who were exhausted to the point of regretting their decision and considered turning back while there was still the chance. Sort of like hitting the wall in marathon running. Only when you had seen the elephant—and kept going—could you fully appreciate the enormity of what you had undertaken.

"If I were to yield to inclination," wrote emigrant Mary Walker, "I should cry half the time without knowing what for."

In 1849, John Walker wrote: "One man returning; says he can't go all the way. Has money enough; loves his wife more than gold."

But we were anxious to begin our hike.

When we asked the woman behind the counter how to go about an ascent of Chimney Rock, she looked at us sternly and then told us it wasn't possible.

"Excuse me?" I asked.

"Climbing Chimney Rock is not a good idea," she said.

"Why not?" I asked. "Can't you at least climb up to the base of the tower?"

I stared at her. I'd heard of so many people scrambling up this rock that I couldn't believe that people were now barred from doing so. The American look-but-don't-get-too-close-or-you-might-get-hurt-and-sue-us mentality seemed to have hit a new low. The rock was right there, visible through the window over her right shoulder—beckoning—and we were all suited up and ready for a rigorous hike. Even Oakley seemed to sense adventure in the air.

"You can go out behind the visitor center and get a good look at it," she offered, pointing to the glass doors at the back of the building that offered fine views of the rock about a mile distant.

"But we want to *climb* it," I said. "Can we?"

She hesitated a long time, looking down at her fingers on the desk in front of her, before saying, "Well, you *can*, but . . ."

I said nothing.

Then she finally blurted out: "But there are so many rattlesnakes that it's really not a good idea."

Now, I'm the world's biggest chicken when it comes to rattlesnakes, and it's always a comfort to me to find a fellow chicken when it comes to these frightening reptiles. Just a few minutes before, in fact, I'd read of an early emigrant who was bitten by a rattlesnake in this vicinity. His treatment was reminiscent of what Dr. Gunn might recommend: "The brethren"—these were Mormons—"immediately applied some tobacco juice and leaves, also turpentine, and bound tobacco on his leg which was considerably swollen. We laid hands on him and Luke Johnson administered a dose of lobelia [a medicinal plant] in number six [a liquid medicine] after he had taken a strong drink of alcohol and water. The lobelia soon vomited him powerfully. He complains of much sickness at his stomach and dimness in his eyes. He appears to be in much pain." Following the quote, the curators of the exhibit editorialized: "In spite of his treatment, Fairbanks survived."

But I also know that unless you do something foolish like put your hand in crags that you can't see or surprise a snake as you come around a corner and step on it, they'll leave you alone, especially if you're making a lot of noise and they hear you coming, which is something our family cannot help. But, still, rattlesnakes are a primal fear of mine, and I was interested to hear this woman out. Leah, who heard the exchange and knew of my fear, rolled her eyes and walked away.

"Have you *seen* rattlesnakes on the trail?" I asked.

"Well, no."

"Has anyone been bitten by a rattlesnake here at some point, aside from that guy in the nineteenth century?"

"Well, no."

"Has anyone ever reported coming close to being bitten by a rattlesnake here?"

"No, but you never know."

She grudgingly told us that the state of Nebraska owned the rock itself and had an easement through private land so that it was permissible to climb the rock—just not advisable—in her opinion.

I figured that we could handle the odds, and I finally coaxed her into telling us where we could find the trailhead. I could feel her glaring at my back as we left.

We got back in the car and drove a half mile down an unmarked dirt road that ended at an old cemetery, the kind you see in old Westerns, a handful of lonely looking headstones set up on a solitary hilltop, no doubt filled with the bodies of all the people who had been bitten by rattlesnakes, I told Leah.

"Oh, please," she said. "You and that woman should join a support group: Terrified of Rattlesnakes Anonymous."

We loaded a daypack with water and a snack, put Balloo on a leash so he wouldn't surprise a snake, and then charged off down the trail making as much noise as usual. The trail wound for about a mile through tall sage brush, prickly pear, and yucca plants whose spiky leaves lined the edge of the trail and kept poking us in the shins.

As we drew close we realized that while the rock itself is not terribly tall, the ascent up the base is indeed steep. We met a group of hikers who were about to begin a three-day wagon train adventure, a tourist jaunt, and had been taken here to get in the mood. Their guide, a toothless, bearded cowboy with a long blond beard and wearing a filthy slouch hat, cautioned us all to stay to the bare rock, since the sand and gravel has a way of working loose and causing a landslide that will cascade down on others—you along with it.

We scrambled our way up, sometimes crawling on all fours and all the while buffeted by the prairie winds that snatched at our clothing and threatened to fling us to the prairie below. The heat of the sun was intense, causing us all to squint in the brightness, but the view from atop was magnificent and well worth it: the tall cliffs of Scotts Bluff visible twenty-five miles to the west, the green ribbon of the North Platte meandering east and west, the only green anywhere. The land was almost exactly as it had been in the 1840s, save the handful of homes and businesses that dotted the small communities along the North Platte. This was such an obvious corridor that it wasn't hard to picture a string of wagons, their white canvas covers shining brightly in the sun, kicking up dust from their wheels as they progressed westward.

We found we couldn't rest for long, though. There was no level place to stand that was out of the wind, and we had to keep a firm hand on Oakley, who kept trying to pull away and would likely go tumbling down the hill in a flurry of stones and cactus spines if we let him go. We crouched against the base of the rock spire for a few minutes before deciding to head back.

Going down was even more difficult, since the wind was at our backs, giving us unhelpful nudges as we felt for footholds in the loose soil, and the dog was tugging at his leash.

But we made it off the rock and back to the car without incident, neither snake bite nor scraped knee, and then pressed on for our next intended campsite: Scotts Bluff, our last stop in Nebraska.

One of the benefits of road trips is the chance of spontaneous discoveries, the delight in stumbling over people and events that couldn't have happened if every night's campsite was predetermined and every day's events mapped out in advance. You simply can't know what you'll find. Back in Alexandria, Nebraska, for example, we had discovered that the annual reenactment of the Pony Express ride—from Sacramento, California, to St. Joseph, Missouri—would be passing our campsite on the same day that we hiked at Rock Creek Station. On the way back that afternoon we pulled to the side of the road at a place where a ranger told us two riders would pass the mail saddle (the "mochila"). And sure enough, a few minutes later a grizzled old cowpoke showed up in his battered Silverado towing a horse trailer. He wordlessly saddled up his mare, mounted, and waited. The kids sat on the car's back porch on the opposite side of the road and watched, their hair blowing sideways in the dry breeze, all of us staring up the road to the west. And then, kicking a plume of dust, a rider emerged from behind a hill about a mile away and came loping up the road. The rider hopped off, tossed the mochila to the new rider, who then galloped off for the next switch some miles later. The whole exchange was an impromptu history lesson, in the company of several ranchers who told us stories of horses and life on the Nebraska plains. One man, in an incongruously high voice, said he had been a rancher all his life. He was about eighty years old, thin as a stem of buffalo grass and wearing tight Wranglers over a pair of well-worn but handsome cowboy boots. His hands and face were leathery and brown, and his eyes twinkled beneath the brim of his worn Stetson. He said he enjoyed writing poetry about ranching life. In his reedy voice he recited one about the beauty of a foal being born on the prairie in spring.

The pageant at Ash Hollow was another such experience—unplanned and all the richer for it.

But the drawback of spontaneity on the road, of course, is you never know where you'll end up camping for the night. Our experience at Cahokia, Illinois, is testament to that.

And so was our arrival at Scottsbluff. (The town of Scottsbluff is usually written as one word; the bluffs themselves as two.) Our guidebook led us to what it said was the only campground in town, which turned out to be a Cahokia-esque dirt lot called Riverside Zoo in the middle of the industrial part of town, parched and shadeless, strewn with trash, and absolutely charmless. We didn't see any animals, who, if they were there at all, had the good sense to stay out of the merciless sun. The host came out of his trailer blinking in the sunlight and spoke as if he hadn't seen a customer in years. He said he had plenty of spots. We demurred.

A woman at the town's chamber of commerce directed us to a reservoir about ten miles outside of town, which turned out to be so infested with biting flies and swarms of mosquitoes, and exposed to the full force of the prairie wind whipping up the surface of the water in whitecaps, that we couldn't even set up camp without all of us being driven almost to tears. Even the kids, who were usually happy just to be turned loose with their bicycles or looking for critters in the trees and at the waters edge, were unable to relax and began fighting and whining. I didn't blame them. The bugs and wind were driving us all crazy. We got back in the car and headed out—we knew not where.

After a brief meeting on the side of the road just outside the exit to the reservoir, Leah and I decided to try one last place that was mentioned obliquely in the guide, a work-in-progress campground in the neighboring town of Gering. We were so exhausted from our morning hike, and the drive from Ogallala, that this *had* to be it or we would reach an all-time low in morale. We didn't have a backup plan, since we wanted to hike Scotts Bluff the following day and view the remnants of the Oregon Trail at its base in Mitchell Pass, which were supposedly the most well preserved in Nebraska. We were hungry, tired, dirty, and our senses of humor had long since been swept away in the dry wind or carried off in our blood by the mosquitoes.

We had some difficulty finding it; no one in the town seemed to have heard of it. But after a half-hour drive through the town we eventually drove over a hill and there it was, just what we needed after more than a week of camping in primitive spots: a brand-new campground (with showers!) and a smooth patch of grass for our tent that had commanding views of Scotts Bluff about a mile to the west. The sun was just setting over the bluffs, the sky filled with brilliant hues of orange, red, and indigo, and the cliffs of the bluffs were ablaze in saturated color—bright red and deep purple that seemed to deepen with each passing minute.

The kids burst from the car for the playground, focusing their second wind with amazing energy, while we set up the tent, finding that we needed to brace our poles with duct tape and wooden dowels because the constant wind was taking its toll. Fortunately, we had plenty of cold beer in the cooler, so, after warming a bottle on the stove for Oakley and putting a pot of water on for pasta, Leah and I slumped on the picnic table with cold ones in our hands, happy to sit in silence and watch the dazzling sky.

• • •

The following morning dawned clear, and we awoke to the joyful trilling of a western meadowlark perched on a fencepost and singing his heart out. We once again resolved to begin our climb early to avoid the worst heat of the day: this time of the more formidable Scotts Bluff. We managed our morning routine with efficiency. It was my duty to be the first one from the tent to make the coffee, using the water in the pan to warm a cozy bottle for Oakley. Once the coffee was ready Leah would emerge and rustle breakfast while I gathered lunch fixings, water, sunblock, and hats, and tried to help the kids find their shoes and socks. They usually went barefoot, their calluses long since hardened to leather, but on hikes we insisted they wear socks and shoes. On the drive to the bluffs I glanced at the headlines in the Scottsbluff *Star-Herald*: LOCAL NATIONAL GUARD SOLDIERS HEADED OVERSEAS: SAYING GOOD-BYE FOR NOW, and LOUSIANA GOVERNOR ORDERS NATIONAL GUARD TROOPS TO NEW ORLEANS (in the wake of the carnage left behind by Hurricane Katrina). Two days before, in the *Omaha World-Herald*, I had read a story about the unflagging Republican support of President Bush's war: HOUSE REJECTS LONG TIMETABLE: NONBINDING RESOLUTION SAYS 'ARBITRARY' WITHDRAWAL IS NOT IN AMERICA'S INTEREST. The reporter classified it as a preelection attempt by Republicans to get Democrats "on record" about the war. Every day's news brought sobering words from Iraq, of course: the countless revenge murders, the roadside bombs, the posturing by American politicians that the chaos was being reined in and the irrepressible forces of democracy and freedom would prevail. Whenever reading the headlines, I always tried to put myself in the mind-set of the 1840s and tried to recall their headlines: the debate over expansion into the territories, including Texas and Oregon, which was Polk's campaign promise (which carried the day); the simmering unrest over the slavery issue and whether new states would be open to slavery or be free; and what to do about the ever-growing "Indian problem" as more land was taken. Despite 160 years of distance, these were the same issues, really: complex, heartbreaking conflict responded to with hyperbole and shrill nonsense. It gave me modest pleasure to use these newspapers as tinder to start our evening campfires.

The cliffs of Scotts Bluff rise six hundred feet from the prairie and are capped in a plateau of grass, scrub pine, and junipers that has been a sacred site for Native Americans for eons. They called it *Me-a-pa-te*, "the Hill That's Hard to Get Around." The site remains one of profound beauty, despite the best efforts of the National Park Service to make it "accessible" to all travelers, namely, to those in cars who want to experience the views without so much as lowering their windows and allowing the AC to escape. Visitors can pull their cars to a stop at a guard shack, pay the modest entrance fee, and then drive straight up a road that ends at a parking lot on top. You don't have to leave your car to enjoy the views. At such places, one can't help but be reminded of Edward Abbey's vision of all national parks: that they be closed to automobile traffic entirely and existing roads given over to hikers, bicyclists, and shuttle buses for those who are either too old or too handicapped to make a human-powered visit. It would be a worthy goal, and Scotts Bluff National Monument would be a good place to start.

Walking trails meander along the rim of the cliffs. Birds of prey reel along the bluffs, diving and screeching. Songbirds fill the trees. And the views are breathtaking.

There are several competing stories of how the bluffs got their name. The most popular version details how a fur trapper name Hiram Scott, a member of William Sublette's 1828 expedition, was injured in a skirmish with Indians near the Sweetwater River, several hundred miles upriver from here. Following his injury, Scott was too injured to ride, so Sublette ordered two comrades to take him in a bull boat—a small craft built of willow saplings and buffalo skins—and escape down the North Platte River, where they would be met at the high bluffs along the North Platte a week later by a rescue party. The trio paddled downriver for several days, but then the boat capsized and all their supplies were washed away. Scott was too injured to continue, so the pair ditched him in the wilderness. And then Scott managed to drag himself, perhaps ten miles, perhaps twenty, no one knows for sure, to the high bluffs of the original rendezvous. No one was there; the rendezvous never occurred, and Scott died of a combination of his injuries and starvation. A year later, the following spring, a skeleton was found at the base of the bluffs by some of Sublette's hunters. As a tribute to his stamina, they called them Scott's Bluffs.

Washington Irving related a version of this tale in his narrative of the adventures of Capt. Benjamin Bonneville, William Shaw's inspiration to head west.

"They determined, therefore, to abandon him to his fate," Irving wrote of Scott's fellow travelers. "Accordingly, under presence of seeking food, and such simples as might be efficacious in his malady, they deserted him and hastened forward upon the trail. They succeeded in overtaking the party of which they were in quest, but concealed their faithless desertion of Scott; alleging that he had died of disease.

"On the ensuing summer, these very individuals visiting these parts in company with others, came suddenly upon the bleached bones and grinning skull of a human skeleton, which, by certain signs they recognized for the remains of Scott. This was sixty long miles from the place where they had abandoned him; and it appeared that the wretched man had crawled that immense distance before death put an end to his miseries. The wild and picturesque bluffs in the neighborhood of his lonely grave have ever since borne his name."

The version that is most likely closest to the truth, however, because it was reportedly passed on by Sublette himself to one of his men (who then published the account in the New Orleans *Picayune*), suggests that the men did all they could to save Scott, only abandoning him when they had lost all hope of saving him. According to Sublette, the three men, following the capsize of their bull boat, reached the bluffs together, half starving and dragging Scott in a makeshift litter, only to find that a man named Bruffee, who'd been designated to rendezvous at the bluffs, had never appeared with a rescue party. After considering their dilemma, they did what they had to do: they ditched Scott, who was obviously dying anyway. There was no need for a second rescue party, because they knew he was dead. Nonetheless, when his bones were discovered a year later they named the bluffs for him.

The visitor center included portions of the poem, "The Wanderer's Grave," written by the traveler Rufus B. Sage, who passed through here in 1845 and whose *Scenes in the Rocky Mountains* was published in 1846. It is about as bad as any poetry has any right to be, but a few lines bear repeating, since it's the earliest written reference to the legend of Hiram Scott. Sage crooned, in his melodramatic iambic doggerel, of Scott's solitary death scene:

> No willing grave received the corpse
> Of this poor lonely one;
> His bones, alas, were left to bleach
> And moulder 'neath the sun!
> The night-wolf howl'd his requiem,
> The rude winds danced his dirge;
> And e'er anon, in mournful chime,
> Sigh'd forth the mellow surge!

And on and on for forty lines. I left the building howling a quiet requiem of my own for the sins of hack poets.

Not surprisingly, and not for the first time, we were the only ones on the walking trail that leads from the back of the visitor center up a two-mile-long meandering trail that has been carved into the cliffs. We all had a good swig of water at the base of the bluffs (there was none at the top), and we were carrying only about a gallon and a half for all of us, and then started our hike, Balloo on his leash and giving us looks of indignation that clearly meant, on a scorcher such as today, he was not a hiking dog and belonged on the lap of a little old lady seated in front of an air conditioner.

At one point the trail cuts straight through the cliff in a tunnel one hundred yards long. Hikers have scooped their fingers into the soft limestone making swooping shapes. We placed our own hands into the imprints of hundreds of hands of all sizes. It was an odd sort of graffiti, not at all offensive, and reminiscent of the marks of the passings of the emigrants who made similar signs in cliffs along the trail.

We made good time, and I jotted in my notebook about the birds we saw. Jonah identified a huge black-and-white bird with an obnoxious squawk in the top of a scrub pine as a magpie. I wasn't sure how he knew this, and when I asked him he just shrugged, and said, "It's the bird that likes shiny metal," but I verified it in my birdbook and found he was right. (Only later did I remember that one of their *Tintin* comics includes a scene in which a magpie steals a key to a firehouse so the firefighters can't save Tintin from a burning building.) Leah said the little birds of prey we saw swooping along the cliffs, their iridescent blue-gray wings sparkling in the sun, were American kestrels, and I noted the presence of a western towhee and a blue grosbeak in the tops of the junipers. We had Oakley in the back carrier, and by the time we reached the top we were thankful it wasn't a whole lot farther than the two steep miles. A backpack that weighs thirty-some pounds is tiring enough; one that weighs thirty pounds and incessantly throws its weight from one side to the other while pulling at your hair provides an added challenge.

At the top of the bluffs, finding the shade and cool breezes a welcome relief, we overheard a ranger telling a story to a group of schoolchildren about why Scotts Bluffs are significant to the Native Americans. An Indian youth of about thirteen years old named Worm had a vision there, he said, when he climbed the bluffs alone and spent three days without food or water. Worm saw that he would one day lead his people and become a great man, a warrior. People would eventually call this skinny kid, who was known for pranks and laziness, Crazy Horse.

Crazy Horse, the ranger said, came back to the bluffs several times during his life, and in his last vision at the top of Scotts Bluffs he saw that he would die soon, at the hands of the whites, but that he would come back to his people in stone. Overhearing the story, we made it a point to remember to stop at the Crazy Horse Memorial in South Dakota on our return trip, in which a team of sculptors is slowly turning a stone mountain into a depiction of Crazy Horse that stands hundreds of feet tall looking out over the Black Hills not far from the faces of Mount Rushmore.

We spread a picnic of sandwiches out under a juniper and had our lunch. Afterward we wandered the trails that skirt the rim, looking at the smudge of peaks on the western horizon. Supposedly you can see the snowy cap of Mount Laramie, 112 miles away, on a clear day, but today it was too hazy. But once again we found this was not the ideal place for Oakley because of his interest in investigating the very edges of the bluffs. On the hike down the heat of the day had grown so intense that we had to carry Balloo much of the way because the surface of the path burned his paws. We realized this guiltily when we noticed he kept walking in the slender patches of shade along the trail's edge.

We were soon back at the base and following the route of the Oregon Trail through the improbably narrow Mitchell Pass. A sign along the trail said that British explorer Sir Richard Burton had passed through here in 1860 and commented that THE SHARP, SUDDEN TORRENTS WHICH POUR FROM THE HEIGHTS ON BOTH SIDES, AND THE DRAUGHTY WINDS—SCOTTS BLUFFS ARE THE PERMANENT HEADQUARTERS OF HURRICANES—HAVE CUT UP THE GROUND INTO A LABYRINTH OF JAGGED GULCHES STEEPLY WALLED IN. WE DASHED DOWN THE DRAINS AND PITCH-HOLES WITH A VIOLENCE WHICH SHOOK THE NAVE BANDS FROM OUR STURDY WHEELS.

As we emerged from the path at the base of the bluffs and walked west, following the well-worn trail we saw one of Burton's storms approaching across the valley ahead of us, a band of wind and rain scouring the roads and farms to the west in a black band. Five minutes later we were hit with a blast of wind and spray, but no real rain, which seemed to hover in the air above us, perhaps evaporating before it reached the ground. Just as quickly it was gone, replaced by a riffling breeze. We walked in ruts that were still so compacted that nothing grew. All around was grass and sage, but in the swales themselves, just dry mud.

As we returned, the sky clouded over and we were met by an equally strong wind storm from the east, patches of sun shining selectively on the bluffs beyond. An arresting sight: the brilliantly illuminated yellow-and-orange bluffs against a charcoal sky. The birds were suddenly quiet and the only sound was the howl of wind in the grass and the junipers. Leah remembered we hadn't put the fly on the tent when we left that morning.

13

DEATH IN THE AFTERNOON

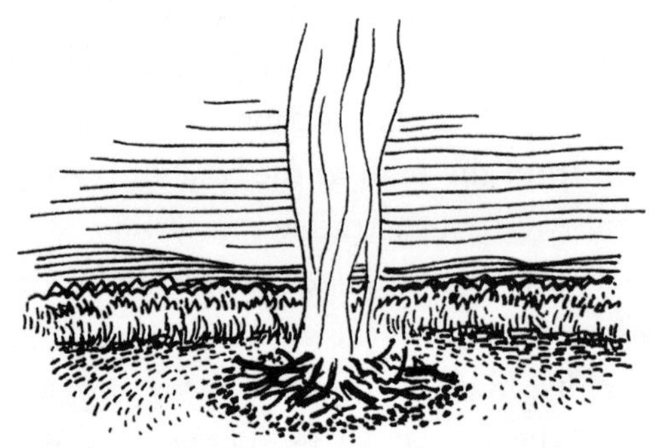

IN THE FIRST FEW DAYS OF AUGUST 1844, following their brief resupply and rest at Fort Laramie, the Independent Oregon Colony fairly flew along the trail, covering some twelve to twenty miles each day. They had begun to feel keenly the delays of the Kansas rains, since they now had barely a month to reach the Blue Mountains, the final barrier to the Columbia River Gorge region, before the first snow hindered their passage. They would have to cover more than seven hundred miles as the crow flies, clear across the full width of what are now the states of Wyoming and Idaho. This would require an average daily run of more than twenty-one miles, an impossible task. Yet they hurried on, hoping the snows of September would fall later than usual.

The emigrants had another reason to hustle. They were afraid that the four thousand or so Sioux Indians they had encountered camping at Fort Laramie might follow along behind for a few days and then ambush them for their equipment and stock while they were outside the range of the fort. And while very few attacks occurred on emigrants in the 1840s—none, in fact, occurred during the summer of 1844—they were nonetheless feeling vulnerable and the rumors of Indian attack, however unfounded, were a powerful motivation to move quickly. As a precaution, Shaw had ordered everyone, on leaving Fort Laramie, to pay no outward attention to the Indians. "If some of the men gave out signs of being afeared, the Indians would follow and attack us," Shaw said.

The Reverend E. E. Parrish allowed himself to find genuine delight in the send-off the Indians provided on August 1. "The Indians, men, women, and children, visited our camp. They are the nicest looking and best behaved Indians we have seen. They had five splendid banners, four of which were waving all the time. They were richly dressed. They wanted presents of tobacco, powder, lead, etc. The men sat down and all smoked a little from the same pipe." John Minto was among the men seated with the Indians and sharing their peace pipe.

On August 11, James Clyman mulled over their predicament, their need to hurry while at the same time needing to stock up on provisions, in his typical rambling way: "[G]rass scarce and nearly dry even on the moist Situations & we begin to find our delay on Kaw [Kansas] river was a great detriment to our traveling here bringing us through this dry region in warmest and dryest part of the Season our Stock begins to look bad and loose their activity and yet we have not arrived at the worst part of our long tiresome Journey our own subsistence dose not look so precarious as the forrage for our stock our horse in particular."

On August 13, the last of the buffalo were taken. Parrish wrote: "We are now in the midst of a buffalo range. After we leave this region it is said to be doubtful whether we will meet any more on the route."

A few herds of buffalo could still be seen, but Shaw and Morrison were anxious about allowing hunting if it meant delay. But the hunters, under strict orders not to bring in too much game as to delay the progress, made the most of the dwindling herds, shooting those that crossed the trail and drying the meat in the camps over smoky fires and in strips from their wagons. They also shot at deer, bighorn sheep, grouse, and whatever vermin they could find along the trail.

"The country all the way is a rich game park," John Minto said, "and swarming with the animals that prey upon game, the large wolf and grizzly bear being most seen." This had the beginnings of a dream come true to Minto, who had worn out the pages of a copy of Samuel Augustus Mitchell's *School Atlas* that he had owned while living in

Pittsburgh and working in the coal mines. "I saw in it a half page description of Oregon—about its heavy forests towards the north, and its open country towards the south, abounding in game and wild horses . . . [T]hat page was thumbed until it was very dark. I would take it up as I came out of the coal mine, and look at that old book." (Minto's school atlas, while inspiring to gaze at, would have presented a puzzle for any would-be emigrant; the page on Oregon Territory, and the river route that crossed the Indian Territories that would ultimately become the Oregon Trail, was wildly inaccurate. Rivers shown on the map simply didn't connect in a way that they did in reality. Not until John Charles Frémont's 1842 surveys would useful maps be available for westward-bound emigrants. It was Frémont's map of the Platte River Valley and South Pass that the Independent Oregon Colony used on their 1844 journey.)

The other animals now in proliferation were prairie dogs, whose burrows dotted the high country by the millions. "Dog towns" were everywhere, covering anywhere from one hundred acres to more than dozens of square miles, their yaps—signals of danger to each other—a source of constant humor to the emigrants. One emigrant said, "The Plains were completely honeycombed" with the dogs' "villages" or "doggeries," and another commented that a prairie dog "resembled a dog, but partook more of the nature of the rabbit."

But the holes also contained a hidden menace, the warnings of which would issue from underground as emigrants approached: the raspy rattle of the prairie rattler. Rattlesnakes and prairie dogs, in the words of historian Merrill J. Mattes, achieve a sort of "subterranean harmony" by sharing holes dug by the prairie dogs. Most of the time, the snakes serve as benevolent guards watching for the dogs' predators, the coyote and, in the 1840s anyway, western timber wolves, which were seen in huge numbers early in the history of the westward expansion until they were eliminated by fearful pioneers and, later, ranchers protecting their stock. When hungry, about once every three weeks, a snake would take a prairie dog as its dinner. Since prairie rattlers tend to be territorial, they check their own population growth, to the full benefit of the prairie dog population, which thrives despite losing an occasional villager. Other than these brief instances of necessary violence, the prairie dog-rattlesnake relationship continues to be a peaceful one.

In a pinch, prairie dogs could be a source of food to emigrants running low on stores. But hunting them could present an unusual challenge. Capt. Howard Stansbury, who surveyed northern Utah in 1849 and 1850, explained the frustration a hunter would feel after shooting a prairie dog and expecting to put it immediately into the stew pot: "When shot, they fall back into their holes, where they are generally guarded by a rattlesnake. . . . Several were shot by us . . . but when the hand was about to be thrust into the hole to draw them out, the ominous rattle of this dreaded reptile would be instantly heard."

Unexpected prairie dog holes could also prove life threatening to hunters chasing buffalo on horseback, "threatening to break the horse's leg and the rider's neck," Mattes wrote.

While the trail was smooth and amenable to swift passage, one reason why the emigrants couldn't cover even more ground (even covering twenty miles a day means, at three or four miles per hour, an average of only four to five hours of travel) was that some event invariably occurred that required stopping the whole train. Often, this reason for stopping was to bury a fellow traveler.

E. E. Parrish's journal records the carnage. On August 4, he noted the passing of a Mrs. Seebern and, on August 11, a Mrs. Frost—both to typhoid. He also noted the ongoing concern that maybe he, too, would be among those to succumb. On August 6: "My health is not much improved. I can hardly write." And on August 9: "My health is poor, but I hope the good Lord may bless the means so that I may soon get out." (Like many others at this point in the journey, he was wagon-bound.) On August 11, Parrish even offered a deal to the Lord if allowed to recover his health, "and I promise my life to his service." (He would live to fulfill his bargain.)

On August 15, the emigrants were preparing to cross the North Platte near present-day Casper, Wyoming, for the cutoff to the Sweetwater River, when a child, John Nichols's teenage daughter Elizabeth, began to deteriorate rapidly from the effects of typhoid.

Once again, John Minto's services were required. He recalled preparing to go to bed that evening when, "Mrs. Sally Shaw and Mrs. Morrison came to me and told me they needed my help very much.

They said John Nichols' daughter was dying, and it would be necessary to bury her during the night."

The digging of a grave, a child's especially, at the end of a long day of travel, must have been a particularly heartbreaking and painful exercise. Her dying would be attended with little ceremony, save a few lines read from the Bible, and a burial would also be rushed because of the need to keep moving. But Sally Shaw appealed to Minto's sense of honor and decency, and also likely knew that a childless man would be less likely to give up hope in the journey when asked to perform such a task: "She said she was aware that all men and boys were probably tired; but there was a great difference between them when asked to dig a grave, when they needed sleep." Minto obliged, fetched a pick and shovel, and reported to the Nichols's tent.

"I did so," he wrote, "and found a girl, just budding to womanhood, drawing her last breath. Four or five good mothers were around the rear end of the wagon. Through the space between I saw the calm, pure, marblelike face, as the last breathings, with a slight struggle, left the upper portion of the breath and neck motionless." Standing with his hands on the shovel, Minto was moved to tears. "From my eight years in the coal mines, I had seen men and boys maimed, crushed, or burned by machinery, falling roofs, or fire damp [a flammable gas], but nothing of that kind affected me like this death scene."

He added: "We dug Miss Nichols' grave in loose soil and stones, near where she died, and buried the body. As dead brush and wood were plentiful near, we burned some over it to kill evidence of what we had done, that the grave might not be violated." This was a common practice in the early days, but the Indians would soon grow wise to it, finding that evidence of a fire was also often evidence of a grave or a cache of goods for which emigrants intended to returned. (Another trick was to bury goods beneath one's tent so that the footprints of an overnight's activities would conceal the disturbed earth.)

The girl's cousin, B. F. Nichols, also a teenager, recalled: "It was the most pathetic scene I ever witnessed. The father and mother stood at the brink of the grave and looked for the last time at the form and features of the little one, whose loving smile had been the sunlight of their existence. She was a very bright little girl and beloved by all who knew her and it was exceedingly hard to leave her alone on the almost trackless wild."

Nichols did not mention Biblical scripture in his eulogy to his young cousin. Instead, he quoted from Greek mythology a passage about the sacrifice of Ion, son of Apollo. Clemantha asks him if they will meet in the afterlife, and he responds: "I have asked that dreadful question of the hills that look eternal—of the clear streams that flow forever—of the stars among whose fields of azure my raised spirit has walked in glory. All were dumb; but as I gaze upon thy living face I feel that there is something in the love that mantles through its beauty that cannot wholly perish. We shall meet again Clemantha."

Nichols then added: "To die amidst loving friends and kindred, surrounded by all the comforts of a quiet home, elicits the sympathy of all, but who can fathom the depths of grief and despair of those heart broken parents as they turn and gaze for the last time upon the little mound of upturned earth that covers all the earthly remains of their loving and beloved little daughter, knowing as they did, that they would never return to plant a rose or strew flowers upon the lonely grave."

The following day, Parrish wrote: "John Nichols' child Elizabeth died last night. She had lain long in the fever."

This was the first child to die on the journey, and the effect it must have had on the mothers in the group, while not recorded in the diaries and recollections of Minto, Parrish, Shaw, and the others, must have been profound, and leaving the girl's grave that morning, just a few short hours after she'd drawn her last breath, must have been horrifying to the girl's mother. To have left the grave unmarked, hidden, in fact, in the desolate, windswept Wyoming high country, must have wrenched every instinct as a mother and as a small-town Protestant accustomed to a three-day grieving ceremony in the comfort of family, friends, and neighbors.

A hint of the agony experienced by emigrant mothers exists in a recollection some thirty-five years later made by Martha Morrison's daughter, Martha Ann, who John Minto would marry a few years after arrival in Oregon and who was about the same age as Elizabeth Nichols. Each year the emigrants would gather around a campfire to trade stories about the overland crossing, and each year the men related their adventures: the game killed, the Indians (real and imagined) repelled, and the excitement of the rolling wagon train. And the women, mostly to each other, would tell the real story: of the suffering. In 1878, during such an event held in Salem, Oregon, Martha Ann Minto (née Morrison) clearly recalled the events of August 15, 1844: "Some of the women I saw on the road went through a great deal of suffering and trial. I remember distinctly one girl in particular, about my own age that died and was buried on the road. Her mother had a great deal of trouble and sufferings. It strikes me as I think of it now—of course I was a girl, too young then to know much about it—but I think how the mothers on the road had to undergo more trial and suffering than anybody else. The men had a great deal of anxiety and all the care of their families, but still the mothers had the families directly in their hands, and were with them all the time, especially during sickness."

Earlier that summer, in June 1878, Martha Ann Minto put it more bluntly, when she rose to speak following the stories of several men, and said: "Some of these men talk as though they enjoyed themselves extremely at pioneering. When we came to Oregon in 1844 I do not think it was very funny. It was not to me."

She described going barefoot and having so little to eat during the last several months on the trail as to be malnourished and starving, and having clothes worn thin by overuse. "I will have to tell you, I expect, of the first pair of shoes I had in Oregon," she added. "As I was going along the road one day—a very muddy road to travel—I met a young man of my acquaintance who was a shoemaker. Very shortly after that I had a present of a pair of shoes. They told me afterward that he took the measure of my foot in the mud."

On the morning of August 16, following the burial of Elizabeth Nichols, the emigrants crossed the shallow waters of the North Platte River for the last time. Where the North Platte cuts through the red buttes at what is now the city of Casper it is flowing almost exactly due north, straight from the western side of the snowy peaks of what is now known as Colorado's Front Range. When the emigrants reached this point, having followed the river around the Black Hills of the Laramie Range, traveling first northwest, then west, and then southwest through the buttes, they then had to jump off—west across an arid, lifeless valley—to join the Sweetwater, which runs east-west toward their passage through the Rockies: South Pass. But to reach the Sweetwater they would have to travel overland, without water, for at least a day. Not everyone made it. Parrish noted that his group of wagons reached the Sweetwater on the evening of August 15, an hour after dark. John Minto and the Morrisons, however, failed to cross the fifteen miles between the North Platte and the Sweetwater on the August 16, and camped instead along a stream called the Sandy, barely a trickle across the parched valley. The family didn't reach the Sweetwater until the following day.

Ordinarily, the arrival at Independence Rock was marked by considerable celebration. The rock served as a beacon for travelers in decades past. For Indians it was a sacred site, comparable in its place in their lives with Australia's Ayers Rock—Uluru—which rises as curiously, if higher, from the Australian outback as Independence Rock does from the desolate Sweetwater Valley.

The Rock supposedly got its modern name on July 4, 1830, by a band of fur trappers led by William Sublette as a tribute to the nation's independence. Later groups of emigrants found the Rock's location an important milestone: if they reach the Rock by Independence Day, they would safely cross the Blue Mountains in eastern Oregon before the snows fell. They would pause for a day or two to celebrate the occasion with fireworks and refreshing baths in the crisp waters of the Sweetwater.

The Rock is hump-shaped piece of granite 1,900 feet long, 700 feet wide, and 128 feet high and oriented along a southeast-northwest axis. It has a shallow saddle in the middle such that its profile suggested various odd shapes to travelers. Some said it resembles a sleeping turtle or an apple cut in half and placed flat-side down. In 1832, John Ball thought the Rock looked "like a big bowl turned upside down," and estimated that its size was "about equal to two meeting houses of the old New England Style." Another traveler thought that "Independence Rock was like an island of rock on the grassy plain," and Civil War soldier Hervey Johnson reported that it looked "like a big elephant [up] to his sides in the mud." From a distance, J. Goldsborough Bruff said the Rock "looks like a huge whale." Like other gold rushers, Bruff found it was "painted & marked in every way, all over, with names, dates, initials."

Its surface has been worn so smooth by the winds and blown sand as to shimmer in the sun like burnished metal. Following the custom of fur trappers, emigrants also developed the habit of leaving their names chiseled into the surface; more than five thousand names of early emigrant were carved into it between the 1830s and 1870s when overland travel was eclipsed by the transcontinental railroad. Travelers continue to carve their names into the Rock—some were dated as recently as 2005—but the more modern names are crude and ugly by comparison, more like graffiti than a memorial to an arduous overland passing. It's clear that those who took their time crossing the continent also took their time etching their names. Many of the early names still exist, the most beautiful being those etched in the 1800s, tidy letters replete with serif fonts, mostly on the southeast corner and in other nooks and crannies not exposed to the scouring effects of the westerly winds.

In July 1841, the Jesuit traveler Pierre Jean De Smet camped at Independence Rock, duly carved his name, and recorded in his diary the first mention of the Rock's alternate name, commenting: "On account of all these names, and of the dates that accompany them, as well as of the hieroglyphics of Indian warriors, I called this rock on my first journey, 'The Great Record of the Desert.'"

A year later, John Charles Frémont also paused at Independence Rock and wrote, in his typically detailed way: "Except in a depression in the summit, where a little soil supports a scanty growth of shrubs, with a solitary dwarf pine, it is entirely bare. Everywhere, within six or eight feet of the ground, where the surface is sufficiently smooth, and in some places 60 or 80 feet above, the rock is inscribed with the names of travelers. Many a name famous in the history of this country, and some well known to science, are to be found mixed among those of traders and of travelers for pleasure and curiosity, and of missionaries among the savages." After calculating the barometric pressure to determine the height above sea level of the Rock, he carefully calculated the latitude and longitude with his sextant trained on the sun. He did not mention whether he, too, hoping for a bit of historical posterity, carved his own name in the Rock. He did, but it has since worn away.

• • •

But the Independent Oregon Colony did not pause for celebration at Independence Rock. It was August 17—they were a full six weeks behind the customary schedule—by the time the last of the wagons passed the Rock at about noon that day, and they paused only long enough to water the stock in the Sweetwater, which runs within one hundred yards of its southeast corner, and likely search out a handful of the most obvious names.

By this time, Henry Sager was too sick to walk and had joined Naomi, the baby, and Catherine, who was still unable to walk because of her broken leg, in the wagon. Dr. Theophilus Dagon, who had been consulted to review Sager's splinting job on Catherine's leg, took up the management of the Sagers' team, turning them loose to be fed and watered that day, and hitching them back to the yoke when the group pressed on.

"He offered his services and was employed," Catherine Sager recalled, "but though an excellent surgeon, he knew little about driving oxen. Some of [the family] often had to rise from their sick beds to wade streams and get the oxen safely across."

That afternoon a small group of buffalo passed close to the wagons, and Sager rallied. "Though feeble," Catherine Sager said, "father seized his gun and gave chase to them. This imprudent act prostrated him again, and it soon became apparent that his days were numbered. He was fully conscious of the fact, but could not be reconciled to the thought of leaving his large and helpless family in such precarious circumstances."

By the middle of the afternoon, the company continued another five miles west and camped that evening at Devil's Gate, an enormous split in the rock through which the Sweetwater passes. The trail skirts the gate itself, passing just to the south through Rattlesnake Pass, since the river cuts through the narrow canyon with no room to travel on either side. That evening Morrison took off with his gun after a bighorn sheep, while John Minto slipped off to go fishing. "I took my fish gig and passed most of the day chasing fish in a deep hole within the west end of the big cleft of the Devil's Gate." The cliffs rise vertically above the river for several hundred feet, the sheer walls making it impossible to pass without walking and swimming through the water. Minto, however, was content to spend the rest of the day fishing. "The deepest place was the north side of the pool, and by going into that I scared out the largest fish to the shallows, and then I threw my three-tined gig or fish spear. For the first hour I had little success, but at length I could throw it from twenty to thirty feet and strike a fish from ten to fifteen inches long. I got a fine lot, besides a day of boyish sport."

The following day Minto was leading the Morrisons' wagon in the lead of the group and was in a reflective mood, awed by the spectacular scenery. He had spent the previous day fishing in one of the most dramatic fishing holes in all of Wyoming, and today he was in charge of leading his boss's team as group leader for the day. The rumpled granite mountains of the Rattlesnake Hills formed a reddish gray wall to his right, the sparkling waters of the Sweetwater burbled alongside the trail. And because of the altitude, the morning was fresh and cool, smelling of sage.

These were the same hills that John Charles Frémont and his cartographer Charles Preuss had sketched and recorded in their 1842–43 expedition, information that Minto (and the others) likely used. The annotated map shows the bold cliffs of Independence Rock and Devil's Gate, and the wriggling line of the river carving a swath between the rocks, and then sweeping curve of the Sweetwater Valley just to the west. A note on the Rattlesnake Hills reads: "Ridges and isolated masses of naked Granite destitute of vegetation."

It's the last ascent of the Rocky Mountains. Where the Sweetwater River drops from the Wind River Range—at South Pass, the smooth saddle where the Oregon Trail traverses the continental divide—Frémont and Preuss had written two notes, one to the east and one to the west: "Waters of the Atlantic" and "Waters of the Pacific." The Sweetwater was the last of the water that flowed to the Atlantic that the emigrants would see.

"It is not possible to avoid being impressed by our surroundings," Minto wrote as the wagon train proceeded due west along the Sweetwater. "I am in charge of the lead team. I am walking along talking with the two oldest girls of Capt. Morrison"—one of whom he'd already confessed in his journals to knowing in his heart that he'd someday marry—"in front of the wagon, answering their questions about the mountains; drinking in the joy of it all myself, while keeping my cattle steady."

Minto was in this heroic mood when, cracking his whip to direct the team toward a shortcut through a patch of sage, he noticed a hare crouched in the shade of a sage bush. "I never stopped the motion of my whip," Minto said, "but put more strength into it, and brought the lash across the head, back of the long ears, and the game little animal is quivering in death. The grand landscape is out of mind as quick as a pistol shot, and I am glowing with interest in my own feat. It is not far below the skin of any youth to where the man that kills other animals for a living still is." Minto tossed the dead hare onto the wagon for the stewpot, only to find, later that evening, that he'd been upstaged by Captain Morrison, who'd shot a bighorn sheep that day and was proudly promising fresh roasted mutton to all. Minto's prize was left for the wolves, he admitted ruefully.

On the afternoon of August 27, the Independent Oregon Colony crested South Pass. Just to the north the snowcapped peaks of the Wind River Range, shrouded in clouds, jutted to the sky. To the south, the broken badlands of the Antelope Hills, unexceptional except for their solitude and barrenness, appeared as jumbled, sandy bluffs. The pass itself had prompted John Charles Frémont two years before to quip, "From the impression on my mind at the time, and subsequently on our return, I should compare the elevation which we surmounted immediately at the Pass, to the ascent of the Capitol hill from the avenue at Washington."

He was not impressed, but that was the whole elemental beauty of South Pass: you were keenly aware of the formidable wall of the Rockies, since the Wind River Range presented a frightening wall of gray-black peaks just a few miles to the north, while the impassable badlands to the south would have taken weeks to cross, and there was no water. South Pass is a geological accident, a smooth ascent with ample water sources on either side. The whole of the crossing, from the Sweetwater on the Atlantic side to Little Sandy Creek on the Pacific side, was less than ten miles and the vertical rise only a few hundred feet.

"Approaching it from the mouth of the Sweet Water," Frémont added, "a sandy plain, 120 miles long, conducts, by a gradual and regular ascent, to the summit, about 7,000 feet above the sea; and the traveler, without being reminded of any change by toilsome ascents, suddenly finds himself on the waters which flow to the Pacific Ocean."

• • •

Frémont, his survey mission accomplished, chose to press on into the Wind River Range and attempt to find the highest peak of the Rockies so he could name it after himself. He failed to do so, but he was amazed by the drama of the mountains as he turned north from South Pass. "The scenery becomes hourly more interesting and grand, and the view here is truly magnificent; but, indeed, it needs something to repay the long prairie journey of 1,000 miles."

William Shaw, as he passed over South Pass that afternoon, would have remembered that Capt. Benjamin Bonneville had been equally impressed by the forbidding character of the Wind River Range. Irving wrote of Bonneville's experience there in 1833: "The Wind River Mountains are, in fact, among the most remarkable of the whole Rocky chain; and would appear to be among the loftiest. They form, as it were, a great bed of mountains, about 80 miles in length, and from 20 to 30 in breadth; with rugged peaks, covered with eternal snows, and deep, narrow valleys full of springs, and brooks, and rock-bound lakes. From this great treasury of waters issue forth limpid streams, which, augmenting as they descend, become main tributaries of the Missouri on the one side, and the Columbia on the other; and give rise to the Seeds-ke-dee Agie, or Green River, the great Colorado of the West, that empties its current into the Gulf of California."

The Independent Oregon Colony hurried west, of course, striking the Little Sandy Creek later that day.

The Reverend E. E. Parrish had traversed South Pass a few days before, remarking on August 23: "Today we passed the highest ground on the route, summit of the Rocky Mountains and immediately commenced going down hill toward the west, leaving the eastern waters forever and commenced the use of the western waters, which we shall use the balance of our time. Atlantic water forever gone and Pacific water to be our future drink. This road this afternoon has been fine all the time, a continual plain." He also noted that with the rise in elevation, the mornings and evenings were cool, and he often noted ice in the water buckets at dawn.

All the while, a few days behind Parrish and his group, Henry Sager, still in the convoy that included the Shaw and Morrison families, was rapidly fading.

On the evening of August 28, the group "made a short drive," according to Minto, and crossed the shallow, swift waters of the Green River, setting up camp beneath a large stand of cottonwoods.

"Nature refused to stand any more," Catherine Sager recalled, "and he became bedfast but being conscious of the helpless condition of his family—out upon a long and perilous journey far from home and relatives going to a strange and savage country—being aware of all this he made a determined struggle for life. Alas, to no avail."

He lay in the wagon, barely able to move, and turned to Catherine, who lay next to him, and said, "Poor child! What will become of you?"

Catherine recalled William Shaw coming to the tent that evening. "Captain Shaw found him weeping bitterly. He said his last hour had come, and his heart was filled with anguish for his family. His wife was ill, the children small, and one likely to be a cripple. They had no relatives near, and a long journey lay before them. In piteous tones he begged the Captain to take charge of them and see them through. This [Shaw] stoutly promised."

Shaw also remembered the scene. "He called me to his wagon just before he died, and asked me if I would see his family on to Oregon," Shaw recalled. "I told him I would do the best I could."

Catherine also remembered what Henry Sager said to Naomi that night, which were probably the last words Sager said before slipping into a state of semiconscious delirium that lasted the rest of the night. "Although a child at the time the conversation made an impression upon my mind that time has not affected," she recalled. "This is the advice he gives his sorrowing wife. 'Go to Dr. Whitman,'"—the missionary who had crossed the Rockies in 1836 with his wife Narcissa and set up a mission, Waiilatpu, near present-day Walla Walla, Washington, to work with the Cayuse Indians—"'and I am sure he will befriend you.'"

That evening, as the rest of the families were settling in, Sally Shaw approached John Minto. He recalled, "At this camp I was again called upon for extra duty on account of the sick. About bedtime I was appealed to by Mrs. Shaw to sit up part of the night with Mr. Sager, who was very ill; and she said that Mrs. Sager was nearly down sick herself, but would see to giving her husband medicine"—likely laudanum—"if I would watch in his tent and inform her at the time, to administer it. The sick man was either wholly or partly unconscious from high fever, and did not during the night ask for anything. On the two or three times I wakened her, his wife responded each time as though she was in fear that he was dead. She would call him by name and he would receive the medicine, yet seem hardly conscious. There was no one to relieve me, and I kept vigil all night, suffering from inability to help this life, which seemed to be burning away."

Their treatment of Sager in his final hours fits squarely with what Dr. Gunn recommended for someone intractably suffering from bilious fever in his book *Domestic Medicine* (presumably after the patient had been copiously bled and flushed with clysters), had Naomi bothered to thumb through Sager's worn copy: keep the patient comfortable, the surroundings quiet and dark, and don't talk too much. "The misfortune in the country is, that many persons who come to sit up with the sick, talk so incessantly as to prevent the sick person from having the repose necessary for promoting a speedy recovery: —and it may be important to remark, that whenever laudanum or opium is given, the person must be kept undisturbed and perfectly quiet."

By morning Henry Sager was dead. It was a cloudy dawn, and a cool breeze riffled the waters of the Green River.

Shaw, Minto, and Morrison dropped a large cottonwood tree, and then split it lengthwise, carving out the pithy core to shape a crude coffin. Minto doesn't say who dug the grave, but it was probably him, since he'd dug most of the others. The sandy soil of the river bottom was loose, though, and by the middle of the morning they had placed Sager's body in the coffin and lowered it into the hole, not marking the grave in any way so as to disguise it from looters. If anyone read a verse over the grave, it wasn't recorded. The man most capable of providing a eulogy, the Reverend E. E. Parrish, was ahead of the Sager, Shaw, and Morrison group of wagons by two days and was camping a few miles away, also on the banks of the Green.

"I well remember the anguish of his wife at the thought of leaving him there and the fear that the high waters would wash away the grave," Catherine recalled of the funeral.

William Shaw noted simply: "One man died on the Green River by the name of Sager."

14

THE GREAT REGISTER OF THE DESERT

As we crossed the border into Wyoming, the land continued to rise steadily. Each town we passed registered a slightly higher elevation so that by the time we reached Fort Laramie National Historic Site in eastern Wyoming, at the junction of the Laramie and North Platte Rivers, we were over four thousand feet above sea level and still climbing. This spot is a pilgrimage site to Oregon Trail enthusiasts because of the significant contribution it made to the fur trappers and the overland emigrants from the 1830s through 1890. And its sprawling buildings reconstructed to minute detail still convey the same sense of isolation, so it's not hard to envision the sense of relief the emigrants must have felt to arrive at an outpost of civilization in this lonely country.

But, really, we had grown so weary of historic sites that we couldn't quite bear the strain of having to make a full-blown homage visit: camping for a few days, peering into carefully preserved (and lifeless) buildings, and listening to people in period clothing speak in folksy tones about the candles they were dipping or the flax seed they'd eaten for breakfast. It wasn't just the kids who'd developed an aversion to too many living-history lessons. The bringing to life of history is every reenactor's challenge. The fort's buildings have all been painstakingly reconstructed, and they present an impressive accomplishment of historic accuracy and detail. But life in the fort in the old days—the brawling fur traders; the free-for-all, multiracial orgies; the drunken reverie played out each evening to the strains of jaunty fiddle music—sounded like much more fun than what we found in the stolid buildings of today's Fort Laramie. When Francis Parkman visited Fort Laramie just two years after the Independent Oregon Colony, in 1846, he described a lively, raucous place: "Numerous squaws, gaily bedizened, sat grouped in front of the apartments they occupied," he wrote in *The California and Oregon Trail*, "their mongrel offspring, restless and vociferous, rambled in every direction through the fort; and the trappers, traders, and *engagés* of the establishment were busy at their labor of their amusements."

Doing our best, we sat in the fort's saloon and drank sarsaparilla sodas, but after more than a month on the road we too felt like restless and vociferous mongrels and longed to be free of the watchful eyes of the docents. Acting on the urge we all felt, Oakley broke from the saloon at a run and, after splashing through a drainage ditch, led me on a high-speed ramble throughout the fort, cutting between buildings and straight through off-limits exhibits, ducking velvet ropes at full speed, so that I got a full tour of the premises in about one-tenth of the time as was likely recommended. By the time I caught him we had seen about enough anyway.

We pressed on for Ayres Natural Bridge, now a state park, which was a hidden jewel along the Oregon Trail, a place where the emigrants began to get a glimpse of the spectacular West.

Just past Douglas, Wyoming ("Home of the Jackalope"—a jackrabbit with antelope antlers), we turned south off the highway onto a dirt road that ended right at the base of one of the dozens of jagged peaks that make up the Black Hills. Their dark gray peaks, though not tall, perhaps twelve hundred feet, were virtually bare, except for tufts of sagebrush, and steep, and appeared to have been violently rent, as if from broken glass. We could see great streaks of white-and-gray granite, the stratified layers that formed the jagged cliffs, and beyond, the snowcapped peaks of the Medicine Bow Mountains that John Charles

Frémont had explored in 1843, following his journey to the Wind River Range the previous year.

In the 1840s, the site was also an oasis to emigrants who had long since grown weary of the parched landscape. The Trail passes within a mile of this deep canyon and travelers, having heard of the magical lure of the place, would take side trips into the canyon to marvel at the bright color and lushness. We were only too happy to discover that the park remains a veritable oasis of lush greenery. La Prele Creek is a shallow sparkling stream that drops straight from the Black Hills, cutting a deep swath through brilliantly red rock cliffs. The reason for the site's name is that at one point the creek cuts straight through a cliff in a tall arch, some thirty feet high and fifty feet wide, that was carved by eons of erosion. As we entered the park itself, dropping into canyon along a twisting road, we noted how green the grass was and how carefully manicured the entire campground was, as if a landscaper from Long Island's North Shore had escaped the suburbs and was hiding out in the Wyoming high country, unable to resist his hedge trimmer and lawnmower. We set up our tent at the base of the arch on a carpet of green grass within ten feet of the sparkling creek.

After the open space of the prairie and mountains, the canyon had a strange energy. We were encapsulated, sheltered from the weather, but there was also a strong feeling of vulnerability that comes with being inside a narrow canyon, as though we were being watched. It was beautiful, but it was eerie.

Indians feared the place, since a young brave supposedly fell from the top of the arch and was killed in the creek. It was thereafter considered taboo to enter. Consequently, trappers and early explorers used the canyon as a safe harbor from Indian raids.

Before the modern road was built, the arch was difficult to reach because of the overgrown brambles that surrounded it. The earliest written record of travelers visits was left by New Orleans newspaperman Matthew Field, who, with Steadman Tilghman, a wealthy Baltimore doctor, and Scottish nobleman William Drummond Stewart, stopped here in 1843. "Rode off in advance of the camp with Sir William to visit a remarkable mountain gorge," wrote Field on July 12, 1843, "a 'natural bridge' of solid rock over a rapid torrent, the arch being regular as tho shaped by art—30 feet from base to ceiling, and 50 to the top of the bridge—wild cliffs 300 feet perpendicular from us, and the noisy current swept along among huge fragments of rock at our feet. We had a dangerous descent, and forced our way through an almost impervious thicket, being compelled to take the bed of the stream in gaining a position below."

Tilghman himself was impressed, writing, "The 'Natural Bridge' is perhaps one of the greatest curiosities we saw in the whole of our interesting expedition. It is at the extremity of a valley formed of an immense chasm, with rocky sides—and a perpendicular height of 300 feet—through which flows a beautiful crystal stream."

I had just dropped onto the grass and was marveling at the beautiful sound that a cold can of beer makes when the sun, wind, and dust have turned your throat as dry and parched as trail ruts—*Pfffsst!*—when up sauntered a tall, skinny man in a foam-fronted baseball cap that read, "Born to hunt, forced to work." He was wearing a plaid shirt, and the cuffs of his tight jeans came within a few inches of the tops of his shoes, showing his white socks. He was walking on the tips of his toes, so that each step was a quick bounce. If he owned any teeth, he wasn't wearing them. I lowered the can.

"Just so you know," he lisped, "there are raccoons here the size of dogs."

This was the Helpful Neighbor. Every campsite has one, ready to lend a hand and offer to haul wood for you or give advice on the best fishing hole or tell you exactly how to light a fire. Unlike in the suburbs, there are no fences or doors that surround each campsite, of course. When you're camping you can't get rid of Helpful Neighbor just by thanking him and closing the door behind you. There's nothing stopping him from settling in and rendering advice on everything. This fellow's name was Charlie. And he spent the next half hour offering helpful information, running back and forth between our site and his own, which was only a few steps away. He was soon followed by an enormous woman with breasts the size of watermelons. Her name was Tracy, and she was as bossy and huge as Charlie was skinny and frail.

"You'd better not leave any of that food out tonight," Tracy bellowed in a voice that echoed against the canyon walls, pointing to our cooler and food crates like a general. "The 'coons here are mean."

I realized with horror she wasn't wearing a bra, and her pendulous breasts swung dangerously with each command. She barked an order at Charlie, who skittered back to their campsite as though he'd been whipped. I suddenly suspected why her meek companion didn't have any teeth. This woman was obviously in charge and she looked capable of great violence.

They were from nearby Douglas and were just up for a few days to "enjoy the outdoors," she said.

"You're here for a few *more* days?" I asked.

"Nope—leaving tomorrow," she said, "but if you need anything, just let me know." She strode back to their picnic table where they had a little campfire. Their car was a tiny dust-covered Geo Metro hatchback with wheels the size of a wheelbarrow's.

Five minutes later Charlie was back, this time carrying a hatchet. He offered its use for gathering firewood, which I realized would be convenient, since we had neither hatchet nor saw, and there didn't seem to be any dead wood in the immediate vicinity.

"Thanks," I said, "that's very nice." When I reached for the hatchet, though, he kept a firm grip and said he would come with me.

"Oh," I said, briefly picturing the headlines in the local paper the next day: CAMPGROUND MASSACRE: PRISON ESCAPEE HACKS EASTERNER TO DEATH IN BLACK HILLS; TOWN SHERIFF SAYS, "HE SHOULD HAVE KNOWN BETTER THAN TO WANDER OFF WITH THIS GUY."

He seemed harmless enough, though, and, if anything, capable of only killing someone with puppylike kindness. "Okay," I answered, telling Leah I'd be back in a few minutes, adding in a whisper, "Call the cops if I'm not back by dark."

I survived wood gathering with Charlie, and we enjoyed a blissful evening, falling asleep to the burbling of the creek. Aware of the creek's proximity, however, and remembering how Hannah Louïse Sager escaped from her tent the night her baby sister was born, Leah and I were careful to position ourselves across the mouth of the tent that night so that Oakley didn't go on a midnight ramble himself.

The following morning, just after six o'clock, we were awakened by angry shouting and the slamming of car doors. We could hear Tracy tearing into Charlie for something—her booming voice drowning out the burbling of the creek. She was obviously furious.

"Do you think they've lost their keys?" I asked Leah in my morning croak. "They won't be able to leave."

"Oh no," she groaned.

"It's *my* fuckin' CD!" *Slam!* "Guns 'n' Roses is *mine*!" Slam! After each outburst I could hear Charlie mumble something, and then this would be followed by another violent tirade from Tracy. I peered out of the tent window and saw him sitting on a corner of the picnic table and grinning toothlessly. He was taunting her.

It was a rude awakening, but at least they hadn't lost their keys. They tore off a few minutes later, their tiny Geo careering dangerously on two wheels as it rounded the corner, Tracy behind the wheel and Charlie sitting meekly in the passenger seat.

We enjoyed a few days of relaxation at Ayres Natural Bridge. The kids played in the creek, we visited the town of Douglas for milkshakes at a vintage lunch counter, and Leah spent a few quiet hours painting the red cliffs in her sketchbook. Oakley's favorite adventure was to escape from our site and go into the caretakers' garage and sit on their ATV. On the morning of our first full day there, we were just wondering where he'd gone when Oakley and one of the caretakers hove into view mounted on the machine. Oakley was sitting on the man's lap, his hands on the handlebars, with a grin that seemed to wrap all the way around his head. The caretaker, a wizened little man who, with his wife, was responsible for the careful grooming of the park, explained that he'd found Oakley sitting on the machine and thought he'd take him for a ride. Despite his mischievousness, people were often charmed by Oakley's friendliness and offered to give him whatever he asked. Since he wasn't shy, he often earned shares of people's dinner, the use of their kids' toy tractors, or, in this case, a ride through a Wyoming canyon on the most amazing invention that a three-year-old could imagine. The man's name was Wendell Manning, and he said he grew up in Ohio and "escaped West" as soon as he could and has never been back. "I just love it out here," he said. He and his wife live here year-round, despite the fact that the park closes in September and the winter's snows often mean they can't leave the canyon for days on end. The two of them have been here since 1970. Manning said he spends winters carving replicas of wagons: buckboards, chuck wagons, sheepherder's wagon, prairie schooners, and Conestogas. He showed me his collection, which was displayed throughout his house, and I admired the craftsmanship and imagined the long stretches of winter time that allowed this sort of detailed work. The solitude of their home in the canyon was absolute.

Later that day, after giving Oakley a cozy bottle, I put him in the three-wheel stroller and wandered the paths of the canyon. The red cliffs were ablaze in color; the sky lapis lazuli. It was like exploring a well-landscaped Garden of Eden.

Taking the car the following afternoon I found where the Trail crosses the road and tried to find the grave of a boy named Joel Hembree, a nine-year-old emigrant who in July 1843—a year before the Independent Oregon Colony passed here, and just a week after the visit by Field, Tilghman, and Stewart—had been killed near here when he fell from his family's wagon and the wheels passed over his chest. He was standing on the tongue, his hands on each of the oxen's rumps, when his feet slipped and he fell to the ground, the wagon passing over him. He was buried in a coffin made from a drawer from the family's bureau. I stopped the car and, using my old brass Army Corps compass for direction, wandered up and down the faint lines of ruts that cut across the range, carefully following the directions in Franzwa's *Maps of the Oregon Trail* guidebook. I didn't find the grave, which was moved in the 1970s by preservationists to a site away from where a rancher wanted to build a dam. The grave was actually discovered by this rancher in 1961, when he was moving rocks and noticed an odd-shaped pile. Upon examination he noted the following: "1843 J. HEMBREE." As was common in those days, the number "4" was reversed. The rancher contacted a historian, who tracked down the name, identified Hembree as a member of the 1843 Applegate emigration, and found a diary entry from an eyewitness to the accident. "He fell off waggon tung & both wheels run over him," it said.

The accident occurred on July 18. The company camped that evening at La Prele Creek. The boy was still alive but unconscious. He lingered throughout the night but finally died at two o' clock the following afternoon. He was buried on July 20, and the company moved on that same afternoon.

I read that when his body was reburied, the excavators built a new pine box and dug a grave atop a grassy hill. I never discovered the grave, but I found myself, not for the first time, choked with emotion as I wandered the tall grass and thought about the boy and his grieving parents burying their son in the middle of this lonely place. The only sound was the rushing of the wind in the grass. Even the birds were silent that afternoon.

On our final day at Ayres Natural Bridge, we decided to hike to the top of one of the Black Hills, which are mostly Bureau of Land Management land and are therefore accessible to all. After striking our tent early that morning and enjoying a last meal in the shady cool of the canyon, we drove to the main road, cut through a rancher's gate, closing it behind us, and parked in the company of about twenty-five Black Angus cattle gathered around a water trough. They regarded us with suspicion, huffing their noses and staring at us with their enormous watery eyes, but keeping their distance. We, too, were wary, since we noticed at least one bull in the herd and wanted to be sure he didn't think we were interested in mating with his companions. We skirted the herd and followed the fence line south where the hill rose steeply from the range. Right at the base we discovered a full skeleton of a cow, its skull and other bones picked clean and bleached white by the sun. The kids gathered a pile of bones to keep and that we would pick up on our return.

As we began to climb, Leah and I both found that we were short of breath. We were over a mile high here, and, unlike the slow pace of the emigrants, had come up into the high country fairly quickly over the past few days. We were paying the price. The children seemed unaffected and proved strong hikers that morning, spiritedly dashing up the hillside and through the sagebrush like a herd of jackalopes. We made it to the top after an hour and enjoyed a snack and drink of water, wondering at the views of the forbidding Medicine Bow Mountains to the south and the jagged peaks of the Black Hills that stretched east-west to the horizon.

Back at the bottom we picked up our pile of bones and, after I mounted the skull on the car's grill, we took off for our next stop about two hours away: Independence Rock. U.S. Highways 25 and 220 follow the banks of the North Platte River through this part of Wyoming, curving northwest and then southwest as the river cuts through the red buttes of Casper (Dick Cheney's hometown). We sailed through Casper, despite the fact that we were told an impressive Oregon Trail Museum there was one of the very best, picking up the two-lane highway that cuts across the most barren lands we'd yet seen. The largest ranch in Wyoming, the Pathfinder (named for John Charles Frémont), owns most of the land here, and we could see, in addition to numerous prong-horned antelope, groups of Angus scratching at the parched earth along the highway.

Independence Rock was a psychological milestone to the emigrants; it was where they felt the transition from one "road"—the Platte River Road—to another, that which led over the Rockies and down the other side.

Emigrants who passed before may have thought Independence Rock resembled the shape of a turtle or a cut apple sitting on a plate. To me, though, as we approached the Rock on US 220, the swooping, sensuous curves suggested nothing but the hips and shoulders of a woman lying on her side—an enormous snoozing desert nymph. As we pulled into the parking area on the west side, Finn said it looked like a "giant's toe" and Jonah a "sleeping turtle."

Our arrival at the Rock coincided with that of a group of about two hundred or three hundred teenagers wearing period clothing, who lay about in the shade of the visitor center buildings, their faces red and flushed, gasping. I asked them why they were dressed like this and why they looked so weary.

"Martin's Cove," one girl answered.

"Excuse me?"

"We just hiked Martin's Cove—pushing the carts—twenty-four miles—three days," was all she could manage before closing her eyes and heaving another great sigh.

A chubby boy with bright red cheeks sitting next to her croaked, "I've got blisters on top of my blisters."

I learned from one of the few adult chaperones that they were Mormons from Coeur d'Alene, Idaho, reenacting an epic survival story from the Mormon migration. The kids had just completed a three-day reenactment, pushing loaded handcarts through the desert near Devil's Gate, just a few miles south of here, as a way to connect with their ancestral roots. Their buses sat idling at the curb, and they were using Independence Rock's water pump and patches of shade to full effect before hitting the road for their twelve-hour homeward journey.

In October 1856, a group of Mormons, the Martin company, passed Independence Rock and Devil's Gate, where the Sweetwater River passes through a cleft in the rock hills when they were forced to stop for the night. Like most Mormon migrations of the era, they were pushing little handcarts, which were loaded with their meager belongings, instead of driving oxen, in an attempt to reach the growing community of Salt Lake before winter closed in. This was a method the Mormons had perfected. They found they could travel faster and also avoid the crowded and overgrazed Oregon Trail, which was the route followed by Gentiles. When the Trail followed the south bank, they followed the north, and vice versa. The Martin company had departed Iowa desperately late in the season, and their stores were virtually gone by the time they reached the Sweetwater. They were underdressed and were on the verge of starving, when, on the evening of October 19, 1856, a terrible winter storm hit, dropping some eighteen inches of snow in a few hours. They were trapped, and huddled together as close as possible in a desperate attempt to keep themselves warm on the open prairie.

Brigham Young, who by this time had set up a Mormon establishment at Salt Lake, had heard in early October that a party was still traveling to Salt Lake, and he knew they would not make it in time. He sent out a rescue party to bring supplies to the Martin Party, which was by this time spread out over sixty miles, between the red buttes, near present-day Casper, and Devil's Gate.

The rescue party arrived with supplies, but the group was so weak, and there were so many children, that swift passage was impossible.

"There were old men pulling and tugging their carts," reported rescuer Daniel W. Jones describing the scene he saw when he arrived with supplies, "sometimes loaded with a sick wife or children, women pulling along sick husbands; little children six to eight years old struggling through the mud and snow. . . . The provisions we [had] amounted to almost nothing among so many people, many of them now on very short rations, some almost starving. . . . The company was composed of average emigrants; old, middle-aged and young women and children. The men seemed to be failing and dying faster than the women and children."

On the night the storm hit, fifty-six people died of the combined effects of starvation and exposure in the little cove of rock now called Martin's Cove. They remained trapped for days. Survivors told horror stories of being trapped in an area where they couldn't bury their dead. That night, as the group huddled to keep warm and one by one their companions died, the dead were dragged over a snowy berm and buried in the snow. Survivors described the sight of hungry wolves feeding on the fresh corpses.

Throughout our journey, I was continually amazed by the Mormon devotion to their history. This was the latest example, and I began wandering the groups of kids asking questions.

"Did you push the carts?" I asked a group of wan-looking teens.

"Yes!" said one girl, who was still wearing her sun bonnet despite sitting in the shade.

"Did you get help from the adults?"

"Nope—the ma's and pa's don't push," she said.

We had arranged with the state of Wyoming for special permission to camp for three days at the Rock. There is not a proper campsite here, only a turnoff in the road with a few signs about the Rock's history. The Rock stands alone in a vast bowl, more than twenty miles in each direction to the closest store and an hour's drive in either direction for any real town. After leaving the Mormons, we drove down a dirt road to the back side of the Rock, over a cattle grate and through a barbed-wire fence, and set up our tent on the east side of the Rock so that we were completely screened from the highway and its visitors. We also hoped it would serve as a giant wind break against the forceful western winds that were screaming across the valley from the Rattlesnake Hills beyond. From this side, the landscape was identical to what it was in Frémont's day, save the barbed-wire fences of the Pathfinder Ranch running away for miles to the east, since we couldn't see the highway and no trees have sprung up around the banks of the Sweetwater in the intervening 160 years.

When Frémont camped here on August 1, 1842, about a mile downstream from where we were, he noted the barren, treeless landscape. "There was no timber of any kind on the river," Frémont had written, "but good fires were made of drift wood, aided by the *bois de vache*." We too saw buffalo chips, but they were not from buffalo per se but from what Edward Abbey referred to disparagingly as "slow elk"—Black Angus beef cattle. We had clearly entered cattle country.

Neither did we find any firewood, but Finn and Raven happily trotted off with the three-wheel stroller to collect a pile of the flaky cow chips, which dotted the ground like rounded landmines and had dried to the consistency of dense, stale bread. Finn and Raven were wearing their pioneer hats and cut quite a picture: Raven in her pink-flowered bonnet and not wearing a shirt so her tanned body glowed golden in the sun; Finn, wearing his felt crusher with the stampede string looped under his chin, and his long blond hair blowing out in the breeze. I watched them wander off together along the base of Independence Rock, bending over now and then and tossing their quarry in the stroller. After about twenty minutes they returned triumphant, the stroller piled high. Never before was a father as proud.

Leah had wandered off and discovered the Sweetwater River and announced that we all needed to come swimming. The river was fantastically beautiful. None of us took off our clothes; we waded in and rolled around in the water fully clothed, splashing and playing. It was the most pleasant temperature. We scrubbed the sand from our hair and ears and rinsed out our clothes. We lay on our backs looking up at the sky and floated along in the gentle current.

That night, as the stars came out in the most impressive display we'd seen yet since this was our first night camping in such open country, we had a blazing campfire of buffalo chips and a handful of sage and juniper branches we had found. The temperature dropped precipitously as the sun fell below the Rattlesnake Hills, so we huddled around the roaring fire. I had become expert at baking cakes in the Dutch oven, but this was my chance to match my skills to the emigrants, since I would be using *bois de vache* for the first time. The trick was in managing the heat. It's easy to burn a cake to carbon within minutes, but, after mixing a basic cake recipe and oiling the bottom and sides of the heavy pan, I carefully separated the coals from the main fire, and placed the oven on top. I then scooped up a bunch of coals and placed them evenly on the heavy lid. Twenty minutes later the sweet smell of cake mixed with the smell of the campfire, admittedly acrid as a result of both sage and cow chips, and the kids were clamoring for a slice.

As we were eating our cake, we could hear the antelopes snorting in the dark as was their habit when strangers approached and camped in their territory. They would come to within several hundred feet of our campfire and watch us, pawing the earth and letting out occasional snorts that sounded like forceful sneezes. This same curiosity had been their undoing when the emigrants went hunting. But we had no guns, and we enjoyed seeing their lurking shadows and glowing eyes.

I pointed out to my fellow Scorpios in the family, Finn and Raven, our constellation rising low in the southern sky: Antares the brightest star. The Little Dipper was right overhead, its brightest star Dubhe pointing to Polares behind us. These would have been the same configuration of stars that Frémont used to pinpoint his position at the Rock in 1842.

It was a magnificent night: no noise of highway traffic or coal trains, the only sound the crackling campfire and the rush of wind and huffing of antelopes; above the twinkling stars, and, next to us in the dark, the comfort and closeness of this giant rock.

The following morning we scaled the Rock and hunted around for names, hoping to find some trace of the Independent Oregon Colony. I knew it was unlikely; they had barely paused at the Rock on their journey, stopping only long enough to water their stock in the river before pressing on to Devil's Gate five miles to the west. But still, there's something about all those names, many dating to the 1840s and '50s, that inspires something of the treasure-hunt mentality. The oldest name we found was on a boulder facing east, just a few yards from where we pitched our tent: Jas. Bacon-47.

"It's like walking in the footsteps of ghosts," said one tourist, recorded by the author Levida Hileman in her book about Independence Rock and Devil's Gate, *In Tar and Paint and Stone*. Hileman indexed all the extant names on the Rock during a survey prior to publication of her book in 2001. She found some two thousand names. She says that the Indian pictographs mentioned in Matthew Field's journals from 1843 have since washed away. When I reached Hileman by phone, she said the significance of the Rock to the Indians was similar to that of the emigrants. During the course of her research, she interviewed a Shoshone woman about the drawings Field saw. The woman said they were likely messages from one Indian to others coming later about the number of days' journey to certain hunting grounds.

Around 10:00 a.m. I put a snack and bottle of water in my knapsack with my bird book, laced up my hiking boots, and then trotted off southward toward a range of granite outcroppings about a mile south of Independence Rock. I wanted to get a bird's-eye view of the Rock in relation to the Oregon Trail and see it in context alongside the Sweetwater River and in the middle of the big valley cradled by the Rattlesnake Hills. As I trotted over a little bridge that crossed the Sweetwater, doing my best Famous Shoes imitation to make the most of my scant time alone, I startled a group of about ten Angus bulls who were lingering in the river. They snorted and bolted, which is always a funny sight, an animal of that size making sudden movements. When they saw what had startled them, they grew curious and started trotting after me, lumbering along the riverbank and then splashing across. It made me run a little faster.

I trotted along a fence line of the Dumbell Ranch, seeing their brand on a fencepost. To strengthen the gateposts, someone had built a Spanish windlass, using what looked like a cow's femur as the twisting pole.

Within a minute I saw a stag bolt from the trail ahead of me, bounding across the range in great leaps. He stopped about a half-mile away on a rise to look at me, before bounding away behind the hills I was hoping to climb. When I got to this spot I could see his prints in the sandy soil.

As I started to ascend the rocky hill, and despite being a mile away, I could hear voices of people climbing the Rock. I turned and looked through my binoculars and at that instant heard a frustrated scream that I recognized as Oakley's. I could see the five of them, Leah restraining Oakley from some dangerous stunt, climbing too high, perhaps.

I scrambled over huge granite boulders the size of dump trucks to the top of the rocky hill. The ridge itself is like a globular drip castle, all rounded and bulgy. I was perhaps five hundred feet higher than the surrounding valley. I sat at the top and ate my snack, looking out over the Sweetwater Valley, the river a serpentine wriggle, and the Rattlesnake Hills. From this distance, the Rock clearly appeared as the anomaly it is. A result of exfoliation, it had heaved to its current position on this otherwise barren and featureless valley, many millions of years ago. It's easy to see why the emigrants came this way: the geology is a veritable east-west highway.

Trotting down the north side, I thought of all the warnings people give about rattlesnakes and how you don't want to surprise them. Coming from up high, I couldn't help but surprise a snake. As a result, I thought a snake was hiding behind every bush, and as I hopped on a rock I heard a dry rattle at my feet and did a panicked dance, hopping from one foot to another as the rattling got louder. I looked down and saw a dry juniper branch stuck to my laces. I descended safely.

When I met the river I surprised a duck hiding in the grasses of the bank. It quacked and hurried off, surprising a large fish, which scooted across the shallow river to the bank. I was reminded of the children's book, *A Fly Went By*, a series of misunderstandings that leads to one animal scaring the next.

I crossed the river without removing my shoes and sloshed back to the campsite in time to make lunch.

That afternoon we met a photographer, a fellow name Jim Henderson, who was cataloguing the names also, except he was using a specialized photography technique that he had developed expressly for this kind of work. He was heavily laden with gear. Several camera housings draped from his shoulders, and he was wearing kneepads because of all the time he would spend stooped on the rock.

Faded and weathered pictographs are hard to record with traditional photography, Jim told me. Natural lighting produces inconsistent color and harsh lighting conditions that prevent color photographic films from capturing faint pigment colors. To combat this, Jim developed "cross-polarization" photography to draw out the pigment and the irregularities in an etching that might be invisible or illegible to the naked eye but becomes visible through the filters. As a result, he does most of his photography at night so he can precisely control the level of lighting required. Funded by grant money, he has spent the past five years recording the etchings and markings of emigrants along the entire Oregon Trail—all two thousand miles of it. He expects to be involved for at least another year, he said, perhaps more. Jim also mentioned another study by a Yale graduate student to document the entire Oregon Trail using imagery technology that could pick up flakes of ferrous metals that shed from wagon wheels, thereby showing precisely where the wagons had passed.

This is the sort of obsessive behavior that I was coming to understand was common in Trail-inspired historians. His knowledge of the Trail was dizzying, and we happily traipsed behind him as he told stories and pointed out beautiful inscriptions.

Jim spent hours climbing around with us that day. He even showed us a hidden cave on the southern side of the Rock that was full of names, as legible as the day they were made, their serif fonts a marvel of penmanship and parsimony: BOWER JULY 11 AD 1847 and D. HOLADAY JULY 6TH 1856 and CHAMBERLAIN JULY 19 1849.

Modern names, some dated as recently as this summer, were sloppy and crude, obviously rushed. They were graffiti. You could trace the significance of the Rock to travelers by the dedication of their inscriptions. I asked Jim why he thought the early etchings and signatures were so carefully done. He said he thought they wrote the way they knew how to write, serifs and all.

But I didn't think that was it. The overland emigrants had a more refined sense of quality than we have today. These Renaissance men and women of the nineteenth century, who were comfortable in their bodies and physically skilled with hand tools, wouldn't dream of leaving their names in a slapdash manner. They were leaving their marks for posterity, and there was ceremony to observe. Besides, they had made the journey of their lifetimes, and this rock represented one of only three places on the Trail where every single overland traveler would pass between 1840 and 1861. South Pass and the North Platte corridor were the other two. The modern names were just people stopped along the highway to stretch their legs.

From the top we could clearly see trail ruts, sweeping away to the east along the green ribbon of the Sweetwater, and running straight west toward the cleft at Devil's Gate. The Trail fades into the shoulder of the east side of the highway, only to reappear fifty yards beyond.

That evening, as the sun set beyond the Rattlesnake Hills, we stood on top of the Rock in the warm wind as the sky turned into swirling hues of orange, red, and purple—and the stars came out, one by one.

15

EATING DUST

A Week on the Trail

BACK IN THE WINTER, when our trip across the country retracing the route of the Independent Oregon Colony was still months off, I had attempted to secure a week of time on a wagon train so that we could experience what it really felt like to travel, as a family, in the 1840s. I had thought that spending the summer traveling by car was hopelessly lame, and that even if we punctuated our driving with strenuous hikes, into the Rockies and along old Trail ruts, and camped along the way, we were still traveling in a machine that offered no connection whatsoever to the one experienced by the overland emigrants of the 1840s.

It started as a rumor, a group of people that swept into outback towns in Wyoming and Montana driving wagons and riding horses and were gone before anyone could ask their names. I had searched for them on the Internet, but all I found were schlocky tourist outfits that took passengers on wagon rides through pretty country, to be sure, but tended to be equipped with air-filled rubber wheels and served fine cuisine around the campfire to the tunes of paid musicians. These were what author Tony Horwitz described as "farbs" in his book about Civil War reenactors, *Confederates in the Attic*: people who wanted to get close to history without really feeling it. In other words, they were posers.

We needed authentic: the dust, the rattling of the wooden and steel wagons over stones and through ravines, the full effect of the blistering high-country sunshine in summer, the full misery.

Finally, after weeks of fruitless searching, I got a phone number—area code Wyoming, a good sign—from a museum curator in Missouri, who said he thought these guys were the real thing. This was a group of reenactors who each year spent part of their summer vacations retracing sections of the historic trails that cover the western United States: the Cherokee, Mormon, California, Overland, and, of course, the Oregon Trail. When I rang the number I heard the gravelly voice of the Old West, the kind you hear in dialects of old westerns. From his mouth the word *pretty* was "purty" and *creek* was "crick."

This was Ben Kern, the outfit's leader, also known as the "wagon master," and he said he had done all of the country's trails by wagon—"and the cutoffs"—and believed himself to have traveled more miles of trail than anyone else in history.

"Even more than Ezra Meeker!" he crowed.

Meeker was a young man in 1852 when his family went west to Puget Sound from their home in Indiana. More than fifty years later, in 1906, when he was still "hale and hearty" at seventy-six, he turned around and did it again, retracing the old Oregon Trail in reverse with a team of oxen and a covered wagon, telling stories of the pioneer days and earning a living by selling postcards and giving lectures. He walked and rode all the way to Missouri, raising money and erecting stone monuments along the trail, and eventually arrived in Washington, D.C., where he met President Theodore Roosevelt. He is a legend amongst trail enthusiasts.

Ben Kern said we were welcome to join him for a week this summer. They would be retracing a section of the Overland Trail in southern Wyoming, crossing the continental divide at Bridger Pass at more than seven thousand feet.

"Through some mighty purty country," Kern added.

While not part of the "Oregon Trail" per se, the Overland Trail was an alternate route that was established when the U.S. government set up "stages" along the route west to protect against Indian attacks. It runs straight across southern Wyoming and was used from about 1861 to 1869, when the transcontinental railroad eclipsed overland travel by animal. By the 1860s Indians were openly hostile to emigrants, since the overland travelers had destroyed much of the grazing land along the fertile Platte and Snake River Valleys and were making a sizable dent in the available game. Over the previous twenty years, there had been numerous attacks and counterattacks, mostly over the sorts of tragic misunderstandings like that at Ash Hollow involving the hotheaded young firebrand John Grattan.

"There's one other thing," I said to Kern that afternoon during our phone call in March. "I have a few children, um, four actually. Can they come?"

There was silence for a moment. "I reckon," he said. "We've had kids before. Long as you keep track of 'em."

"And I have a dog," I added, but I wasn't sure he heard me, since it sounded like the mountain wind was whistling through the mouthpiece of his cell phone, "a very small one."

We had arranged to meet along the side of State Highway 130, which cuts across a high, windswept tableland west of the Medicine Bow Mountains, on the morning of June 25. They would have arrived the following evening and be camped just off the highway. "You'll see our wagons," Kern had said.

That morning we had stopped at Devil's Gate, where the Church of Latter Day Saints maintains a visitor center, for a hike along the Sweetwater River. I particularly wanted to see the bucolic waters of the river where it cuts through the cleft in the rock of Devil's Gate proper, where John Minto had spent an idyllic afternoon fishing and where so many other emigrants marveled at the tall cliffs and the sparkling river.

We were not disappointed. The emerald waters poured from between the cliffs in deep swirling pools. We swam and climbed along the rocks until, where the river is squeezed at its narrowest and deepest, we could go no farther without risking the safety of the children. Jonah almost caught a green snake, but it slipped beneath the water and out of sight.

We saw numerous pioneer names etched in the rock or written in axle grease—some dating to the 1850s.

Back at the visitor center, I was cornered by an earnest elder wearing church-issue white shirt, black tie, black pants, and name tag who repeated the history of the Martin's Cove disaster and the Church's efforts to maintain the site as a connection with the Mormons' difficult past.

I was officially on "Oakley duty," since Leah had taken Raven to the bathroom, but whether it was this man's persistence or my weariness, I let my attention wander for a moment and Oakley slipped away—around the corner of the building. I finally broke free of the elder, who looked alarmed when I explained Oakley's Houdini-like tendencies, and, to his credit, he made immediately for the river. When I reached the corner of the building, I saw that Oakley had indeed vanished. We then spent the better part of a half hour searching the buildings and riverbank until a woman emerged from the office holding Oakley's hand. He was smiling innocently, and he was chewing something.

He had been hiding under a desk.

"He was eating cat food," she explained.

To the Mormons' great relief, we got in the car and sped away, humiliated yet again by the bizarre insouciance of our child, bound for Rawlins, Wyoming, about an hour's drive, where we would get a few last-minute supplies before our rendezvous with the reenactors. We would be fed on the journey, but we had been encouraged to bring "liquid refreshments."

U.S. Highway 287 actually crosses the Continental Divide twice in this short distance, once to enter the Great Divide Basin, and once to emerge from it on the southern side. The Basin is like a giant crater where the Divide splits, forming an enormous bowl and covering some five million acres of land known as the Red Desert—a unique high-desert ecosystem that is home to the largest migratory game herd in the Lower 48. We saw groups of pronghorn antelope everywhere, but we didn't see the storied elk herds. We didn't stop to explore; the thermometer on the car dash read 102 degrees.

After stopping at a supermarket in Rawlins we pressed on, southward toward the town of Saratoga, and, cresting a hill, we saw the white canvas covers of a circle of wagons just off the highway. An American flag streamed from the back end of one. A group of animals, mostly mules, judging from their ridiculous-looking long ears, were grazing close by in corrals of portable electric fencing. As I pulled to a stop and opened the door, we felt the full blast of the wind rip through the car. It was a harsh, dry wind, and there was no shelter from it here whatsoever. There were no trees. It swept unimpeded for miles across the open prairie. The only plant life was low sage scrub and an occasional tuft of brown grass. The desolation of the spot was complete.

As I shut the car off, Leah suddenly panicked.

"Twain, you don't know anything about these people! They're a bunch of kooks reliving the glory days of the West. This could be a disaster," she said. "If we join them, leaving our car here, we'll be trapped. For a week!" She paused for breath. "We're vegetarians! I doubt they even know what that means."

I stayed silent. This had been building all morning, but I had assured her that I had told them we didn't eat meat and that Rod Henderson, the "Trail Boss" and Ben Kern's partner, would be doing the cooking himself and had assured me we wouldn't go hungry. He had a kindly chuckle like Barney Rubble—*kew! kew!*—but Leah hadn't spoken to any of these guys. I could understand her position, yet here we were. We'd come all this way.

I couldn't calm her down. In fact, I made the mistake of suggesting that she stop "obsessing" about vegetarianism.

"Obsessing?!" She was furious, so I kept quiet and let her fume.

Usually, she's the one to charge off on new adventures, and I'm the one who tries to serve as a hapless sea anchor, attempting to slow the force of her pull into some crazy adventure, but I was witnessing a mother lion's protective instinct. Save his escape that morning, Oakley had been better, not throwing as many tantrums and enjoying being outside. The open air and the mountains could absorb his energy like the suburbs of Charleston can't. But his behavior was unpredictable.

We couldn't get out of the car and talk about it, our usual tactic to avoid the ears and unsolicited input from the kids, since we would then have to introduce ourselves to the reenactors, who were seated in the shade of their wagons about one hundred feet away, and staring at us.

The kids were similarly entrenched. Usually they jumped free of the car even before we shut down the engine, but they hadn't budged. They must have picked up on Leah's stress.

"Would you like to call Diana?" I asked.

Diana is a close friend from Maine, where we lived for a dozen years before Charleston, and I figured that Leah could use a soothing voice from far away who could hear her out. I knew Leah wouldn't quit; she couldn't live with herself, as she is susceptible to being labeled a chicken. But a familiar voice would be a great comfort. In the meantime, I said, I could go introduce myself and see about settling in.

I approached the group sitting in the shade and said hello. They were all wearing rancher clothing, mostly vintage Western: sweat-stained Stetsons, J. Peterman–style canvas overcoats, Wranglers, battered boots with spurs, and pearl-button shirts. They smiled pleasantly, even touching the brims of their hats, but didn't say much in return, only nodding their heads. They didn't get up to say howdy or shake my hand or offer a beer. They sat where they were and looked up at me mildly. I felt like an idiot, standing there with a goofy smile on my face, having just pulled up in an overstuffed station wagon with a load of kids. I may as well have been from Mars.

They had been on the trail for a week, and it was clear they'd developed that foxhole bond. I was an intruder. Worse, I knew they had seen my South Carolina license plate. I was from Back East and therefore couldn't be trusted. They gestured vaguely to a tent on the far side of the circle of wagons and said Ben Kern was inside.

The tent was a buckaroo-style canvas pyramid with a single wooden pole in the middle—the kind that's built less for rain than to withstand wind and dust storms. Through the flaps I could see a pair of old cowboy boots attached to a person with an old cowboy hat covering his face. He was either dead or taking a nap, so I left him alone.

I wandered around for a few minutes, saying hello to people who met my eyes, but it was clear these folks didn't know I was coming, and if they did, they didn't care. The Trail Boss, Rod Henderson, the one with the Barney Rubble laugh, was off shuttling cars and wouldn't be back for a while, they said. As I walked back to the car, wondering what I could say to Leah by way of comfort, I noticed she and the kids were gone.

I found them inside a covered wagon and was suddenly greeted by a rake-thin old man with teeth like a donkey. He stuck out a tanned hand.

"My name is Nebraska Bob," he said, "and this is my home."

He gestured for me to climb up into his wagon, which I did and where I found the kids all sitting on the side benches next to Leah, who was wearing a fixed smile that said, *He's cuckoo!*

We proceeded to get Nebraska Bob's life story: He'd grown up on a ranch ("not a farm; we don't call them farms in Nebraska") that has belonged to his family for generations. His son now operated the homestead ranch, the fifth generation. This wagon had belonged to his great-grandfather. He'd raised several kids, and he read his Bible every day. He pointed to a worn-out Bible on the wagon seat, its cover long-since missing, its pages creased and rumpled, making it look like the kind you see chained to public phones in Manhattan.

"What's your religion?" he asked. "Which church do you go to?"

I dodged the question and asked him more about himself and his wagon.

He had the whispery rancher voice that I had come to associate with the men of Nebraska and Wyoming who spent their lives outside: hushed, folksy, and entirely without pretense. This was the voice of the wind through sagebrush. The voice sounded familiar, comforting even. It took a moment to place it, but then it became clear: Ronald Reagan. I was sitting in a covered wagon in the Wyoming high country and speaking with the voice of Ronald Reagan coming from a man who said his name was Nebraska Bob and whose favorite subject was the Bible. Not surprisingly, his second favorite subject was Nebraska, and his conversations invariably included a discussion of the superiority of Nebraska's geography.

As we thanked him for the tour of his wagon and spilled out of it, he caught my hand.

"You need church," he said in a voice that mingled with the wind. "Your kids need church. It's a big responsibility having a family. They need the Lord!"

This could be a long week.

• • •

When we dropped from the wagon, an old man with a shuffling walk—his legs like a pair of parentheses—was coming toward us, raising a rooster-tail of dust because his feet never left the ground. He grinned broadly at me, exposing two gold-rimmed front teeth, and extended his hand. He pulled me close, peering deep into my eyes. He held my hand firmly and grinned at me wordlessly for several seconds. He had a wispy white beard and sparkling eyes with an intense gaze. His large hands were callused, his knuckles swollen and ragged; in fact, they looked as if they'd been trampled by a herd of buffalo, yet his grip was solid and unyielding. The most filthy, worn-out-looking cowboy hat I had ever seen appeared to be molded to his crown, and he was wearing tight black Wranglers secured with a belt buckle the size of a wagon wheel, and the same pair of boots I had seen protruding from the buckaroo tent. This was Ben Kern. I liked him instantly.

He apologized for not greeting me upon arrival. They'd been up since 4:00 a.m. and at his age—he was seventy-nine, three years older than Ezra Meeker when he'd crossed the country the second time, he pointed out—he'd had to take a nap or he'd fall asleep standing up.

"Like my mules yonder," he said, pointing to a pair of huge mules close by, their heads hung and their eyes half closed against the blazing sunshine, giving them a stupid expression.

Ben shuffled off to his truck and pulled out a spare buckaroo tent for us to use so our modern tent didn't pollute the traditional look of the camp. He said dinner would be served in an hour or so, and that we were to make ourselves comfortable. He introduced us to a woman in a long pioneer dress with a flower pattern and a cotton shirt with ruffled sleeves. This was Candy Moulton, who greeted me with the same enthusiasm he had, shaking my hand and Leah's and saying hello to each of the kids in turn.

Oakley was never shy about meeting people. Wearing his ten-gallon hat, he peered up at her with a huge grin and held out his hand. He always aped the meaningless greetings people give each other at such encounters: nice to meet you, how're you doing?, and so on. Except he didn't use actual words, just what they sounded like to him—a bunch of sounds offered in a cheerful tone.

"Rabida-rabida-rabida," he said to Candy, taking her hand and giving it an enthusiastic shake. "Hoo-ya-ya-hoo-ya-ya-ya."

Without a pause, she grinned back at him and returned the compliments just as heartily.

Candy helped us set up our buckaroo, and made us all feel welcome. She had accompanied Ben on numerous trail crossings and had written about many of them in Western magazines and books. She lived on a ranch with her family close by and was a walking encyclopedia of the Westward Expansion. I would learn during supper (from someone else) that she had recently won the prestigious Spur Award from the Western Writers of America for her biography of Chief Joseph.

After setting up our camp, we shuttled the car to the nearby town of Saratoga, where we could pick it up the next day for yet another shuttle. We would learn that these sorts of reenactments require nightmarish logistics. Rod and Doris, with the assistance of a retired archaeologist from Utah named Carl, would run support vehicles, meeting us at our campsites with the trailer that carried the porta-potty, a huge water tank, the horse feed, and all our food. Since we were crossing mostly private land, Ben has had to make certain concessions that landowners insist on, despite sacrificing elements of authenticity.

That evening, the awkwardness of the afternoon evaporated. Every man in the group, without fail, took off his hat when introduced to Leah. And Oakley wandered amongst them as if they were old friends, and he was their compañero. He shook hands again and again, offering the same hearty greetings to each in turn.

We were met cheerfully by Rod Henderson, the Trail Boss, and his wife Doris, and then fed a substantial meal of spaghetti. Leah leaned against me and whispered, "I feel better."

We also met Mike Schaffner, who was a dead-ringer for Teddy Roosevelt: the same round spectacles, the same brushlike moustache, and the same big grin. His horse Sparky was a huge black stallion that had been a wild mustang on the Wyoming range until he was captured and broken.

"Broke by that man right there," Mike said, pointing at a large Indian with long black hair. This was Vic, retired from the BLM where he'd worked his entire career, most recently managing the herds of wild mustangs that still run free on the Wyoming range.

Vic had few words but a big smile. When I had wandered the camp looking at all the wagons, I had come across Vic's. His mules were towing two wagons, a normal size prairie schooner and a "kooster," a two-wheeled wagon towed behind the four-wheeled one. What's this for? I'd wondered aloud. He'd just grinned, pulled the flap aside, and showed me an enormous cooler the size of a coffin. It was full of ice and beer.

Another Mike—I never did learn his last name—had a way of speaking out of the corner of his mouth, spitting out words like carpet tacks, that was both charming and cool as hell. If it came from anyone else, it would have seemed menacing, especially so because of the gravelly whisper that suggested years of smoking. But from Mike there was warmth in the voice. He'd described the recent birth of his grandchildren and lovingly said that, while his wife had gone up to be with their daughter for the birth, he was happy to wait until they could hold their heads up and find their way in the world.

"They don't do much when they're little pups," he said. "But we'll have a good time together when they get a little older." I didn't doubt it. He was from Sheridan, Wyoming, and recently retired after twenty-six years in the coal mines.

We also met Quackgrass Sally, a California transplant who operated a ranch in Montana north of Beartooth and Absaroka Ranges. Her last name never surfaced either, which I learned was sort of an in-joke with this group: not to ask one another's last names but to bestow a silly nickname. She had a big gap-toothed grin, a pair of Pippi Longstocking pigtails, and said her namesake was "a poisonous plant up in the Dakotas." She didn't say how it had been given.

We also met John and Jenny Stephenson—Wyoming natives—whose reserved manner I had originally mistaken for unfriendliness.

The most physically impressive figure was Cowboy Larry, a huge man with shoulders as broad as the back end of a wagon and meaty hands the size and weight of skillets. I felt like a child greeting him, my hand swallowed in his. He had a thick brushy moustache that entirely covered his mouth. He had been a "bulldogger" in college, someone who wrestles steers for sport, which meant he was regarded as just about the toughest kind of creature that existed in Wyoming. Bulldogging was supposedly born in 1903 when a cowpoke grew frustrated with a belligerent young steer that wouldn't go into its pen. The ranch hand, an Oklahoman named Bill Pickett, leaped from his horse, bit the steer on the lower lip like a bulldog, and then wrestled him to the ground where he could rope him. Ever since, bulldogging has been one of five major events at today's rodeos. Unlike bronc riding, which requires having a small and sinewy physical build, bulldogging requires bulkiness and brute force. Bulldoggers are the linebackers of the rodeo.

Each meal Larry piled jalapeños on his plate and proceeded to devour them like popcorn. That evening I tried one, carefully lifting my lips as I bit down, and my eyes instantly teared. I felt every bit as meek as I must have appeared standing next to him. Cowboy Larry would make the Marlboro Man shrivel in his Wranglers.

After supper the kids wandered along the abandoned railroad tracks that ran nearby, catching horny toads and bringing them to us for inspection, their fat little bodies immobile in the children's hands.

"Do your kids know about rattlesnakes?" asked Wyoming Mike, spitting the words from the corner of his mouth. He did not seem to be an alarmist or a safety maven like that woman back at Chimney Rock, so I must have flinched.

I said they did, but I'd warn them again.

"A bite from a prairie rattler won't kill 'em," he said, "but it would make 'em real sick."

"Have you seen any recently?" I asked.

"There was one outside my tent last night," he said.

"Outside your tent?"

"Yep, he was settin' in a hole about like this." He cupped his hands to form a circle about the size of a dinner plate.

"What did you do?"

He squinted his eyes a little and then said, "Let's just say he's still in that hole."

I learned later that he'd shot it with a pistol.

I hustled off to warn the kids—to make a lot of noise and not to put their hands in any holes.

After the dishes were cleaned up and the stove put away, everyone retreated to their tents. The sun was still fairly high in the sky. It was only a little after 7:00 p.m. yet everyone was clearly headed to bed. We hustled the kids into the tent also, not wanting to keep everyone awake with their noise. The kids were exhausted anyway and were soon asleep, but Leah and I lay awake for a while reading, since it was still broad daylight.

After it got dark, we spoke about the day. We were both worn out.

"Are you okay?" I whispered.

"Yes," she said. We were both silent for a while. We could hear the horses breathing close by, and the wind riffling the canvas of the buckaroo. "I want to be Quackgrass Sally," she said. I thought the same about Cowboy Larry.

We woke to the jingling of spurs and bridles and the shuffling of hoofs at 4:30 a.m. A few minutes later we heard Rod on his bugle, doing his best to huff out the strains of reveille, but it sounded sickly, like a dying elk's last lament, and was only recognizable because he'd warned us the night before what the tune would be. He broke into laughter—*kew! kew!*—and gave up on the bugle, saying, "Time to get up!"

It was still dark and freezing cold. We quickly got dressed, putting on everything we owned, covered on the outside with our blue raincoats to cut the wind. Team Wenzel was ready.

The stars were still twinkling when we emerged from the tent and moved around to keep warm. It had been made clear to us that, while we were welcome to observe everything, we were to keep clear of the horses and mules during feeding times. This was serious business.

We all huddled around the breakfast table eating breakfast burritos in the half-light of dawn—the jagged silhouette of the Medicine Bow Range looming, immense purple giants, to our east. Each of us was given one serving. After helping Leah serve the kids, I wolfed mine hungrily, looking forward to eating another four of five of these little treasures, when I realized that was it. Rod and Doris were packing up the chuck wagon. Breakfast was over, and everyone was moving for their horses, securing harnesses, lifting the wagon tongues in place, and climbing into their seats. I was famished, and it was only 6:30 in the morning—another six hours 'til lunch! A refrain from an Edward Abbey story rung in my cold ears: "Cowboys ride on a hard belly."

We were split up into two wagons: Leah, Jonah, and Finn in Ben Kern's stagecoach, and Oakley, Raven, and I with Nebraska Bob. I lifted Oakley and Raven in, and climbed into the seat to Nebraska Bob's left. Raven sat between us, and Oakley sat on my lap. A moment later, at 6:55, I heard Ben say, "Git up!" and his mules started to walk. He peeled out of the circle and started rattling down the dirt road that led to the highway. Each of us soon did the same, Nebraska Bob taking up the rear.

The noise the wagon made as it bumped along the road can only be described as horrendous. The steel rims of the wheels scraped over every bare rock with a shriek, far worse than fingernails on a chalkboard. The steel bands beneath the seat could only charitably be described as springs, since they did little to absorb the shock of each rut, rock, and divot in the trail. The backrest of the seat came halfway up my back, barely covering the lumbar, so we were forced to sit up straight. Within ten minutes, my back was stiff and I was shifting my weight to ease the growing numbness in my rear end. I pushed Oakley to the foot well, which was fine with him, since he could stand with his hands on the front of the wagon and watch the horses. Nebraska Bob told us their names were Speck and Skeeter, names that Oakley enjoyed saying.

As the sun rose over the mountains, we crossed the highway and joined the Overland Trail proper, a section of trail that sees little service in the way of motor vehicles. Cowboy Larry and Mike Schaffner were the scouts, riding in the saddle, while the rest of us sat in wagons. They would effortlessly hop off their mounts when we approached a gate, and then one of them would wait as we passed through so that he could shut the gate behind. There were six wagons in all, and it was a fine sight from the rear, seeing them roll away to the west in the morning sun along a trail that led through mile after mile of tall sagebrush.

Nebraska Bob waxed on about religion and the superiority of Nebraska's land for over an hour. His views were typical of the Christian extremist movement: keep out the Mexicans by building a big fence across the border, make those who are somehow legal learn English by declaring English the "national language," steamroll the A-rabs in the Middle East and teach them English, too. *His* ancestors were Norwegian and had assimilated without fanfare, blah, blah, blah. The funny thing was, he was so darned good-hearted and gentle, that his potentially combative words sounded absolutely harmless coming from his mouth. I told myself he was likely parroting Fox television or his preacher.

Besides, he was giving us a ride, and I was happy to absorb his rants with little objection. It was too beautiful a day. The cool air was pungent with the herbal aroma of sage, which covered the hills like a silvery-green carpet.

"[T]he whole air is strongly impregnated and saturated with the odour of camphor and spirits of turpentine, which belongs to this plant," Frémont wrote as he passed near here in August 1842. "This climate has been found very favourable to the restoration of health, particularly in cases of consumption; and possibly the respiration of air so highly impregnated with aromatic plants may have some influence."

After an hour of rolling along, the air was still cold, but the sun was soon warm on our skin and we could shed our jackets. Raven and Oakley discovered that they could have free run of the back of Nebraska Bob's wagon as we rattled along. We had been issued small bags of trail mix, and by 8:00 a.m. the two had eaten our whole supply, ferreting out the chocolate chunks and happily flinging the peanuts overboard.

We were warm and happy; the smells and sights of the open land were thrilling.

Inspired, I hopped off the back of the wagon—I knew better than to try and leap from the side of a moving wagon after reading of so many people injured by falling under wagon wheels—and trotted behind for a while. I could keep pace with an easy stride and thereby shake off the cramps in my back. Oakley and Raven would kneel in the back of the wagon grinning at me as I jogged along in an easy lope like Famous Shoes.

By 10:00 a.m. we had descended a steep hill that turned out to be the rim of the North Platte River Valley, about one hundred miles upstream (south) of where the original Oregon Trail emigrants of the 1840s turned west and joined the Sweetwater River. We were soon clomping over a little bridge to our campsite, where Doris, Rod, and Carl had already set up the chuck wagon for lunch. Ben circled the wagons in a grassy field, and by 11:00 everyone had removed harnesses, staked out their animals, and were cycling them to the water trough.

This would be our rhythm for the next six days: up before dawn, moving by 7:00, and set up camp by noon—finished traveling for the day. We would then sit around the campsite all day in the shade of our wagons.

It didn't seem like such an ambitious pace, but we could easily cover fifteen to twenty miles this way, which was as much as the early emigrants ever did in a single day driving oxen. Horses and mules travel at almost twice the rate of oxen at four or five miles per hour. Ben's use of mules and horses on this particular trail was historically accurate, too. By the time the Overland Trail was in use, in 1861, the stages were a day apart and could supply horses with grain, unlike the 1840s, when horses were only used for saddle work because of their inefficiency digesting trail scrub.

I understood why Rod and Ben had each suggested an ample supply of liquid refreshment: there wasn't a whole lot to do besides sit in the shade and throw back a few, but if Leah or I did this we wouldn't be much use caring for the kids. We were just wondering what to do with the next ten hours of daylight when John Schaffner walked up from the river. He was soaking wet from his boots to his hat.

"Just had my cowboy shower," he said, water running off the end of his nose and into his moustache. "Did my laundry and had my bath at the same time." He was grinning his TR grin.

Evidently he'd walked right into the river fully clothed and rolled around in the swift current for a while until he thought he was clean enough. "I left my hat on the bank, though," he said.

We did the same, rolling around in the cool water, which absorbed another hour, but it was a tedious afternoon. The only other excitement was when Oakley discovered a tin of horse salve in the stagecoach. We had been letting him play in it, not thinking there was anything he could get into, when he came walking toward us with his hands in the air. They were bright green from his fingertips to his elbows, and he had a worried expression on his face. It was nontoxic; in fact, Ben said it would ensure his hands wouldn't get sore the rest of the trip.

The trailer that Rod and Doris hauled behind their truck served as the center of the camp. It carried our drinking water, which offered easy access to all to water the horses and to fill our canteens for the day. Next to the water tank was the porta-potty. The walls were thin. When someone was using it, and someone else was filling their water bottle from the water tank, it sounded like the water tank was being filled from one end and emptied from the other.

The porta-potty offered other joys. Oakley discovered the toilet paper inside, and he also found that if he locked the door behind him he could unroll a whole roll of paper onto the floor before Leah or I managed to jimmy the lock and stop him. Everyone found this amusing the first time he did it. They laughed so hard he did it again and again, but people suddenly stopped laughing when Rod and Doris reported the toilet paper supply was running low. Instead, they started giving Leah and me terse "just-so-you-know" reminders when it looked like Oakley was headed for the trailer with a mischievous gleam in his eye.

That evening at dusk the sky above us was filled with diving and swooping birds. At first I thought they were bats, but they were too large. I asked John Stevenson. As a professional taxidermist (I found out later that he is considered one of the most well respected in the country), he was a virtual catalogue of knowledge about animals: tracks, habitats, their food preferences, and seemed to know every bird and their calls. He identified the swooping birds we saw as nighthawks. They flew around and around our campsite, their dark silhouettes clear in the evening sky, using their whiskerlike face feathers to eat mosquitoes.

Tuesday was a rest day. Since the journey required careful planning with private landowners and the shuttling of cars, these days of doldrums were necessary. And we were being led by a near-eighty-year-old. We decided to hop in the car and escape the camp to explore Saratoga. John Schaffner had recommended a Western store that would have a goodly supply of local country music, and a slouch hat for Leah, who decided that a baseball cap was insufficient shade for this high-altitude exposure to the sun. We spent an hour wandering the sleepy streets, ducking in and out of the shops, when Leah reported that Oakley was missing.

"He was right here," she said, "and now he's gone." I had been in a bookstore with the other three kids, and she had been waiting out front. Oakley stepped around the corner of the store and simply disappeared, she said. She was adamant that he was only a few steps away. We wandered the shops and back alley for a few minutes, making inquiries of storekeepers whether they'd seen a blond three-year-old on the run.

No one had. Fifteen minutes passed. Then a half-hour. By this time we had reconnected with John Schaffner and several locals joined in the search. We fanned out, searching backyards and asking people all over town. The town was small, perhaps only one square mile, surrounded by featureless scrubby hills. He couldn't have actually gone anywhere, unless he'd been abducted, but that didn't make sense since he had such a penchant for deliberately escaping. Yet, where was he?

We called the police. The sheriff showed up in his Ford Bronco and started a grid search of the neighborhood. After an hour he still hadn't appeared, and several people were in an outright panic. Leah and I were embarrassed, but neither of us really believed anything bad had happened to him. We knew he was hiding. He'd done it so often before.

And sure enough. After more than an hour, we were just coming together at the corner where he'd originally disappeared, when a man and his teenage daughter walked out of a house with Oakley in their arms. He was smiling. His face was covered in chocolate.

"He was playing with some toys in our living room," the father explained. "We just got home, and there he was. We don't lock our door; he must have walked right in."

Relieved, humiliated, angry, helpless, frustrated. We felt the same complicated mixture of feelings that parenting often invokes, again questioning whether it was foolhardy to bring an oppositionally defiant toddler on such an adventure, again feeling that we were inadequate parents.

We returned to the camp ashamed and defeated, but, despite repeated admonishments about running away, Oakley was unfazed and wandered the camp happily all that afternoon—under our watchful gaze.

"You can't run away, Oakley," we said again and again. "We were scared."

And he always responded the same way: "What." It wasn't a question. It was a statement. "What." As in, *you just said something, and it sounded sort of interesting, but I'll be darned if I know what it meant.*

He didn't get it. I often told his therapist that these incidents had forced me to change my parenting tactics with him. Unlike my other children, who I attempt to nurture and relate to in a deliberate way,

Oakley required something baser. It was my singular mission to simply keep him alive until he was eighteen. Fed, sheltered, and very well loved.

That evening we were treated to a full-scale hee-haw around the chuck wagon. Candy brought some pioneer clothing from her home for Leah and Raven, long flowing skirts that made them look every bit like pioneers. John Schaffner dug a long pit and set up a half-dozen Dutch ovens over a charcoal fire and made a feast of peach cobbler, biscuits, corn bread, and potatoes. He and Candy's husband Steve, who had joined us for the dinner, took turns singing songs and reciting cowboy poetry. John Schaffner recited several of his own, in a rambling, rhyming free verse, and several by the renowned cowboy poets Henry Herbert Knibbs and S. Omar Barker.

Schaffner recited poem after poem from memory, waving his hat and arms for expression, mimicking lassoes thrown and broncs ridden, often leaning back on his heels or leaning way down low, smiling, frowning, and wrinkling his face in mock pain. It was a whole-body performance.

His own, "Full Moon in the Cow Camp," bears repeating.

When the cattle's bedded down and the stars are shinin' bright.
When the full moon lends its glory to the beauty of the night.

The campfire pops and crackles in the evenin' breeze.
The cowboys gather round the wagon in a-takin' of their ease.

Coyotes are heard a-howlin' not so very far away.
The cowboys talk in rhyme and rhythm of the happenin's of the day.

The night guards on their horses softly singin' as they circle round,
The sleepin' herd of longhorns out there on the beddin' ground.

The night's so calm and peaceful the cowboys can't help but feel,
The closeness of a God in Heaven and know He's really real.

This little cowboy gatherin' keeps a-goin' til the embers are but a glow.
The bedrolls are out there waitin', but no cowboy wants to be the first to go.

One by one the heads start in to noddin', and some cowboy gives in
at last.
The other cowboys follow suit in headin' for their soogans for the night
is fadin' fast.

As they settle quickly into bedrolls nobody says a word.
Now, all is quiet in the cow camp 'cept for the night guards singin' to
the herd.

Such a peaceful time out on the prairie with the cows and cowboys
sleepin' in the night.
When the full moon's softly glowin' and the stars are shinin' bright.

Candy's husband Steve Moulton belted out a few tunes while playing his guitar. The most popular was a song about a dying cowboy who wanted to have his hide tanned after death and made into a lady's saddle: "So I can ride between the two things in this world I love the best."

Next morning there was a dispute over breakfast between Nebraska Bob and Doris. She and Rod had made breakfast burritos again, and apparently Nebraska Bob "didn't care for them" and had asked for toast instead. Doris bit her tongue and searched around in the wagon for some bread, which after a few minutes she located and began to toast over an open flame on the stove. Meanwhile, Nebraska Bob had forgotten about the toast and had polished off his eggs and was just cleaning his plate when Doris presented him with the toast.

"Oh, no thank you," he said, "I'm done with my breakfast." Doris fumed, but she didn't say anything, and everyone chuckled as they washed their plates and started for their wagons. He was oblivious, and these sorts of things happened again and again with him. It was soon clear that he'd cultivated a reputation as a bit of a Gomer Pyle, innocently frustrating those around him. He was always last to harness his team, he allowed his horses to follow too closely to the wagon ahead of him, and consequently Ben was always riding him. He was the scapegoat. People criticized him for keeping his horses too skinny, and he countered that theirs were too fat. I kind of felt sorry for him, yet he was so unaware of his effect on the group, that you also couldn't blame them for being irritated with him.

I rode in Ben's stagecoach that day with Finn, Jonah, and Raven. The vehicle was an exact replica of one that had ridden the Overland Trail in Wyoming in the 1860s, and I found it offered its own set of discomforts that were different from riding in a wagon. You were cut off from the outside in a way that you're not in the front of the wagon. You can only see out the side windows, so the effect is similar to riding in a train. You long to see the trail ahead. And the springs, such as they were, offered very little in the way of shock absorption. Each rock was jarring. And the wheels were the same steel-rimmed horrors of Nebraska Bob's vintage prairie schooner. The seats were padded, but they were also narrow and very upright, which offered the rider a proper Victorian experience. If you slouched at all, you slid to the floor when the carriage hit a rock or a bump, so we all just lounged around on the floor. As we rattled along, mile after mile, Jonah started to complain of queasiness. His face looked green. He was getting seasick from the swaying and jerking. Only by hanging his head out the window in the fresh air was he able to keep down his breakfast. I tried reading aloud to the kids, but the noise of the wheels was such that it was hard for them to hear me, and it was equally hard for me to see the type, since the book wouldn't hold still. I gave up after only a few minutes, and we rode along without speaking for the rest of the morning. We didn't need typhoid to feel miserable.

Unhappily for us, it was a longer ride that day. We stopped for lunch and a bathroom break—"a pause for the cause," as Cowboy Larry called it—for only ten minutes before rattling on. During another such pause, Candy pointed out the individual mountains around us: the Sierra Madres to the south, of which Bridger Peak is the tallest, Mount Zirkel in Colorado, and behind us, Kennedy Peak, and Coad, Sheep, and Elk Mountains in the Medicine Bow Range.

After lunch, I was invited to join Ben up on the driver's seat for the remaining ride into camp, and the kids all gave me resentful looks from the windows as I scrambled up on the high seat, giddy as a schoolboy to be free of the coach. As we started rolling, it was thrilling to be outside in the fresh air again. I could also study how Ben handled his mule team. He was constantly talking to them: "Get up, Jake! Get up!"

Of his team, Jake was the lazy one. You could see him start to lag behind Pete when the trail inclined, and then Ben would crack his switch on the animal's rump, not hard, just a firm reminder.

I learned from Ben that he'd been married three times, either outliving his wives or outliving the marriage; it wasn't clear which. Born on a homestead in western Nebraska, near Courthouse and Jailhouse Rocks, Ben had learned to work horses from his father. He had lived his whole adult life in Wyoming, working mostly as a ranch hand. He was happiest when he was seated on a wagon, following historic trails through land that had not been marred by development.

Throughout our ride the rest of that day, Ben kept extolling the beauty of the land. "Mighty purty country," he said again and again, in between curses at Jake the mule. We hadn't seen a single house or paved road all day. He knew all the landowners between the Pacific and Missouri where the Oregon Trail passes.

"When I want to cross their land, I don't call them on the phone or nothin'," he said. "I go to their house and look them in the eye. I explain about what I'm doing, and they always give me permission to cross their land."

He said he had recently had a casket built for himself.

"It's got a map on it of all the trails I've done," Ben said as we rattled along. "More than twenty-thousand miles of trail, but there's room for one more: west-to-east on the Oregon Trail and then on to Washington, D.C., just like Ezra Meeker."

I wondered where he kept it.

"In my bedroom," he said.

Our camp that evening was just over a high ridge, which required us to descend a frighteningly steep trail. Sitting way up on the stagecoach, teetering along as the mules picked their way downhill, it became clear what a masterful driver Ben was. He maintained meticulous control of his animals, speaking to them all the while, giving them the rein they needed to find their own way but at the same time communicating to them that each second he was demanding their full attention. Cowboy Mike had earlier explained to me that mules are not only smarter than horses, they care about their own survival. This means they won't run down a steep embankment, like a horse will, and risk breaking their necks. (This is also why the Grand Canyon park staff uses mules on their dizzying pack rides into the canyon.)

"Mules don't want to die," Cowboy Mike had said. "They pick their way carefully and you get a more comfortable ride in the process." But they're also like rebellious teenagers, he said, that never outgrow their interest in trying to get away with something.

"You let your guard down for a second, and mules will exploit it. They're smart as hell, and they'll make you pay for your inattention."

I felt my heart in my throat as Ben guided the mules down the embankment. The track was so narrow that even the slightest deviation would have sent us sprawling, the wagon tumbling end over end down the hillside. The brake, which is nothing but a foot lever that clamps a rubber pad onto the wheel rim, did little to slow the speed of the team. The wheels simply locked up and the coach skidded. All the control was in the efforts of the mules at keeping their weight pressed back against the harness.

The camp was an old homestead that had been abandoned some time in the last decade and taken over by a cattle ranch. It sat on a plateau on the north side of a ridge overlooking a vast valley to the north and west: a spectacular setting. We wheeled into a circle, set up our tents, and then wandered the old buildings. There were prairie dogs and rabbits everywhere, their burrows dotting the field. It was too high in elevation for rattlesnakes, Candy told me, so I let my guard down and allowed the kids to wander freely. Within a few minutes, Jonah had caught a baby bunny in his hands and was cradling it in his hands for people to pet.

That evening Vic and I developed a quiet joke that would serve us well throughout the rest of the trip. Since I had filled one of Rod's coolers with beer, and he had his coffin-size cooler in the kooster, we took to being sure we each had a beer in our hand in the long hours of the afternoon. It was always a wordless, and remarkably efficient, exchange. One or the other of us would point at the cooler and the other would invariably smile and give a single nod in response.

I wandered the derelict buildings with Nebraska Bob, going into a decrepit wooden structure with a dirt floor and windows high up by the roof. Inside, a brick fireplace, piled with old ash, stood against one wall, its bricks crumbling. A trailer home had been set up next to this structure. Nebraska Bob surmised the old building was the main house. In the old barnyard, which was still fenced in with a high split-rail, I found John and Jenny Stevenson standing next to a corral. I was thinking what a sad place this was, shabby and crude, wondering who on earth was exiled to live in this godforsaken spot, when I asked them what they thought of it.

"De-luxe!" John exclaimed.

He and Jenny had just wandered the whole property and figured out the entire economics of the outfit. I told them I thought the place was a dump. John smiled and started pointing out what he and Jenny had determined.

This was a hugely successful ranch, he said, which maintained eight hundred head of cattle in its prime. He knew this for two reasons: one was the natural spring that bubbled up from the ground, the one feature that made this spot possible to begin with. They'd found it just down the hill, and it was still giving water.

The real reason they knew this was such a successful ranch was a single clue they had noticed in the barn. In the barn there were four stalls. In each stall were two feeding chutes. This meant the farm had supported four teams: eight horses. With eight horses you could work four hayricks, which could support eight hundred cattle! Jenny pointed to a rotting hayrick in the field above.

There was also an enormous chicken coop with an insulated roof, which had housed hundreds of chickens, he said; a hog house; and the building with the dirt floor was the blacksmith shop, he said, not the house.

"The house was there," he said, pointing to where the ugly trailer was sitting. "It probably burned and they put that trailer on the old foundation." The circular corral was used for breaking horses; it was small, only about thirty feet across, so you could keep control of the animals. There was a screened meat-drying house.

He pointed out all the metal fittings on the gates and fences and in each of the buildings. They were all shaped by hand here at the blacksmith shop, he said. It was only so sad and forlorn looking now that a huge conglomerate had bought the property and folded it into their larger ranch, covering hundreds of thousands of acres, one of the largest operations in Wyoming. The actual homestead was no longer needed as a base of operations. The economy had moved on.

But the spirit of the people who had lived out their lives became evident with each sweep of John and Jenny's hands. Jenny had grown up on such a place, a smaller ranch farther north, but she knew the time and dedication required to squeeze money from the Wyoming scrub. And these were the ghosts we were looking for on this trip. Each fitting of the corral fence, each board in the barn, each shingle on the roof had been placed by someone who saw promise in this land. It was not the lush Willamette Valley of Oregon. By the time Wyoming was settled, all that land was gone. But the people who'd settled here—some three generations, according to John and Jenny—were inspired by the same dream that drove so many families west.

"De-luxe," John said again. A few minutes later the sun dropped below the western hills.

In the morning, I was back with Nebraska Bob. He was feeling sprightly because he had found a passage in the Bible that he wanted to share with me. Something that proved I needed to think more about the Lord, he said.

"Psalm 127," he said, handing the reins to me as we rattled along in the morning sunshine and flipping open to the page he had dog-eared.

He read aloud: "Children are a gift from the Lord, the fruit of the womb, a reward. Like arrows in the hand of the warrior are the children born in one's youth. Blessed are they whose quivers are full. They will never be shamed contending with foes at the gate." He looked at me squarely and closed the book.

"That's you," he whispered. "You are a young man, and you have many children. They're a gift from the Lord."

I was touched by his affection, and I had to agree with the spirit of his message. He was sharing his wagon with my family, and I told him how much I appreciated his kindness.

• • •

Our day's ride was a short one. We rode about eight miles to the base of the deep valley we had overlooked the previous evening at the old homestead. By 10:00 a.m. we were circled in a patch of scrub above a small reservoir about a mile from the base of a tall hill. It was a dispiriting location, barren and ugly, and exposed to the full force of the unremitting sun and whipping wind. I looked at the children: their faces were chaffed and their noses peeling; their lips were so dry that the skin was coming up in flakes. Their hair, grown shaggy and unbrushable, resembled stiff straw. And they looked exhausted: their eyes were sunken and haggard looking. Despite our best efforts to get them to drink water frequently, it was impossible to keep them well hydrated in this sun and wind. We had now been on the road exactly a month. We had camped every night so far, and the effect was taking its toll.

That afternoon, while I was shuttling the car to the end of the trail with Cowboy Larry and Rod, Leah took the kids down to the reservoir and let them play in the water. When I got back, she said Ben had had a bath, too. He had stripped himself of his cowboy togs and put on a bright red swimsuit that was several sizes too large for him, and, still wearing his floppy hat and his boots, began to wander down to the pond for a dip. Oakley then joined him; he, too, was wearing only his bathing suit, tall hat, and boots. He looked up at Ben, Leah said, and yammered in his enthusiastic way as they made their way together to the water's edge.

Only Ben's hands and face were tan. His pale body shimmered in the sun. He sat on a rock and removed his hat and boots and waded into the water, where Candy and Quackgrass Sally scrubbed him all over with a bar of soap. Afterward, Ben and Oakley sloshed up to the wagons and stood in the shade. Ben popped open a beer, and Leah got Oakley a bottle of cold milk. They stood together in the shade, both with their hats tipped back and an elbow propped on a wagon wheel.

What wasn't funny, she said, was that unbeknownst to her the water contained alkali, and she had let the kids play in the water too long. When the wind dried their skin, it began to crack—painfully. They all started crying in pain, and she couldn't figure out what the problem was until she saw the hairline cracks in their ashy skin. She covered their bodies in moisturizing lotion, but this stung painfully. They screamed louder, all four of them crying in pain, until the lotion took effect.

To make matters worse, while I was away Leah had overheard Quackgrass Sally making disparaging remarks about our family, and Leah was upset.

Evidently, while I was gone, the group had been sitting in the shade of the wagons as they were wont to do, whiling away the afternoon by drinking beer and telling stories, when Quackgrass Sally suddenly launched into a mocking tirade directed at us. What she didn't know was that Leah was sitting on the edge of the group, taking it all in. For several minutes, Quackgrass Sally was openly ridiculing us: for having too much gear and apparently for being soft. Leah also said that Quackgrass Sally had mimicked me, aping my behavior after I'd eaten the hot pepper the day before and exclaimed loudly about its force. I had joked, apparently too deadpan and she'd missed the humor, that if I ate enough of the jalapeño peppers my moustache might grow as substantial as Cowboy Larry's. Quackgrass Sally thought I was serious, and was appalled at my idiocy, and she now was making full use of it to inspire her vitriolic routine. Her whole performance had made it sound like I was a sniveling girly-man from Back East, and that Leah and I just weren't cut from the same coarse cloth as they were.

I knew how we must have appeared to this bunch: showing up in our overstuffed car with four kids and a dachshund. It was a rebuke of the gravitas of driving animals on the open range.

They were all feeling low. To escape the brutally strong sun, and to nurse the tender spirits, we gathered the kids back to the tent for an early bed time. We would feel better in the morning, I told Leah. We all slip sometimes, say things we don't realize are hurtful.

As I lay awake in the tent that evening, I thought back about the Independent Oregon Colony and reflected that it was exactly this sort of trifling incident that threatened to undo these fragile groups as they made their way west. Petty insults, gossip, personality clashes, careless words. Cornelius Gilliam had been hotheaded and, like Quackgrass Sally, had a loose tongue that forced the group apart and threatened their progress. When Gilliam resigned, William Shaw and Wilson Morrison stepped in to provide firm leadership. They had to keep the group together for the next five and a half months. We couldn't even get along for a week!

I slept fitfully that night, imagining ways I could get revenge on this woman who had insulted my family, but by morning, as the eastern sky swirled in lavender and orange against the sage-covered peaks, the bad feelings had evaporated.

It was to be another long day. We had some twenty miles to cover, and our day would include crossing the Continental Divide at Bridger Pass—some seven thousand feet above sea level. We would see no roads, and we would spend the entire day out of sight of any signs of civilization, Ben said, relishing the historic virginity of the open country.

The first part of the trail included two exceedingly steep hills. The day before, Ben, Mike, and Cowboy Larry had been discussing how to manage them. The teams would need help getting the wagons up. Their hooves would likely slip on the loose stones as they reached the steepest parts and leaned against the weight of the wagons. A running start wouldn't help much because the hills were too high, the run too long.

So they decided that Cowboy Mike would get his wagon up first, since it was relatively light, and he had a strong team of three young mules. He would then unhitch the team and return to the base of the hill, where he would secure a tow line onto the tongue of the other wagons. Cowboy Larry would also take a lariat rope, secured at one end to the horn of his saddle and the other to the wagon tongue. They would go up one wagon at a time: Cowboy Larry and his steed in the lead, serving as a kind of tugboat on a long line; next would be Mike driving his three mules; and then would be the wagon team harnessed as usual to the wagon tongue. They would repeat the process until each wagon was up, and then they would do the same thing on the second hill.

To lighten the load, and to take a break from riding in the wagon, we had volunteered to walk for the first few miles that morning.

The first run proved efficient. The stagecoach made it up without incident. John and Jenny's wagon, too. The horses and mules charged into the hill, their heads lowered against the strain, as the drivers lashed their whips, snapped their reins, and made a lot of noise.

"Get up! C'mon, boys! Get up!" Mike roared as he ran up the hill behind his team of three mules, again and again until all six wagons reached the top of the first hill.

On the second hill, all hell broke loose.

They were towing the last of the wagons, Nebraska Bob's, up, and were halfway to the top, when the cinch on Cowboy Larry's saddle suddenly snapped. The cinch dropped to the ground and the loose buckle began slapping against the hind legs of Larry's horse. It was terrified and started bucking wildly, trying to shake whatever was hitting its legs. Fortunately, Larry had realized in an instant what had happened and instantly released the tow rope on the saddle horn. In the next second, as the saddle came loose and dropped to the ground, he slipped off the rump of the bucking horse, dropping clear of its flying hooves. If he had had his tow rope tied instead of looped, or if he'd reacted slower, he and the saddle could have ended up tangled in the horse's feet and then being dragged under Mike's team of mules, which were charging up behind.

Meanwhile, as Larry's horse bucked and kicked itself clear of the saddle and ran off, Mike and his team of mules hadn't slowed their ascent. To stop in the middle of the hill, he had realized, would result in a dangerous backslide that could cause the wagon and teams to jackknife in a nasty tangle of rope, harnesses, and scared, thrashing animals. They all made it to the top. No one was hurt.

"But things got a bit Western there for a while," Mike said later.

Leah and I and the four kids trotted ahead while the teams rested at the top of the second hill. Raven was wearing her sunbonnet and borrowed vintage skirt and, with the wagons rolling behind her, appeared to be walking straight out of *Little House on the Prairie*. Oakley was in the three-wheeled stroller, which Ben had taken to calling "the Mormon handcart" (a reference to the notorious handcarts the Mormons used on their 1847 migration), and Balloo ran alongside in the slim shade it cast, making the most his four-inch legs. Finn joked about hitching Balloo to a rope and having him tow Oakley up the next little hill. Had Balloo understood, we doubt he would have laughed along. We walked about two miles that morning before the wagons caught up to us and took us on board.

We climbed higher into the mountains all that morning, meeting up with Rod and Doris and the feed trailer for lunch and a quick watering of the animals along the trail. As we approached Bridger Pass, we were joined by two mounted cowboys who were employed by the ranch we were passing through. The landowner had given permission for us to cross, but she sent her men out "to be sure you all close the gates," they said as they loped alongside us, shrugging and offering embarrassed smiles as apologies for the distrust of their boss.

Late in the afternoon we turned into a narrow canyon, and Ben circled the wagons in a tight circle on a narrow plateau above a trickling creek. With one or two of the kids I had taken to helping Nebraska Bob set up his portable electric fence and disassemble his harness. He showed us how to arrange the harness on the wagon tongue so it wouldn't get tangled. As we were setting up our tent, we heard a surprised shout from over near the creek.

"Snake!"

Jenny was walking one of her mules to the creek to be watered, picking her way carefully through the tall sagebrush. A prairie rattler was still issuing its aggressive noise from one of the larger bushes. A moment later, after Leah and I had gathered the kids to be sure they didn't get too close, we watched John Stevenson stride to his wagon and return with a long-handled shovel. Apparently this snake had messed with the wrong woman.

From about one hundred feet away, we watched as John walked around the bush and poked at the snake. He would extend the shovel into the bush, and then we'd hear a loud "*Clang!*"—followed by another angry rattle. The snake was striking, again and again, at the blade of the shovel, as John attempted to wear him out. After a few minutes of this, we saw John slowly extend the shovel into the bush and then bear down on the shovel with what looked like all his weight. He moved his hands back and forth in a grinding motion and then a moment later drew the shovel out. The snake's head was on the blade. In one motion he flung the head across the creek. He then leaned over, reached his hand into the bush, and pulled out the body of the snake, which was still writhing, holding it up by its tail. It was so large, it reached the ground.

And then we all gathered around. He showed us how, by nudging the tail with the shovel, the snake's reflexes caused it to whirl back and strike, with its headless stump, at whatever was touching its tail. It did this for several minutes. Ordinarily, John said, he would have left the snake alone, especially if we were just passing by. But because we were camping so close, and the canyon was so narrow, it was too dangerous. Knowing our children's exploratory habits, I was grateful.

Someone suggested skinning the snake, I'm not sure who, and before I knew it, John was offering to show me how if I was willing to get a little bloody. I picked up the still-twitching snake, surprised by its warmth and heaviness, and carried it down to the edge of the creek. We then spent the next hour, the three older kids and I, peeling the skin away from the body, scraping off the tissue, and then rubbing salt into the skin. To the delight of the kids, inside the snake's stomach we made a gruesome discovery: a whole prairie dog, the snake's last meal. John also gave us instructions on how to cure it with glycerin when we returned from our trip. (Along with various elk antlers, a cattle skull, and some bones, it hangs in our living room as part of a collection of mementos from our trip.)

There was a fine mood in the camp that evening. Leah and I felt a pang of pleasure when Ben Kern asked if he could use "the Mormon handcart"—Oakley's three-wheel stroller—to transport the horse feed from the trailer down to the horses, a distance of some one hundred yards down the hill. Its sturdy construction and large wheels made it ideally suited to the task. That the stroller was not authentic was forgivable in the name of efficiency. He brushed off offers of assistance and happily pushed the stroller back and forth like a proud mother leading her newborn.

Later that evening, after everyone else was snoring, Leah and I saw the most magnificent sunset. As a light rain shower passed overhead, the sky turned brilliant yellow, the whole canyon lighting up like, as Nebraska Bob would have said had he been awake, the gates of heaven. A dazzling rainbow spanned the canyon.

In the morning, we descended the canyon to where it met an abandoned house that had once served as a station along the Oregon Trail. We crossed a little bridge and pulled into a grassy yard. Two nights before, we had been visited by an old woman who had spent part of her youth here. It had been a cattle ranch then, but she knew countless stories of the stagecoach days, the most lively of which was one about a stagecoach being attacked by a group of Indians in this canyon in 1865. The travelers had arrived at the previous station, only to find that it had been burned by Indians the day before, the lone caretaker murdered. The travelers had then attempted to continue on to the next one, this one here at Sulphur Springs, only to be chased for almost twenty miles. Several of them, including the coach driver and several horses in the team, were killed by gunfire, and at one point the stagecoach had been surrounded. But a young man—his name appears to have been lost—had cut free the dead horses and leapt to the reins, only to have his hand shot off by one of the Indians. This didn't slow his progress, however, and he was credited with saving the other six or eight people by driving the remaining horses successfully through the canyon and arriving at this spot, where they were protected by a band of soldiers. The Indians were then driven off.

I had all but given up riding in the wagon. I much preferred to trot behind Nebraska Bob's wagon, since it was the last in the train. When I wanted to take a break, I developed a way to jump into his wagon without having him stop, by grabbing hold of the tailgate and throwing myself into its bottom. It wasn't graceful, but it was effective, and, by alternately running for a while and resting in the seat next to Nebraska Bob, it made the morning pass enjoyably.

Leah, meanwhile, grew jealous of the fun I was having. She, with Oakley, was riding inside the stagecoach, and this road was particularly rough. To make matters worse, we had been crossing several dry riverbeds with steep sides, resulting in some painful thrashings—not unlike being in a horse-drawn washing machine, she said. Her back was killing her, she said, and Oakley had had enough She demanded that we switch. During a pause for the cause, she, Oakley, and Finn dropped from the stagecoach and, with Oakley in the three-wheel stroller, began trotting along behind.

All went well for about a half hour. But soon the ground leveled out, and there were fewer riverbeds to cross. The horses and mules, perhaps also sensing the end of the road, picked up the pace. Leah and Finn were falling behind. I could see them, but she had said she was happier walking, so I figured she was okay and didn't want us to stop. I thought she'd be embarrassed, in fact, if I had asked Ben to stop and everyone to wait for her to catch up. I then forgot about her as Nebraska Bob and I fell into the easy chatter of horses and superior geology of Nebraska, and, inevitably, the Bible.

We must have traveled another hour like this—covering some five miles—because by the time I remembered about Leah and Finn, it was noon and we were pulling into the dusty parking lot where we'd all left our cars. They were nowhere to be seen. About a half hour later they came huffing into view, their faces red with exertion. They cut quite a picture, actually: Leah's long skirts blowing in the breeze; Finn's long hair steaming out from beneath his felt crusher. I was admiring their fortitude when they made clear that they felt they had been ditched. Evidently, they had run out of water some time ago, and the skirt that I had thought so becoming was "just about the last thing" that one should wear when jogging on a dusty trail in the height of summer, she said. Oakley had shown remarkable good sense, meanwhile, by falling asleep in the stroller.

While everyone busily disassembled their wagons and harnesses and loaded their horses into their trailers, we quickly packed up our car and were ready to go in half an hour. It was clear everyone had a precise system for how things were packed, and assistance wasn't needed. We stood around in the hot sun for a few moments not knowing quite what to say. This group of people who we had known only as pioneer characters suddenly were fading before our eyes, as though in a time warp, suddenly becoming who they were in real life: a banker, a taxidermist, a construction worker, two ranchers, and several retirees. The trip was over, and, hot and exhausted as we all were, we also felt genuine affection for this group. Candy gave us all big hugs. Vic grinned at me wordlessly and pumped my hand. Ben graciously thanked us for our help and grinned his gold-rimmed smile; Rod and Doris cracked jokes about us being the nicest vegetarians they'd ever met.

I asked Nebraska Bob whether he'd do it again next year, knowing it had been a hard trip for him. The night before everyone had talked about picking up at this exact spot to retrace the rest of the Overland Trail where it continues across Wyoming and into Utah.

"Sure I will," he whispered, shaking my hand. "Sure I will."

16

INTO THE VOID

FROM THIS POINT FORWARD, as the Independent Oregon Colony left the Green River and approached Fort Bridger in what is now southwestern Wyoming, Frémont's 1842–43 map would have been useless. It had shown the course along the Great Platte River Road and guided the emigrants to the Sweetwater and to the key geological feature that permitted passage through the Rockies by wagon—South Pass—but from then on, the emigrants of the early 1840s relied almost exclusively on the local knowledge of their guides. For the Independent Oregon Colony of 1844, these people were James Clyman and Moses "Black" Harris, former fur trappers who had been back and forth across the Rockies numerous times over the previous two decades.

Frémont returned many times to go farther than the Continental Divide, of course, creating the most detailed maps of the entire western United States than had ever come before, but his 1842–43 map ended at the Wind River Range. On this map, which Minto, Morrison, Shaw, and others were all carrying, nothing but blank space appears beyond the 111th meridian. The Little Sandy River, which the group crossed on the afternoon after traversing South Pass, peters into white space on the map. The Green River, where Henry Sager died, doesn't even appear.

Most of the earlier maps, the one from Minto's old *Mitchell's School Atlas*, say, or the one Benjamin Bonneville published following his return to Washington, D.C., and New York in 1835 (and which Shaw likely had, along with his copy of Washington Irving's book on Bonneville's adventures), were next to useless. The same can be said of the maps made by missionary Samuel Parker following his 1835 expedition. Their scale was simply too small and too distorted to be effective for day-to-day navigational purposes. It was not until Frémont's second expedition, completed in 1845, that his surveys of the full Oregon Trail and surrounding lands would be linked with those of California and the Northwest region (published by the U.S. Navy's Charles Wilkes in 1844) that a comprehensive, usable map of the territories would be available to overland travelers.

To connect South Pass with the next key geological feature of the westward trail, the Snake River, which runs east-west across what is today the state of Idaho, the Oregon Trail at this point zigzagged southwest and northwest—a patchwork of small rivers and roadways known only to the Indians and the guides. The distance between South Pass and the Snake River is not far, less than two hundred miles as the crow flies, but actually required emigrants to cover almost twice that distance if they were to have ample water and grazing for their stock.

James Clyman observed: "Our rout through this Green River valley has been verry crooked & might be easily made to save about 50 miles by keeping more westwardly as the rout is equally level & the only object of this zigzag road is to pass the trading hous which however is some convenienc as we ware able to trade every extra article we had for mokisens & leather clothing. Exchanged of all our worn out mules and horses."

On August 29, the group followed the Green River south to where it met Fort Bridger, opened earlier that year by trapper-entrepreneur Jim Bridger, the second of the three fur company outposts that existed along the Oregon Trail. The company was desperate to stock up on provisions for their remaining journey. The Morrison family, which started the journey with two fully supplied wagons and an entire herd of cattle, was now running out of supplies, likely because Wilson and Nancy Morrison were supporting those who were less prepared than they.

Morrison traded one of his plows—an item as valuable as any for the settling of Oregon—for a single barrel of flour with a man who commented upon the lateness of the season for crossing to Oregon.

John Minto witnessed the exchange. "He was a man of five nine or ten inches at the most, but strongly framed in breast and shoulders; light brown hair, flaxy at the ends; eyes steel blue or gray." The man had secured the plow to a pack animal and said he was headed to Taos, where he and his young half-Indian wife were hoping to settle. Minto said, "The man [Morrison] was dealing with was very different from those here apparently on show." Presumably Minto meant that the man was not a hard drinker and living for the moment, like the other fur trappers, but seemed centered and serious. It would be a few years later that Minto would recognize the face of the man he'd met in a photograph of a famous scout. It was Kit Carson.

Minto also traded. His clothes were ragged, and his double-barrel buffalo gun was damaged, only firing on one side, and he had been told by Nancy Morrison that she would stitch him a pair of buckskin trousers if he traded his gun for some deerskins. He followed Carson into the fort where he met another legend, Jim Bridger, who impressed him as "powerful built" but "coarser made and coarser minded" than Carson. Minto asked Bridger if he would accept his gun for deerskins.

"Young man, I can't do it. We get few deerskins here," Bridger answered. "I'll give you ten antelope skins; that's the best I can do."

Minto agreed, and he wandered back to Nancy Morrison with the skins, well pleased with himself for his shrewd trade. He didn't record her response, but the reality was, the skins were next to useless for his needs. Proper deerskins don't stretch when wet, and Minto realized his folly the following day when he witnessed another fur trapper trade three rifle charges of powder for one such antelope skin. "That means, I gave a gun needing a twenty-five-cent repair, more valuable than any rifle for killing buffalo on the run, for thirty charges of ammunition; and I am told, this is three times the cost of the skins to Mr. Bridger." Minto had been cheated.

The Sager family had a similar experience at Fort Bridger. It began over an inexplicable distrust Naomi had of the German doctor, Theophilus Dagen, who insisted on staying with the Sager family following Henry Sager's death the day before. Dr. Dagen, who was traveling alone and could therefore offer his services, had even offered to drive their team, but Naomi had hired a young man instead. "Mother was afraid to trust the doctor," Catherine said, "but the kindhearted German would not leave her, and declared his intention to see her safe in the Willamette."

When they arrived in Fort Bridger, the Sager children immediately set about fishing in the stream, using wagon sheets as nets. "That evening the new driver told mother he would hunt for game if she would let him use the gun," Catherine said. "He took it, and we never saw him again." Dagen was now in charge of the Sager wagon.

He presided over a miserable lot. "John and Francis, heartbroken over their father's death, were showing alarming symptoms of camp fever themselves," Erwin Thompson wrote in *Shallow Grave at Waiilatpu*. "Although they were not to become seriously ill, the slightest sign of sickness sent terror through Naomi's mind. Catherine's shattered leg was healing but slowly. Elizabeth was old enough to know fear and discouragement. Although Matilda and Louise were too small to comprehend their plight, the baby [Roseanna] suffered because of Naomi's sickness."

It was at Fort Bridger that John Minto realized what a burden it was to travel with a family. He could cover twice the speed the wagons could, even if he were to strike out on foot. And he was captivated by the young men circling Fort Bridger. The trappers lived in the wilderness hunting bountiful game; they frolicked with Indian women in the forts when they grew lonely, living the most carefree life he had ever seen. On the morning of August 31, Minto asked Morrison if he could be discharged of his duties and leave the train to live the life of a fur trapper.

"I was unsettled part of this day," Minto said, "and in the evening I asked Captain Morrison if he could now dispense with my assistance, telling him that I felt inclined to try a year or two of this trapper's life."

Ever patient, Morrison responded: "I suppose I could do without you from this point on, but I would advise you not to stop here. These men you see are little account either to themselves or their country; they will do you no good, and the time you stay here will be lost out of your life, if you do not lose life itself. I wouldn't stop if I was you."

It was an especially long speech from the usually taciturn Morrison.

"My father could not have bettered this counsel," Minto said. He stayed with the group.

When the group left Fort Bridger, each day's journey was now a race. Beginning at dawn with the yoking of the teams, the day's movements often involved a jockeying for the lead position, where the leader could enjoy the clean views ahead without choking on dust from others. On September 1, Minto was in the lead with one of the Morrisons' wagons, when another wagon from Shaw's company kept trying to edge past. Minto would not yield, and the two drovers exchanged harsh words until Morrison rode up.

"As we came very near the levels of the bear River, one [wagon] drove in between our wagons, and some words passed from me to the driver, whom I would not let pass me," Minto said, "but as we came to the wider valley Captain Morrison signed to me to drive to the left, and then I saw the wagon behind me carried someone sick, and I felt sorry I had not given the lead, and so the least dusty travel."

The following day, September 2, Nancy Morrison asked Minto to spend the day fishing instead of driving. And the same on September 3. He grew suspicious of her motives and confronted her. "I was again by Mrs. Morrison to try for trout, but I remarked in reply, 'It seems to me I could do more to help along than catching a few pounds of fish.'"

Her reply: "John, I don't want to make you mad; but Wilson thinks you drive too fast, and that the cattle will get out."

Minto was petulant at first, and his frustration must have showed. On the one hand, he felt obliged to perform his duties; on the other, he was chafing to make more progress than the cumbersome wagons.

"She saw I understood," Minto said, "and I was hurt; I had not thought of the consequences of overdriving, much less of losing the team by it. I went to my angling submissive and reflective." He rode off on horseback ahead of the wagons to seek out a fishing hole, but it was during this solo jaunt that he found an opportunity that hatched a plan to accomplish both his interests. That night he camped with a family that was well ahead of the main wagon train, along with two young men, also with horses, who were considering striking out ahead of the group. Minto also realized that his would be one less mouth to feed from the dwindling supplies.

"This day was spent by me reflecting rather than angling, and I resolved I would not eat the bread of Captain Morrison unless I could do him service," Minto said of September 5, "but as he had been kind and generous to me, I could only part with his good will and consent."

On September 6, a few days before the group arrived at Fort Hall, Minto spoke to Morrison. "I took occasion to speak to Captain Morrison about going on in advance from Fort Hall. He could see nothing against this, if there was no danger from the Indians—and these people [Indians encountered thus far] seemed glad, rather than otherwise, to see us."

In the company of Daniel Clark, John Minto departed the wagon train on September 6. They were to proceed on to Fort Hall and await the rest of the train. If Minto could trade his gun for a horse, and it seemed that Morrison could do without him from then on, Minto would continue the rest of the way to the Willamette Valley ahead of the wagon train. It's not clear from the diaries what agreement, if any, Minto and Morrison made about meeting up in Oregon, but an agreement must have been made, since Minto would be instrumental in helping the Morrison family survive the last part of the journey.

Since Minto had no horse (the ones he'd been using had belonged to the Morrisons), he trotted along behind Clark's horse at a jog. He hoped to trade his remaining gun for a horse at Fort Hall, still some thirty to forty miles away, judging that they could reach it within two to three days. He carried his gun, a handful of charges, a powder horn, some matches, and a small package of steel fish hooks, all he owned in the world. Minto must have been in phenomenal physical shape to have such confidence in his stamina, trusting that they would find sufficient game to shoot and never straying far from the various rivers that led to the Snake.

Minto trotted behind Clark's horse for four days. On the morning of September 11, as they were beginning their last day's journey to Fort

Hall, they were overtaken by an Indian on horseback. He was leading another horse behind him.

"He looked at Clark's excellent mount, and then at me laboriously walking among the brush to avoid the loose, sandy road," Minto said, "then asked, by signs, if I would ride, and was answered affirmatively. He unloosened his hair rope from his saddle and dashed at the loose animal, catching him at the first throw; made a bridle of the rope by two half-hitches on the lower jaw, took the saddle blanket from under his saddle for me to ride on, and signed to Clark he was in haste and would leave me at the fort. Then we set off at a gallop."

The unlikely pair had not gone far when the Indian noticed Minto struggling to stay upright on the loose saddle blanket and no stirrups, while clutching his heavy buffalo gun in one hand and holding the reins in the other. "He therefore stopped again," Minto said, "put his saddle onto my horse and took the substitute himself, and away we dashed again."

They rode in silence to within a mile of the fort. The Indian then stopped at a small stream and washed his face, and then, to Minto's astonishment, brought out a pocket mirror and combed his hair, "thus prepared for company." As he sat extolling the kindness of this stranger, a young Indian girl walked up holding a pail of ripe blackberries. She gave Minto as much as he could eat. Though she expected nothing in return, Minto gave her a few steel fishhooks as thanks, which the girl happily accepted.

"Such was the treatment received from the first Oregon Indians seen by the writer," Minto said.

Clark arrived soon after and the two walked into the fort to await the wagons.

The wagons emerged from the last of the passes through the Rocky Mountains on September 11, reaching Fort Hall on the west bank of the Snake River, the last of the fur trapper forts along the trail. It marked the start of the most grueling portion of the trail's two thousand miles, following the Snake River Plain. The river curves an arc across the widest part of what is now the state of Idaho. Unlike the Platte, which is flat and wide and is surrounded by smooth terrain for most of its hundreds of miles, the Snake winds through a canyon, which becomes steeper and less accessible as it flows west. It is surrounded on both sides by the roughest, driest country.

Minto, Clark, and S. B. Crockett, who was also in his twenties and without a family, left the company on horseback on the morning of September 16, at a place where the Portneuf River feeds into the Snake. "We started with fifteen pounds of buffalo pemmican, purchased at Fort Hall," Minto said. Nonetheless, as they were leaving, one of the emigrants, a black freeman from Missouri named George W. Bush, gave them a word of warning. "Boys, you are going through a hard country. You have guns and ammunition. Take my advice: anything you see as big as a blackbird, kill it and eat it." It was sound advice. The men saw little game on the scrubby Snake River Plain and would survive by trading fish hooks for salmon offered by the Indians. "We found fish-hooks good small change for the purchase of fish—much better than money would have been," Minto said.

Since they moved swiftly, they often had little time to hunt, several times going for three and four days without a proper meal. At one point they made a meal of raw duck meat. Another time they ate rotten salmon.

The wagons, meanwhile, were engaged in a virtual free-for-all, moving as fast as they could in a race not just against the clock but against their ever-dwindling supplies. No one attempted to stay together unless it happened naturally.

Naomi Sager's health continued to decline with each passing day.

"Mother planned to get to Whitman's and winter there, but she was rapidly failing under her sorrows," Catherine wrote of Naomi's condition after they left Fort Bridger and began following the Snake River. "The nights and mornings were very cold, and she took cold from the exposure unavoidably. With camp fever and a sore mouth, she fought bravely against fate for the sake of her children, but she was taken delirious soon after reaching Fort Bridger, and was bed-fast."

Naomi was never to fully recover. She spent the first two weeks of September in fits of melancholic delirium as the family wagon rattled west. "Traveling in this condition over a road clouded with dust, she suffered intensely," Catherine wrote. "She talked of her husband, addressing him as though present, beseeching him in piteous tones to relieve her sufferings, until at last she became unconscious." Catherine was still riding in the wagon. Her leg wouldn't heal until months later. This close proximity to her mother's last days would inform her later writing of the time with heartbreaking clarity. Catherine frequently recalled her mother's moaning, day after day.

It had become clear to Sally Shaw and Nancy Morrison that Roseanna, the frail infant, would die if she remained with Naomi much longer. "Those kindhearted women would also come in at night and wash the dust from the mother's face and otherwise make her comfortable," Catherine wrote. They took Roseanna from Naomi and set up a feeding schedule amongst other nursing mothers so that the baby would not starve. Still, most thought she couldn't survive.

The trail along the Snake River was rougher than any the emigrants had so far traversed. James Clyman described it as "the more barren, sterile region we have yet passed. Nothing to disturb the monotony of the eternal sage plane." To make matters worse, the river begins to descend into a canyon as it moves westward, making access to the river difficult. Often, days would pass when they could not reach water and had to make dry camp.

The women of the camp tried to shield Naomi Sager from the worst of the dust by hanging a screen in front of the wagon. But this made the wagon "so stuffy that her breathing was impaired," wrote Frank McLynn, in *Wagons West*. "They were traveling through cruel and unforgiving country—slaked and unslaked lime volcanic rocks and fine coarse sand, sometimes mixed together, sometimes discrete, in pure form, with, as the sole vegetation, sagebrush, prairie thorn and liquorice plant, shrubby and thickset."

The day before she died, Naomi also called for William Shaw and asked for further assurances that he would see the children to the Whitman mission. She also asked that he not separate them—that he remember her dying wish was that they stay together. Shaw must have mumbled some agreement, because he made reference in his reminiscences of this promise. Naomi then called her oldest son, John, to her side.

"After giving minute instruction to [Shaw]—she bid farewell to her children saying to John—'Oh my son, be kind to your little sisters,'" Catherine recalled.

Naomi lingered all the rest of that day, moaning all the while and drifting in and out of consciousness. That night, when one of the women came to wash her face, Naomi seemed to have slipped away.

"Taking up her hand," Catherine recalled, "she found it cold and pulseless. She immediately summoned the others." But she wasn't dead, at least not yet.

Catherine recalled that her mother rallied for a moment and blurted out, "Oh, Henry, if you only knew how we suffer." They were her last words, and she collapsed, dying later that night. This was on September 24, when the company was nearing Three Island Crossing, near present day Twin Falls, Idaho, just twenty-six days after her husband's death. The cause was also typhoid, likely contracted while caring for Henry.

There were no cottonwoods to build a coffin, and there was little time to waste on the dead. Several of the men—it isn't clear who, although it likely included Shaw—dug a grave in the sandy soil and lined it with willow boughs. Since Naomi Sager lacked a change of clothes, she was buried in the dress she died in, a blue calico.

"We looked everywhere for a light colored dress of mother's, but it was not to be found," Elizabeth Sager recalled. They wrapped her body in a sheet and lowered her into the grave.

"Her name was cut on a headboard, and that was all that could be done," Catherine said. "So in twenty-six days we became orphans. The baby was taken by a woman in the train, and all were literally adopted by the company. No one there but was ready to do us any possible favor. This was especially true of Captain Shaw and his wife. Their kindness will ever be cherished in grateful remembrance by us all. When our flour gave out they gave us bread as long as they had any, actually dividing their last loaf. To this day Uncle Billy and Aunt Sally, we call them, regard us with the affection of parents."

Shaw cut the Sager wagon in half so it was a two-wheeled kooster that could move more swiftly over the rough ground. Naomi Sager's fine china, with the speckled roses, the cherry chest of drawers, and the rolled carpet were all tossed to the side of the trail. They loaded the few remaining stores into the little cart. Dr. Dagen remained in charge of the team of oxen—and the train rolled on.

17

GHOSTS OF THE PIONEERS

WE WERE NOT FIT TO BE SEEN BY POLITE SOCIETY after our week on the trail. We were dirty—deeply dirty—and emotionally and physically bereft. Consequently, we could not have chosen a better town to recover than Lander, Wyoming: a rough-and-tumble mountain town nestled against the jagged peaks of the Wind River Range. It's set on a hillside, the nine-thousand-foot mountains dark and foreboding behind, with sweeping views of the foothills and expansive valleys to the east.

We rolled into town late in the day and found a Mexican restaurant on Main Street. We parked the car and tumbled into the restaurant in as civilized a way as we knew how, but we had long since forgotten how to use our "inside voices," and we were still wearing the clothes we'd put on that morning at our campsite alongside the Trail. The faces of every patron turned as we walked in and were hurriedly shown a table by a frightened-looking young Mexican girl. Oakley must have felt the closeness of the walls because he suddenly turned feral, crawling on the floor on his hands and knees and making unidentifiable animal noises. We hadn't seen a proper bathroom in over a week, so I made the most of the tiny restroom, scrubbing the kids' faces and hands one by one until they were glowing red. I could do nothing for their gnarled, dread-locked hair, but at least we weren't a health hazard.

Back at the table, the waiter must have sensed our urgency—or he wanted us in and out as fast as possible—since the service was exceptional. During the previous week, Rod and Doris had fed us cheerfully, but they hadn't fed us much, and we were all famished. Soon plates of refried beans and cheese, steaming tortillas, bowls of fresh salsa, and great mounds of rice were piled around us, and we had a high time eating as much as we could. A swarm of locusts could not have done a more efficient job of clearing the plates. Our table manners were abysmal. At one point I noticed Oakley using his knife like a shovel to stuff a pile of beans and rice into his mouth. Everyone else was using their hands, vacuuming their plates in a blur.

We found a campground right in town—The Sleeping Bear—that had showers and laundry and magnificent views of the valley. The sites were small and cramped and full of the usual monstrous RVs, but we didn't care. We spent the next morning cleaning out the car, scrubbing dried milkshake and pee stains and crumbled foodstuffs out of the seat upholstery. We all showered. We did several loads of laundry. And we mailed an enormous parcel back home to Charleston, full of antlers, the snakeskin, books we'd already read or that I'd accumulated for later research, unnecessary clothes, and other random souvenirs. By early afternoon we had begun to feel human again.

That evening we attended a rodeo, sitting in the bleachers with magnificent views of the Wind River Range. It was a warm evening, and it was the perfect diversion. The first event was broncs, the next bulls, and we all delighted in seeing their riders getting tossed into the dust and then scramble to the fence so they didn't get scrambled. After a week with horses and mules, we could all appreciate the skills of those involved, including the pair that lassoed the loose bull or bunking bronc that had rid itself of its rider.

The most exciting event, however, was the Indian Relay. Four teams of Indians had four horses apiece. Each team had one designated rider. They all rode bareback. The rest of the team members were the pit crew. The idea was to race around the dirt track as fast as possible, change horses in the pit, and then go around again, changing each time a lap was complete until four laps had been accomplished. First to cover four laps with the team's four horses was the winner.

It was a spectacle from the beginning. Each person was dressed in his team's jersey, delineated only by color: black and gold, green, red, and purple. The riders came galloping onto the track, loud music blared from the speakers, and the rest of the horses were led by the support crews. All the animals were excited, high stepping and tugging anxiously at their bridles, a wild look in their bulging eyes, nostrils flared and steaming in the cool night air. Their riders were the same. Each was a lithe youth of about sixteen, and they sat on their mounts with an easy nonchalance, as though they were a part of their leaping horses' sinuous bodies. The event may have been disorderly and chaotic, but these young men were first-class athletes, quivering but clearly in control. Horses jumped sideways and reared on their hind legs; they kicked and shook their manes. And all the while their riders sat casually, absorbing every muscle twitch with absolute fluidity.

By the time the race began, the crowd was on its feet, stamping and cheering. The horses took off in a flurry of sand and hooves and screams from the pit crews. It took only about thirty seconds for the riders to circle the lap and reappear around the final bend, the horses absolutely wild and galloping with abandon. And they didn't slow for the change. All the spare horses and support crew were standing directly beneath the stands, just ten feet below the roaring crowd, in a mass of writhing energy. As the horses came charging in, one of the crew merely caught the bridle of the running horse while the rider leaped off—sometimes landing on the saddle of the fresh horse and sometimes taking a single bounce onto the ground before swinging into the saddle and charging off down the track. Several times the new horses were already running by the time the rider caught hold, so it was all he could do to hang on, feet dragging in the sand, and climb aboard the sprinting animal.

One rider, a member of the red team who seemed to be the youngest of the bunch and who was wearing mirror shades, was clearly in the lead. He finished first each lap, but the purple team must have saved their strongest horse for last, because it took off like a flash in the final lap, making enormous strides and gaining rapidly on the leader with each passing second. We were all wildly cheering at this point, our nerves jangling with the thrill, and as the horses rounded the final turn there was no clear leader. Red and Purple were exactly abreast and running full tilt, the riders leaping and thrashing the reins to squeeze every ounce from the animals. In the final fifty yards, in a pounding tumult of hooves and muscle, Purple edged ahead for the win. It couldn't have been more exciting if it had been choreographed.

By the time the animals were cleared and the next event announced, we felt like we'd been in the race ourselves, and it was time to head home. We gathered what was left of our children and drove slowly through town and back to The Sleeping Bear, all of us falling precipitously into the deepest sleep.

In the morning we drove up Sinks Canyon, following the Popo Agie River upstream, and then up the steep switchbacks, straight to the top of the Continental Divide of the Wind River Range. This was where, in 1835, Capt. Benjamin Bonneville, William Shaw's inspiration to head west, crossed "fearful precipices" and "rugged defiles," and then was forced to "clamber on hands and knees" to reach the top. By the time we reached the top, where we parked the car and hiked to a fire tower, we were at more than nine thousand feet. The air was thin and cool, and Leah and I found it difficult to walk too quickly without being winded. It was here amongst these same jack pines and sugar pines that Frémont had wandered aimlessly after completing his survey of South Pass, hoping to find the highest peak in North America so he could name it for himself. He didn't, but he claimed he did, and no one has since been able to determine exactly which peak he climbed and claimed was the tallest. He calculated his altitude at 13,570 feet, but he did not take a celestial observation to fix his position. The peak that bears his name is a possibility, but so are any one of about three or four peaks in the general vicinity. This was also where Frémont encountered a solitary honeybee.

"Here, on the summit, where the stillness was absolute, unbroken by any sound, and the solitude complete, we thought ourselves beyond the region of animated life," he wrote, "but while we were sitting on the rock, a solitary bee (*bromus, the humble bee*) came winging his flight from the eastern valley, and lit on the knee of one of the men."

He was touched by the experience, imagined the bee as the first to cross the Continental Divide as "a solitary pioneer to foretell the advance of civilization," but not enough to spare its life. He pressed it into a large book, and then, after noting the presence of gneiss and feldspar at the summit, began his descent, and his return trip to Washington, D.C. "We had accomplished an object of laudable ambition, and beyond the strict order of our instructions," he wrote.

We hiked as far as a stone fire tower on the Continental Divide, put up in the 1930s by the Civilian Conservation Corps, and at the top reveled in the magnificent views of the peaks that Frémont and his men had ascended. We were in the clouds up here, and snowfields were everywhere even though it was July. We congratulated ourselves for our laudable ambition and returned to the car, huffing and puffing despite many weeks now of strenuous hiking.

We camped that night in the Shoshone National Forest along the shores of a mountain lake. While the spot was beautiful, it was not peaceful. ATVs and motor-cross bikes roared passed our campsite incessantly. The "National Forest" designation means you can do as you please on the land, including hunt, cut timber (with a contract through BLM), and tear around on motorized vehicles of any kind. In other words, you can do whatever the hell you want to on the land, because it belongs to you. The result is a near-Hobbesian state of nature: guns, chainsaws, and ATVs. Strangely, "National Parks" prohibit you from doing any of these things, and the feeling that you're being watched by the Smoky Bear rangers there is inescapable. It's because you are: they will issue citations for picking flowers or pocketing rocks as souvenirs. Neither seems to be a healthy way to interact with nature and wilderness.

The following morning, after a brisk swim in the lake, we descended the ridgeline driving southward toward South Pass. As we rolled west on U.S. Highway 28, the land immediately smoothed, the landscape taking on the shape of long, rolling billows. South Pass itself is as unexceptional as it was important to the westward emigrants. Without the signs at the rest area along the highway, you would have no idea that this slight hump in the land was the key to connecting wagons to the waters of the Pacific.

We got out of the car and walked around the signs, which directed us to look at a set of faint swales rising toward us from the east, carving a gentle arc through the grass and sagebrush. This was the Oregon Trail, clearly visible despite the intervening years. Some half million people passed through here, through the Rocky Mountains by way of this narrow, smooth saddle, between 1840 and 1869.

South Pass was supposedly first discovered by Westerners in 1812 by the Wilson P. Hunt and Robert Stuart party of John Jacob Astor's American Fur Company. But they kept the knowledge to themselves as a trade secret, and it was effectively lost to common knowledge until 1823 or 1824 when it was rediscovered by trapper Jedediah Smith (and James Clyman), who was working for William Ashley.

In 1832, Capt. Benjamin Bonneville became the first to bring wagons over South Pass. In 1836, Narcissa Whitman and Eliza Spalding traversed South Pass with their missionary husbands to become the first white women to cross the Rockies.

The roadside plaque does not overstate the case: THE SOUTH PASS, IN WHICH YOU ARE NOW LOCATED, IS PERHAPS THE MOST SIGNIFICANT TRANSPORTATION GATEWAY THROUGH THE ROCKY MOUNTAINS, INDIANS, MOUNTAIN MEN, OREGON TRAIL EMIGRANTS, PONY EXPRESS RIDERS, AND MINERS, ALL RECOGNIZED THE VALUE OF THIS PASSAGEWAY STRADDLING THE CONTINENTAL DIVIDE. BOUNDED BY THE WIND RIVER RANGE ON THE NORTH AND THE ANTELOPE HILLS ON THE SOUTH, THE PASS OFFERS OVERLAND TRAVELERS A BROAD, RELATIVELY LEVEL CORRIDOR BETWEEN THE ATLANTIC AND THE PACIFIC WATERSHEDS. As I copied these words, the wind whipping at my notebook pages, Oakley was climbing all over the sign like a monkey, and Jonah was trying to tell me about the butterfly in his hand and how its tongue would emerge from behind a flap on its face.

An estimated forty thousand people died and were buried along the Oregon Trail between the 1840 and 1869: from typhoid, cholera, wagon accidents, gunshot wounds, and later, Indian attacks. Graves were dug on the side of the trail, as deep as the soil allowed, and then piled with rocks to deter animals. Most of these graves have disappeared, their wooden crosses rotted away, the bones scattered by animals. Consequently, having one's grave invaded was a carnal fear amongst emigrants. The most notorious emigrant story to this effect is that of William Smith's family of 1846. He and his wife Ellen and their nine children, the youngest of whom was two and the oldest sixteen, and a few members of their company, became stranded in eastern Oregon when they lost their way. They were crippled by sickness, and then they ran out of provisions. The group camped for six weeks, living on the last of the stock, hoping the sickness would pass through the group so they could move again.

Finally William Smith had had enough. He declared that he would "take his little Spring Wagon to holl the littel children and doughter Louisa who had mountin feavre as might say starvation . . . nothing to eate. She was 16 years old." And then Smith suffered a heart attack and died. They buried Smith in the "little Spring wagon." But then Ellen Smith rallied. She loaded her children onto the family's surviving ox, tying the children who could walk to the animal so that their walking would keep them warm against the chill of early winter. Her toddler and her eldest daughter Louisa, who was clearly dying, she lashed to the back of the ox. And they started walking west.

The family pressed on, but Louisa soon deteriorated and she began to plead with her mother that, when died she wanted her grave deep enough so that animals could not reach her body. "[She] told her mother she wanted . . . a grave six feet deep for she did nat want the wolves to dig her up and eat her."

Louisa died shortly thereafter, and Ellen Smith implored the men of the company to dig a grave. But the soil was rocky, and their tools were poor, and they only managed four feet before giving up in frustration. Ellen excoriated the men and demanded they dig two feet farther, but they refused. She grabbed a shovel herself and began digging her daughter's grave, desperately striking at the hard earth until the men—overwhelmed at the sight of a mother digging her child's grave—did as she had requested.

By some miracle, Ellen Smith and her surviving eight children made it to Oregon. She staked a claim of 640 acres, and they cleared it together. Her children grew up and married off, and she lived well into her old age to see numerous grandchildren.

• • •

Henry and Naomi Sager died within three weeks and 250 miles of each other, Henry along the banks of the Green River and Naomi on an unremarkable patch of trail near the present city of Twin Falls, Idaho.

We sped west from South Pass onto a broad plain, parallel to, and often right on, the old Oregon Trail on Route 28, and the land flattened with each passing mile.

I wanted to find Henry Sager's grave. Everything I'd read about his death scene was depressing. He'd died in agony, expiring from typhoid after weeks of debilitating illness that had turned his bowels into liquid and prevented him from absorbing water and nutrients. As he was dying, he also had the knowledge that he'd brought his seven children and wife to the edge of the earth so he could live out his dream of working a free claim in Oregon. I wanted to see what he'd seen on his last day, when he said good-bye to his children, when he cried his apology to Naomi. I wanted to hear the current of the Green River, the dry breeze through the sagebrush. The full desolation. This grave would be alive with Henry Sager, I hoped.

And so it was. We were miles from anywhere—not a house, a building, or anything resembling civilization in all directions—when we rolled across the little bridge that spans the Green River and turned into a parking lot of the Seedskadee National Wildlife Refuge on the west bank. No cars passed on the highway; there was none in the parking lot. We were the only visitors.

We shut off the car and walked along the edge of the river. This was the exact place where the Oregon Trail crossed the Green River. It was here, on this western bank, that Henry Sager died on August 28, 1844.

Cliff swallows dived and wheeled along the surface of the current. A moderate breeze from the west riffled the dark rushing water. The sky was overcast and gray; a storm was approaching from the west, black clouds mounting on the horizon. The river is shallow, perhaps thigh deep in the middle, and the sound of the water flowing over the loose gravel must have provided some comfort to Sager in his final hours. The current was swift and steady, but it was not wild or confused with whirlpools or large eddies. It simply flowed southwest, toward the waters of the Pacific.

I tried to wade across the river, but when I was halfway across and the water reached the middle of my thighs, I realized I was in danger of being swept off my feet. The air was cool, and a swim this late in the day would give me the chills. I returned to the bank and we wandered the tall cottonwoods. These were descendants of the trees Shaw and Minto cut down to fashion Sager's coffin. The sandy soil was loose, as it was in his day. Catherine Sager wrote that the following year, in 1845, a party of emigrants had come across her father's grave and found his bones disinterred—perhaps by wolves, perhaps Indians looking for a trinket—spread around in the sagebrush and bleaching in the sun.

Leah and I and the kids had all separated as we wandered through the sagebrush and cottonwoods lining the bank, but soon Leah walked back to me. She was holding something—a bone—and she quipped that it was Sager's thigh. It could have been. It was the right size. It was old and weathered, and in this arid climate it could have been preserved easily despite the intervening 162 years. More likely it was a cow bone. There were plenty of them around.

She held it up, almost shaking it at me accusingly, and said, "I'll bet Naomi was pissed at him. How could she not have said, 'You drag us all the way out here—and now you go and die on me!'" She handed me the bone, this symbol of the quixotic nature of husband-wife relations, and walked away.

I had read an article in the *New York Times* in April before departing on this trip about the science of impulsivity that made me think of Henry Sager, and it came to my mind again as I wandered this lonesome riverbank wondering about the life of the man whose thigh bone I believed I was holding. Those of us who manage our impulses control our destinies. Those who don't, well—they die horrible deaths in lonely places having brought all their loved ones along, leaving them stranded.

"The people who can binge, gamble or try hard drugs and get away with it have a native cunning when it comes to risk, this and other studies suggest," the article read. "They are prepared for the dangers like a mountain climber or they sample risk, in effect, by semiconsciously hedging their behavior—sipping their cocktails slowly, inhaling partly or keeping one toe on the cliff's edge, poised for retreat." In nineteenth-century Oregon emigrant language, in other words, William Shaw had native cunning and Henry Sager did not. They both attempted the same task—crossing the continent with their families—but Shaw had a few toes on the cliff's ledge. It was a fine line, but he knew when to say when. And that's why he survived.

I choose to think the bone was part of Henry Sager. I was there to find a piece of his spirit, to reach out to him, as a father and husband, to touch and honor the restlessness that drove him to this lonely place. I put it in my backpack. As I write these words, it sits on my desk in front of me with the following words written in black ink on its bleached, porous surface: "7/4/06 Green River Wyoming."

We drove most of that night, after stopping for fireworks and pizza at Kemerrer, Wyoming (home of the first JCPenney retail store), rolling downhill into Idaho and into the city of Soda Springs well after midnight. We had read emigrant diaries that described the beauty of Soda Springs, where carbonated water bubbled up from the earth in numerous blow holes.

"These Springs are a great natural curiosity," wrote James Clyman as he passed through the area on September 7, 1844. "It almost takes your breath to drink a cup of it Quick from the Spring. I had not much more than one hour to make my examinations." (They were moving as fast as they could to beat the snows in the Blue Mountains.) "Several Large Springs of fresh water Break out in the viceinity of these & one hot Spring."

It was a veritable playground for these exhausted emigrants, and we could have used a similar experience. But the modern city of Soda Springs is not what it once was to early travelers. The springs that delighted Clyman and others along the Oregon Trail have been covered by a dammed reservoir, and the Monsanto Company "Slag Pour"—a hideous phosphorous plant—glows day and night like Mount Doom in the background, its molten "lava" visible from miles away.

The only real spring still left is in the center of town, but it has been "captured" and now sprays every hour on the hour. (The town chamber of commerce boasts that it is the "world's only captive hot spring.") The source of the spring is natural hot water, but it's on a timed valve. It was discovered in the 1930s when an enterprising young plumber drilled 315 feet into the ground with the intent of making a naturally heated swimming pool, but the force was such that it proved unfeasible. It shoots one hundred feet into the air. Little mounds of rust-colored carbonate surround the geyser, giving it a dispiriting air.

We had driven around in the middle of the night looking for a campground, only to get hopelessly lost on back roads in the Caribou National Forest. We finally surrendered at about 2:00 a.m. and checked into a dingy motel.

When I told the sleepy clerk what I'd done, he asked, "Did you go right or left at the ranch?"

I vaguely recalled seeing a ranch in the dark and making a right turn.

"Shoulda gone left," he mumbled, passing me the key. The following morning Oakley was up at dawn, and we had found a sad little breakfast place whose parking lot abutted the geyser.

"I want to go home," Leah said when her grayish omelet arrived.

We moved on, but discovered the town of Lava Hot Springs a few miles down the road, which was everything the town of Soda Springs was not. The town is set in a narrow canyon. A bucolic river carves its way through downtown, and public hot springs—the water varying degrees to suit every comfort level—offer weary travelers the chance to restore their sense of hope. The spa is surrounded by a beautiful Japanese garden, with flower-lined pathways carved into the purplish volcanic rock that formed the steep walls of the canyon. It was a magical place and such a contrast to the Soda Springs, which has effectively ruined its natural attractions.

We also rented inflatable tubes and took turns rafting down the river, which goes straight through the middle of town. We soaked in the hot pools, explored the twisting paths, and departed a few hours later, bound for a state park campground on the Snake River, fully restored.

As I pulled the car onto the highway, Leah eased her seat back and closed her eyes. "I've got my groove back," she said.

On August 9, 1862, a string of eleven wagons were threading their way through a narrow pass along the banks of the Snake River, a place where the trail ultimately squeezed through a fifty-foot gap in a jumble of volcanic rock, when a group of Indians on horseback came charging down from the bluffs above. They attacked the emigrants violently, killing one man outright and mortally wounding a young woman. They ransacked the wagons, tearing open barrels of flour and other supplies, and then, cutting the oxen free from their yokes, made off with as much stock as they could. The terrified emigrants were left stranded, with several others of them badly injured, and no stock to move their wagons. The Indians moved east along the river, only to come upon another such wagon train a few miles later, which they attacked with equal vigor, killing three more men and taking this group's stock as well.

The surviving emigrants of both groups limped to a defensive position just west of where the trail passed through the rocks at its narrowest point.

"The ground is covered with feathers, blood, flour, and corn," wrote H. M. Judson, who came upon the carnage later in the day. Darkness forced the groups to camp, surrounded by the grisly specter of their mutilated companions, but by dawn they felt emboldened to attempt to recover their stock.

The leader of the expedition, a man named Kennedy, gathered a group of thirty men and backtracked, eastward, until he found the Indians camped on a creek just three miles away. But they were well armed and drastically outnumbered the emigrants. In the ensuing battle, which resulted in a hasty retreat by the emigrants, five more whites were killed, including Kennedy. The Indians did not press their advantage, however, and the wagon trains were allowed to roll on unhindered by further attack. Apparently all the Indians wanted were the stock. In all, ten whites were killed and a larger number seriously injured.

That the incident occurred is not surprising. By the 1850s, the Oregon and California Trails were seeing tens of thousands of emigrants roll west each year. Lands were overgrazed, and buffalo herds significantly reduced. After decades of mostly peaceful relations, the Indians were striking back. AFTER 1854, EMIGRANTS HAD GOOD REASON TO BE ALARMED, reads a sign at Massacre Rocks State Park, the site of the infamous Indian attack of 1862. WAGON TRAFFIC HAD RUINED IMPORTANT TRADITIONAL INDIAN TRAILS. UNCOUNTED THOUSANDS OF OXEN, HORSES, SHEEP, AND CATTLE HAD OVERGRAZED A BROAD ZONE ALONG THEIR TRAIL,

LEADING TO INDIAN RESENTMENT. WORSE YET, A FEW EMIGRANTS HAD SHOT ENOUGH INDIANS TO PROVOKE A GOOD DEAL OF BITTERNESS.

Oakley and I were exploring a section of trail ruts about a mile east of Massacre Rocks, about the same location where one of the emigrant groups had been attacked. I was pushing him in his three-wheeled Mormon handcart while he had a cozy bottle. I had taken him shopping for groceries in the town of American Falls, and on the drive back I had sought out this spot because of a mention in my guidebook about the massacre and a section of pristine trail ruts. Leah and the three other kids were back at the campsite scrambling on the large boulders that overlook the deep waters of the Snake.

We had chosen the campsite because of its magnificent setting: on the banks of the Snake River where it carves a swath through a beautiful canyon dotted with enormous sagebrush. I wanted to swim in the Snake River—to feel the vibrations of this leg of the Oregon Trail journey—and discovered that, with the exception of the existence of Interstate 86, which carves its own swath through this picturesque canyon, the land appears largely unchanged. I had read frequently of the impassability and harshness of this region.

An 1843 letter by emigrant Jesse Looney to his family back East (carried back East by John Charles Frémont) read in part, "the wild sage will trip you. This shrub was very plentiful and hard on our teams."

And emigrant Peter Burnett had written, also in 1843, "Our route lay down the Snake River for some distance. This road was rocky and rough, except in the dry valleys, and these were covered with a thick growth of sage or wormwood, which was from two to three feet high, and offered a great obstruction to the first five or six wagons passing through it."

Oakley and I picked our way through huge sagebrush bushes, many growing upward of six feet. And the whole river valley, as far as we could see, was similarly carpeted in the silvery-green bush.

We spent three days exploring the riverbank and hiking the trails. One day we rented a canoe and kayak and paddled upriver in the emerald water, the cliffs rising around us as we paddled east. We beached the boats on the opposite bank and had a swim and then wandered along the steep riverbank until we came to the remains of a shack. We had learned from the park ranger earlier in the day that it was lived in by a hermit prospector named River Joe for some thirty years until he died in the 1960s. The cabin was full of signs of his thrifty life: knotholes had been patched with the round bottoms of tin cans, tacked in place with carpet nails; the roof was patched in places with strips of a metal sign; a crude three-plank table stood in the corner; and an old smokestack jutted through the roof. It was hard to believe that anyone had chosen to live for several decades in this miserable shack on the steep banks of the river. But I had to admire the view of the river from his kitchen window: a green ribbon of water flowing west through tall orange cliffs.

"Graves depress me," wrote Paul Theroux in *The Happy Isles of Oceania*. "They're for pilgrims and hagiographers."

He was describing Robert Louis Stevenson's grave on the Samoan island of Upolu. He had hoped to tour the author's grand house to feel the energy of his life only to be shooed away by the island's potentate and told to visit his grave instead. The man was living in Stevenson's house, and he didn't want visitors. Yet the grave was uniquely unsatisfying, offering no connection to the living man.

I felt this same despondency when, after our few days camped along the Snake River, we went in search of Naomi Sager's grave. She had died along the roughest, most desolate part of the trail somewhere along the Snake River between what is now the city of Twin Falls and the town of Glenn's Ferry. But at that time there was very little to mark the location. The actual references in Catherine, Matilda, and Elizabeth's accounts of their mother's death offered vague reference, and their memories had likely faded by the time they'd written the accounts as adults. We pulled off the highway in Twin Falls, Idaho, hoping for some sign of her ghost, an indication that her spirit was still wandering the Snake River Plain.

We saw nothing but mile after mile of car dealerships, gas stations and minimarts, strip mall plazas with wireless stores and Wok-n-Grills, and cash loans on car title stores. Her grave could be anywhere along a thirty-mile stretch of trail that no longer exists, long ago tilled under for commercial hell holes, highways, soybean and potato farms, and, more recently, acres of ugly tract housing with faux Olde English names that ended with a vestigial "e"—like "Pointe" and "Downes." If Naomi's ghost hung around the Snake River Plain after she died, I had no doubt it had long since fled, probably back East, to the farm in Missouri, perhaps, where she had fervently wished she never left.

18

LOVE IN THE TIME OF TYPHOID

SHORTLY AFTER THE DEATH OF NAOMI SAGER, the Independent Oregon Colony crossed the Snake River at Three Mile Crossing—a curve in the river where three islands sit side-by-side across the current, creating a sort of natural bridge. The river here is swift but fairly shallow, only up to the bottom of a wagon bed, which allowed the stock to wade across while still hitched to the wagons. But it is deep enough that the drovers doubled up the wagons, one next to another, to minimize the risk of their being swept away, the mass of the two wagons presenting a more stable resistance against the current.

To cross the stream, the wagon train drovers and the guides effected a clever tactic that used the river's current to ferry themselves from one island to the next until they were across the full width of the river. Descending a steep hill on the south bank, the wagons entered the river at an oblique angle, facing downstream, and were swept diagonally with the current toward the downstream end of the first island. They then turned the team east and walked upstream on the island so they could repeat the maneuver for the crossing to the center island. From this second island they forded across the remaining width of river, skipping the third island, until they reached the north bank of the Snake. The danger of the crossing was its holes: if an ox stepped into a deep hole in the river bottom, still yoked to the wagon, it could drown, and then the whole wagon would likely be rolled and carried off downstream.

As a precaution, a single horseman would lead the way scouting for holes, while two other saddled riders flanked the crossing wagons. The maneuver also required teaming the oxen in groups of four or six animals apiece, sometimes more, to counter the force of the current and control the wagon. Furthermore, if one team stepped into a hole, it swam while the others maintained their footing and kept the wagon moving.

Two years before, in August 1842, John Charles Frémont had lost his howitzer to the swift current here and several of his pack mules almost drowned. "[W]e were obliged to extricate by cutting them out of the harness," he wrote.

There were no accidents, but the Sager children would all remember with clarity how, despite the best efforts of their brother John to seal the cracks with tar, the water spouted through the wagon's cracks as they crossed the deepest sections of the river.

Dr. Dagen proved a kindly caretaker for the Sager children. His queer German accent, and the scorching German-English curses that he fired at the oxen when they failed to do his bidding, proved a delight to the children, and they grew fond of him.

One morning when he was loading the Sager kooster, he put too much weight in the back end and it flipped, all the family's belongings cascading down on top of him. Matilda Sager recalled the incident: "The Dutchman," as she called him, "was loading in the bedding and cooking utensils, when he got so much back of the center of gravity as to tip the cart up, whereupon he set up hallooing and scrambling that was very amusing to lookers-on."

Dagen fashioned a crutch for Catherine from a forked branch and padded it at the fork, so that she was soon able to hobble around the campsite after the wagons were halted for the day. Her broken leg was healing. During the last few days of September, Dagen removed the splint and found the leg thinner than the other, but just as straight. "Your papa did a good job," he said.

The baby, now in the care of Mrs. Eads but frequently passed amongst the mothers for nursing, had been renamed Henrietta Naomi by the Sager girls in honor of their parents. Sally Shaw and two other mothers, Mrs. Nichols and Mrs. Daniels, "were constant visitors to the Sager camp."

The group began to spread out considerably on the journey along the Snake River. John Minto and his two companions were far ahead, traveling by horseback and making much better time. "By now the emigration of 1844 to Oregon had largely degenerated into a free-for-all, with individual riders heading for the Columbia River as fast as their horses would take them, and a general atmosphere of devil-take-the-hindmost," wrote Frank McLynn, in *Wagons West*. "Everyone knew that there was only a month to go before the first snows could be expected; they might well have to pay dearly for those early floods in Kansas."

Since the Shaws, Morrisons, and surviving Sagers did not keep track of the dates of their trip, it's impossible to reconstruct a day-to-day picture of the final month of their journey. Nathaniel Ford's company seems to have been ahead of the Independent Oregon Colony by at least a week, since Minto mentioned passing their train a few days after he departed the Colony just west of Fort Hall, and there is no further mention of the original Gilliam group in Clyman's journal. Like Minto, Clyman departed the company to travel on horseback, in the company of other bachelors, so he could spread advance word about the group running short of provisions. He was also carrying a letter addressed to Dr. Marcus Whitman at Waiilatpu Mission. It was from William Shaw, and it described the fate of Henry and Naomi Sager, with their dying wishes: that he adopt all seven of the children.

A few days later, on October 9, Narcissa Whitman would write in a letter to a family member back East: "It is expected that there are more than five hundred souls back in the snow and mountains. Among the number is an orphan family of seven children, the youngest infant born on the way, whose parents have both died since they left the States. Application has been made for us to take them, as they have not a relative in the company. What we shall do I cannot say; we cannot see them suffer, if the Lord casts them upon us."

• • •

The Reverend E. E. Parrish was also ahead of the Shaw and Morrison company. He and a small group of families found it easier to travel in groups of only two or three wagons apiece, and they were making good time. The day Naomi Sager died, September 24, Parrish and company crossed the Snake at Three Islands Crossing. It was uneventful, Parrish simply marveling at the clarity of the water.

But his jaunty notes belie the suffering of his family from typhoid. Both ten-year-old Rebecca, and his son, Thomas Mapel Andrew Jackson Parrish, whom he called Jackson, age fourteen, were suffering from typhoid and were riding in the wagon as a result of their sickness. And the day before, Rebecca suffered an identical accident to that of Catherine Sager.

"To-day as little Rebecca was trying to get on or off the wagon, she slipped and fell, the wagon wheel rolling over and breaking her thigh," Parrish noted. "A sad accident for her and us all." She cried in pain at each rock in the trail, he said. Ever the optimist, however, Parrish added, "Glad, however, that it is no worse."

On September 29, a daughter was born to the Hawley family, Parrish wrote, while the group was camped just east of Fort Boise. All the while, the emigrants traded freely with—and camped within sight of—groups of Nez Perce Indians. "We are buying fish of the Indians," Parrish wrote on October 2, as they prepared to cross the Snake River for the last time and enter the Oregon Territory. "The price is a load of ammunition for fish." But at least they weren't going hungry—at least not yet. ("The Indians are offering us more fish than we want.")

The only annoyance the emigrants suffered at the hands of the Indians was smoke from the fires they set in the sage "to harvest roasted crickets, grasshoppers, and lizards."

On Thursday, October 3, Parrish and company crossed the Snake into Oregon, chaining all the wagons and oxen together, one behind the other, in a long train to protect against the swift current. "I thank God for the mercies that have attended us through all our difficulties," he wrote.

• • •

The Colony pressed on through the narrow pass along the Burnt River and by the end of the first week of October had entered the broad valley of the Powder River. The "Lone Pine," which for the previous three years of migrations had served as a landmark on the far end of this lonesome valley, had been recently cut down. Someone had thought it would make good firewood, only to realize their folly (the wood was green and unburnable) after it was felled. Steep, pine-covered mountains, the first of the Blues, were now along their left flank, but they would skirt this range until they came to the Grande Ronde River, where the trail ascended steeply into the Blue Mountains for the final push.

"After many hard pulls up and over mountains we landed in the valley on the south side of Grand Rounde, the most beautiful and picturesque spot we had seen on the road," wrote Benjamin Nichols Jr. "Surrounded on all sides by mountains which were covered with green foliage, consisting of pine, fir and tamarack, it formed quite contrast to the sand and sage brush of the plains through which we had passed."

While no doubt thrilled by the sight of the tall trees, the first deep green they had seen since departing Missouri, they also noticed another color at the tops of the higher peaks: white. It had begun to snow.

The ill luck that plagued the Sager family did not dissipate with the deaths of Henry and Naomi. On the last day of September, a few days after crossing the Snake River into Oregon Territory, they were camped at Grand Ronde, at the very base of the Blue Mountains. Once again, one of the children, Elizabeth this time, wandered too close to the campfire, which had been built high to ward off the night's chill, and her calico dress burst into flames, fanned by the night wind. She screamed, and Dr. Dagen leaped to his feet and beat the flames out with his bare hands. She was uninjured—saved, perhaps, by the layers of undergarments—but Dagen's hands were badly burned. It would be several days before he could manage the oxen again.

The group was, by this time, entirely without flour, and the diet of almost all meat began to take its toll on their digestive systems. "Aunt Sally, feeling miserable herself, came every night to see how the Sager children fared," wrote Neta Lohnes Frazier in *Stout Hearted Seven*. "From somewhere she got a little milk, which she portioned out, saving a few swallows for Dr. Dagen, who was very ill. He said later that the milk saved his life." Sally Shaw traded a few old clothes for a skinny milk cow.

While the nights had been cold on their journey across the Burnt River and Powder River Valleys, the days were now cold as well as they gained elevation. Snow was piling up.

"Having so light a load we could travel faster than the other teams," Catherine recalled, "and went on with Captain Shaw and the advance. Through the Blue Mountains cattle were giving out and left lying in the road."

Another evening, when the doctor and Francis Sager, who was fourteen at the time, were having trouble lighting a fire, Francis sprinkled a little gunpowder from his powder-horn directly into the smoldering wood. Flames flashed instantly upward and the powder-horn exploded in his hands. The flare burst in his face, burning off his eyebrows and eyelashes and singeing the hair on his head. He dashed to a spring and plunged his head underwater. When he returned, obviously unhurt and sheepish, Dagen and his siblings burst out laughing at the sight of their brother's face.

"[He] came back destitute of winkers and eyebrows, and his face was blackened beyond recognition," Catherine said.

Another night, shortly after the group had departed Grande Ronde and begun their climb into the mountains, William Shaw was awakened by his wife, who said she thought she heard the faint cries of a child: "Mama! Mama!" Shaw found Louise wandering aimlessly in the woods, wailing uncontrollably. She had found her way out of her bed in the wagon, and no one had noticed. The temperature was well below freezing.

"Taking her up," Matilda Sager recalled, "he placed her in the boys' bed between the Doctor and John. But for his timely aid she would have perished."

Yet all the while, notwithstanding the rough travel, the Morrisons must have found time to enjoy a little frolicking detour of their own. Somehow, inexplicably, in the midst of the dying and dust, Nancy had become pregnant. A child would be born the following April, which meant that conception occurred sometime in August or September. That they had the desire seems incredible. People were actively dying, first the Nichols's daughter Elizabeth, then Henry Sager, and then Naomi. Nowhere in the diaries is there any mention of amorous attention, of course; their evangelical prudishness would have blushed at any such reference. The only such glimpse that such things occurred appears in Minto's diary, in which he describes the wedding night of a young man and woman back in Kansas. The bride's father refused consummation, however, and placed his daughter in the family tent and "the kindly old man sat up all night with a brace of old-time flintlock cavalry pistols to enforce his opposition."

That they were prudes is an understatement. They also felt guilty about, and fearful of, sex, taking great pains to deny its existence. For example, a section in *Gunn's Domestic Medicine* on "The Outward Parts of Female Generation" describes female anatomy first with an apology: "I would omit these parts altogether, were not the slight delineation of them essential to understanding medical doctrines and diseases relating to them." It then proceeds with a prim reproach: "The front [of the vagina] exhibits what is called the MONS VENERIS, which is shielded by nature with a coat of *hair*, as if she aimed at the concealment of these parts, intended for the procreation of the human species."

A section on "Love," however, best illustrates the 1840s pioneer mind-set as concerns carnal matters. "This is one of the master passions of the human soul, and when experienced in the plenitude of its power, its devotions embrace with despotic energy and uncontrolled dominion, all the complicated and powerful faculties of man," Gunn wrote. Lest the reader get the wrong idea, however, Gunn admonished that the power of love be "restricted to its legitimate objects, and restrained within due bounds by moral sentiment," so that it "may be called the *great fountain* of human happiness." Finally, love "concentrates all its pure and sublime energies at the great *fountain of existence*, the throne of the LIVING GOD." Somehow, while death was all around them, the great fountain of Wilson Morrison's happiness—not to mention his sublime energies—had found its way into Nancy's skirts.

• • •

When the Sagers, Shaws, and Morrisons cleared the Blue Mountains on October 15, the view they were offered as they emerged from the dense forests was breathtaking: thousands of feet below them were rolling grass fields and on the horizon, the flat, snowcapped peaks of Mount Hood and Mount St. Helens.

They camped on the Umatilla River on October 15, near the present town of Pendleton, Oregon. "We purchased of the Indians the first potatoes we had eaten since we started on our long and sad journey," wrote Catherine Sager.

"This was Cayuse country," wrote Erwin Thompson in *Shallow Grave at Waiilatpu*, "the Indians among whom Dr. Whitman had established his mission. The emigrants had already met a few Cayuses as far east as the Grande Ronde and had found them to be different from the Indians of the eastern plains."

The Reverend E. E. Parrish, along with his family and their traveling companions, the Hawley and Cave families, were just a few days behind the Shaws and Morrisons. Mrs. Cave was due to give birth any day. They would also turn north for the mission with the intention of nursing their ailing children back to health. When he arrived at the Umatilla campground October 22, he, too, exclaimed at the apparent bounty of the land. "[T]he best kind of bottom land and good grass," he wrote. He noted the presence of hundreds of healthy grazing horses, which all belonged to the Indians, who were tending thriving plots of corn, potatoes, and pumpkins in fenced-in gardens. "This is a fine growing country," he added.

He also noted that the "packers," people on horseback who were provisioning stragglers with supplies from the Whitman mission, reported that the snow in the mountains was now knee deep. "Most deplorable, indeed," Parrish wrote. "We made a fine escape, for which we thank God."

Like the Indians John Minto had met along the Snake River, the Cayuse showed an eagerness to trade. Whitman had been teaching them to farm and raise beef cattle in hopes of encouraging them to adapt to an economic, rather than nomadic, lifestyle. "He was convinced that only by this means could he prepare them for the inevitable advance of civilization that was going to overtake them." In this Whitman was ahead of his time—and he would pay the price.

At Umatilla the Trail split: those who were going straight to the Willamette Valley pressed northwest to the Columbia River Gorge, working their way across the undulating, grassy countryside over land that settlers would soon realize was among the best topsoil in the world and capable of growing just about anything. The Shaw and Sager families would split from the main group here and press north the following day for the Whitman mission, near what is now Walla Walla, Washington.

Shaw rode ahead that evening with the intention of discussing with Marcus and Narcissa Whitman his hopes of leaving the Sager children in their care. He returned late that night and reported to his wife what he'd learned. The Whitmans would take the girls, he said, but they had no use for the boys. Sally was distraught over the possibility that the children might be separated, but Shaw described a scene of bedlam at the mission: "People running in and out all the time, enough to drive a person crazy. Children all over the place."

He was also wracked with his own conflicting emotions. Both Sagers had specifically asked him to keep the children together, but he was barely supporting his own family, let alone another seven children, one of whom was a sickly infant. The Sager children overheard the exchange: Sally's pleading, Shaw's hand-wringing and assurances that he'd do the best he could to convince the Whitmans to take the boys as well. The following morning Catherine asked Sally about the baby. The infant was still a few days behind, up in the mountains, and would be brought to the mission directly by the Eads family. Sally said the infant was so weak that they shouldn't expect that she could survive the trek through the mountains. That morning, after Elizabeth had flung her arms around Sally's waist and pleaded with her to let them stay with the Shaws, Billy Shaw softened. He assured his wife—and the children, too, apparently—that if the Whitmans wouldn't take the boys, that he would. And he would return in the spring for the girls so they could all stay together.

"With this promise in their ears," Frazier wrote, "the four girls climbed into the cart. John and Frank came along behind with the three extra oxen, their old Bossy, and the broken-down cow Aunt Sally had bought. Dr. Dagon cracked his whip and they were off, Uncle Billy leading the way on horseback. The girls, looking out at the back, waved to Aunt Sally as long as they could see her."

They traveled all that day, camped along a creek that night, and then arrived before noon on October 17, looking every bit as disheveled as could be imagined after six months on the trail. Sally Shaw had tried to clean them up and trim their hair, but they must have been a shocking sight to Narcissa Whitman when they appeared on the dusty wagon road that led from the Blue Mountains.

"Here was a scene for an artist to describe!" Catherine recalled. "Foremost stood the little cart, with the tired oxen that had been unyoked lying near it. Sitting in the front end of the cart was John, weeping bitterly; on the opposite side stood Francis, his arms on the wheel and his head resting on his arms, sobbing aloud; on the near side the little girls were huddled together, bareheaded and barefooted, looking at the boys and then at the house, dreading we knew not what. By the oxen stood the good German doctor, with his whip in his hand, regarding the scene with suppressed emotion. Thus Mrs. Whitman found us."

Three Islands Crossing today is largely unchanged in appearance since the 1840s. Standing at the interpretive center on the north bank of the Snake River, I looked across at where the Oregon Trail cuts a deep angle into the bluffs on the opposite bank. The islands themselves appear similarly unchanged with the exception that they are now covered with thick stands of trees. I stood on the deck while the docent pointed out various landmarks: the impossibly steep drop—about a forty-degree angle—to the water's edge, the route they took between the islands, and then the final landing on the north bank where the trail continued northwest.

"The difficulties attending the crossing had been represented as being almost insurmountable; but upon examination we found it an exaggeration," wrote emigrant Joel Palmer of his August 23, 1845, crossing at Three Islands. Nonetheless, he wrote, "Great care must be taken that these teams not be beat down too low and beat over the ripple." To be "beat down too low" meant to be swept downstream; the "ripple" was where the water was shallow. Thus, if you were beat down too low, past the ripple, you were suddenly in deep water with no recourse but to do your best to release the animals and swim for shore as your belongings were swept away forever.

The previous year a regiment of "Buffalo Men," Civil War reenactors who are descendants of an original black regiment, had staged a reenactment here. The men were in their sixties and seventies, "and their horses were old, too," a docent told me. While the horses were in the deepest part of the crossing, on the final approach, one of the horses snagged its foot on some weeds and suddenly spooked, throwing the rider into the swift current. "He would have drowned if they didn't have the Ski-Doos to fish him out," she said.

Two years earlier another incident occurred during a different reenactment. One of the town's citizens, who makes the crossing each year with his team of oxen, was halfway across when one of the oxen lost its footing and slipped into a hole. The animal was forced under, and the wagon lost its forward momentum, was caught by the current, and then tipped. They were all swept downstream, and one of the oxen drowned. It was never released from the wagon. On the same day a colt that had been tied to its mother on the crossing was also drowned.

I asked Dixon Ford, the seasoned ox drover from Utah, about Three Islands Crossing, and he said that in the best of circumstances it is a challenging feat and the skill of the pioneers in handling the crossing was not to be underestimated by modern reenactors.

"It takes two to four teams"—four to eight oxen—"of young, strong oxen to pull a wagon across the Snake, with a drover at each team, and a rope or chain attached to the tongue, and being pulled by an ox team already across," Ford told me. "This way, in the event the [release] pin was pulled to save the oxen, the wagon could still be pulled to the bank."

The exhibits here, as in most of the museums we visited, were strikingly sensitive in their presentation of how the Indian population was treated. This one provided equal space in presenting exhibits on the displacement of the tribes and the Trail of Tears as it did to the emigrants' journey. (Interestingly, these museums stand in contrast to the numerous plantation museums back in Charleston, which barely mention slavery, only offering occasional verbal shrugs, such as, "It was a way of life," or "The slaves on this plantation were actually treated pretty well.")

On our drive through the last part of Oregon—we were hoping to camp in the Blue Mountains near Baker City, Oregon—Leah fantasized about having a date, just the two of us. "A nice restaurant," she said, "where you sit on chairs, not in the dirt, and there's a table in front of you with a knife and fork. And a napkin! And then there's a tall glass of water with ice chips in it."

"And where are the kids?" I asked.

"Babysitter," she said. "And then we'd walk along a harbor somewhere in the—away from this heat!—cool evening breeze and . . ."

"And then you'd fall in the water!" Jonah shouted from the back seat.

"And you'd eat Cheetos!" Raven added.

Leah ignored them. "My hands would not be sweaty; in fact, they'd be clean. And then afterward we'd sit on the park bench under a streetlamp. Just one night like that, and I'd be happy to go back into the woods and be a savage again. Is that too much to ask?"

"And then Oakley would say, 'ARRRRGH!'" Finn yelled, joining the fun.

But Leah's eyes were closed and she was far away from us, on the park bench by the harbor with the cool evening breeze blowing in off the sea.

We camped in a beautiful pine forest in the Wallowa–Whitman National Forest, just outside of Baker City, Oregon, a small city along the Powder River at the edge of the Blue Mountains. The scent of pines and the coolness of the shade felt wildly luxurious after a month of camping in the harsh sunlight and dusty scrub of Wyoming and Nebraska. There was a change in the air, a whiff of something gentler. As we had crossed the Snake River into Oregon we immediately noticed fruit trees lining the highway. Now, there were lupines blooming in the clearings, and the birds were different: flickers and robins and nuthatches. It must have driven the emigrants crazy with anxiety, to know they were almost there yet know they had one of the toughest challenges, a snowy weeklong mountain crossing when they were nearly starving, still to come.

We spent the following morning wandering the wide sidewalks of Baker City while waiting for the car's oil to be changed. This was one of those rare small cities in which you could conduct all your daily business without need of a car, without having to drive from one strip to another. The dealership was across the street from the public library, which was flanked by a beautiful green park with tall shade trees, and through it all ran the crystalline waters of the Powder River. I bought two coffees and some pastries at a sidewalk café, and Leah bought a large bag of fresh cherries at a farmer's market in the park. If Bill Bryson had missed Baker City in his search for "Amalgam"—the perfect American town—in his book *The Lost Continent,* he would need to return and eat some cherries alongside this river.

Today, the pass through the Blue Mountains is almost as spectacular as it was in the 1840s. A twisty, narrow highway, I-84, ascends westward from the Grande Ronde, flanked by stern warnings to trucks about the steep grades and required speeds, through dense forests of towering Douglas-fir and lodgepole pines. (The tranquil scenery actually belies a nasty local fight over the health of the forest: loggers, Indian tribes, and environmentalists all pitted against each other, and the Forest Service caught in between.) This is the Blue Mountains Scenic Byway, which rolls through the dense forests and then spills out on the other side in a tremendous view of the valley that so enticed the overland emigrants. It was too hazy to see Mount Hood that day. The wheat fields spread below like a rolling golden carpet. As we descended, mile after mile of switchbacks, our ears popped from the pressure. We passed several runaway-truck ramps and signs ordering trucks to adjust their speed and gear selection according to their respective weights. At the base of the mountains, where Parrish, the Shaws, and the Sager children had been so impressed by the presence of Cayuse Indians and their little farms, there was an Indian reservation, the commercial center of which was a sprawling casino. The lot was full of RVs and truck rigs and an untold number of cars. Dr. Whitman's efforts at directing the energies of the native peoples to fruitful industry in the capitalist tradition had paid off—all too well.

19

WHAT LIES BENEATH

MONDAY, NOVEMBER 30, 1847, three full years since the arrival of the seven Sager orphans, dawned gray and cold on the Waiilatpu Mission. A chill fog enveloped the Walla Walla River Valley so that the Blue Mountains were not visible to the west. The spirit of the camp matched the weather that morning. A deadly course of measles had arrived with the migration of 1847. The largest such migration so far—it included some five thousand people—it brought with it the disease that had crippled the families of the mission that fall. About seventy people now lived at Waiilatpu, including eleven children, a schoolteacher, numerous hired hands who exchanged labor for food and shelter, several emigrant families who paused to regain their health after the arduous overland journey, and, presiding over it all, an increasingly haggard Marcus and Narcissa Whitman.

The disease had been especially cruel in the Cayuse communities in the neighboring area. Every week saw the death of another Cayuse child, and that morning, in fact, Marcus had administered to the burial of a child in the mission cemetery. Its mother had carried its body to the mission for a Christian burial. Hundreds of Cayuse had died in the previous months, yet no white person had. As Catherine Sager recalled: "I have seen from five to six [Cayuse] buried daily."

The reason was clear: this was a scourge brought by the whites to eliminate the population of the Cayuse one by one. Added to this suspicion was the Indian belief that the doctor who failed to cure his patients must die himself. As early as 1845 Narcissa had written to her parents of "the serious trials . . . with the Indians." Two Indian leaders died that spring, and the Whitmans were duly warned: "[T]hey have ventured to say and intimate that the doctor has killed them by his magical power, in the same way they accuse their own sorcerers and kill them for it." Yet she signed off that letter with the optimism that carried her along the two-thousand-mile journey and gave her the strength to build the mission in the first place. "We are in the midst of excitement and prejudice on all sides, both from Indians and passing emigrants, but the Lord has preserved us hitherto and will continue to, if we trust Him."

The previous day, Sunday, November 29, Marcus had traveled thirty miles south to visit the Cayuse lodges on the Umatilla River, the same communities that had so impressed the pioneers of the Independent Oregon Colony on their descent from the Blue Mountains in November 1844, only to find that the population was wracked by disease. Marcus had been given a dire warning by his friend Stickus, a Cayuse who had not converted to Christianity as so many others had, but who nonetheless nurtured relations with the Whitmans and other white settlers. The Cayuse were blaming him for the deaths, Stickus told Whiman, and the killing of a failed medicine man—the *tewat*—was a longstanding Cayuse tradition. Leave Walla Walla until the measles passed. His life was in immediate danger.

But, returning to the mission that evening, Whitman did not make plans to evacuate the mission, either because he felt he could not leave so many people in need or because he underestimated the threat and couldn't believe that these people, who had grown to be his friends and to look up to him, could actually harm him. He told Narcissa of Stickus's warning, and both Elizabeth and Catherine Sager, now eleven and thirteen years old respectively, overheard. "If things do not clear up," Marcus told Narcissa that night, "I shall have to leave in the spring." Whitman had made a deal—or so he thought—with the Cayuse a week previous: allow him to stay through the winter, and if, come spring, they wanted him to leave, he would shut down the mission, take his family, and depart forever. Nonetheless, the tension and threats continued unabated.

Narcissa had long ago been frustrated by her interactions with the Cayuse, yet she must have underestimated the urgency of the pressing threat. She found them "insolent, proud, domineering, arrogant." But until this point she had not found them violent.

Both the Whitmans were exhausted. In letters to her family back east, Narcissa incessantly referred to the effects of her husband's multi-tasking on their health. "I am so thronged and employed that I feel sometimes like being crazy, and my poor husband, if he had a hundred strings tied to him pulling in every direction, could not be any worse off." In addition to the Sager orphans, the Whitmans had adopted several mixed-raced children, including the daughter of legendary mountain man Joe Meek, Helen Mar Meek, and the daughter of fur trader Jim Bridger, Mary Ann. "I now have a family of eleven children," Narcissa gushed to her parents in 1845, before the measles epidemic and before management of the mission taxed their health. "I get along very well with them; they have been to school most of the time; we have had an excellent teacher, a young man from New York . . . there are two girls of nine years, one of seven, a girl and a boy of six, another girl of five, another of three and the baby [now renamed Henrietta Naomi after her biological parents], she is now ten months." Her brood also included the teenaged Sager boys, John and Francis.

And in all other aspects, the mission had been successful. The center of the mission was a large, T-shaped adobe building whose ten rooms served as dining hall, school, and living quarters for the Whitmans, their adopted children, and several emigrant families. There was also a blacksmith shop and a sturdy bunkhouse that was used to house emigrant families. The mission included a thriving farm with healthy herds of cattle and sheep. The wheat was unrivalled in its quality, and Whitman and his hands had built a gristmill, which was powered by the Walla Walla River and, up in the Blue Mountains where timber was plentiful, a sawmill that supplied lumber for the almost constant construction and building additions.

And the Sager children thrived also. Narcissa Whitman, standoffish at first, had embraced the children and nursed baby Henrietta Naomi back to health. Over the course of the winter of 1844–45, both Narcissa and Marcus Whitman became attached to the children, so that by spring, when William Shaw made good on his promise to check with them, the Whitmans felt resolute in their interest in adopting them all. An adoption and estate agreement was drawn up on June 25, 1845, signed by J. W. Nesmith, probate judge of Oregon, and the property given over to the Whitmans:

> 3 yoke of oxen at $50 per yoke
>
> The fore wheels of one wagon
>
> One cow
>
> One odd steer
>
> One cow (excluding five dollars expended in procuring her from the Indians)
>
> 3 chains and two yokes
>
> 1 ax
>
> 1 screw plate

The total value of Henry Sager's estate was listed as $264.50—or a little over $7,000 in today's money.

The children, even Francis whose rebellious streak would lead to his briefly running away from the mission to live with the Indians, grew to love Narcissa as a mother. Each child recalled the "big-hearted Dr. and Mrs. Whitman" who taught them scripture and encouraged their interest in school. They learned the workings of the farm and delighted in sharing their lives with the Indian communities. "We had our different kinds of work to do," wrote Matilda Sager of her three years at the Whitman Mission. "We had to plant all the gardens and raise vegetables for the immigrants who came in for supplies. We got up early in the morning and we each had our piece of garden to weed and tend. . . . Everything was done in routine." They swam in the river, went on picnics, gathered flowers and herbs for botany lessons with Narcissa. They found the mission full of music and learning and genuine love.

In its eleven years of service, the mission had been built to achieve a thriving industry where natives and whites coexisted in relative harmony. The temperate climate, and a blessedly rich topsoil that remains, today, the pride of Washington State, allowed for a success that emigrants could only have dreamed of achieving. And it was all done with an admirable selflessness. The Whitmans could have achieved great wealth, had they chosen, but instead their goal was to teach the natives the way of the open market—and, of course, to show them, in the full spirited manner of the evangelical Second Great Awakening movement, the benefits of accepting Jesus Christ as their savior.

But Marcus Whitman was no idealistic fool. He understood the need to be cautious and to not allow his sense of charity get in the way of his good sense. He effectively marginalized those who showed a penchant for erratic or destructive behavior, and he rewarded those who were frugal and trustworthy. In a letter relating to mission business, written just three weeks before the events of November 29, Whitman called one such Cayuse man a "worthless vagabond" for his constant abuse of trust. The man was "not worth the food he eats," Whitman wrote to Alonson Hinman at his supply station at the Dalles—a set of rough rapids on the Columbia that marked the traditional end of the overland portion of the journey. (They have since been eliminated by a dam.) Yet by late November, Whitman was worn down and likely saw any attempt to flee, to follow the advice of his friend Stickus and save his skin, as a greater chore and risk than remaining at the mission and simply weathering the epidemic. His medical training would have informed his decision: measles would rip through the weakest of the population, but it would pass.

Another such troublemaker was Joe Lewis, "an unprincipled scoundrel who saw personal gain in spreading discontent." A Canadian Indian—not a Cayuse—who joined an emigrant group at Fort Hall that summer, Lewis seemed to be wandering about looking for trouble when he fetched up at the Whitmans' doorstep that fall. He had been kicked out of the wagon train for stirring up trouble, and within a few days of his arrival, both Narcissa and Marcus had concluded the same thing: he had to go or he would spell their doom by turning the Cayuse against them. But Lewis saw at once that at Waiilatpu he had stepped into an opportunity. The diseased natives were indeed restless and the building resentment of the white interlopers could be harnessed, he thought. If Lewis could drive off or kill Whitman, he would be seen as a hero and would be able to manage the thriving mission.

Marcus Whitman derailed his scheme, at least for a time, persuading a passing emigrant train to take Lewis with them down the Columbia River Gorge as far as the Dalles, where Whitman hoped he would be swept farther west in the river traffic and not return to Waiilatpu. But by late November Lewis must have been too tempted by the tense situation at Waiilatpu, which was also conveniently separate from the growing communities at the end of the Oregon Trail, with their fledgling courts, law-enforcement squads, and their provisional legislature, and so returned to the mission.

"The field was well opened for creating trouble," Catherine Sager recalled, "and Joe Lewis improved the opportunity offered."

The building tension of the autumn of 1847 burst on November 30, with the arrival of two Cayuse on the steps of the Whitmans' house late that morning. Tiloukaikt, a respected leader who had himself lost three children to measles, and another man, named Tomahas, knocked at the front door and angrily demanded medicine for their families. Both Marcus and Narcissa Whitman had been up most of the night tending to the sick and must have sensed the edge to the men's voices. John Sager and Mary Ann Bridger were in the house also; Francis and Matilda Sager were at school in an adjacent building. The remaining children filled the house's beds, both in the living room and upstairs, in a makeshift measles ward.

Pushing the door open, the men stalked into the kitchen, shouting their demands as they approached the living room. But Whitman immediately bolted the door, sealing himself, Narcissa, the children, and access to the other children upstairs, inside. John Sager and Mary Ann Bridger had been fiddling with a ball of twine to make a new set of brooms when the men entered and remained in the kitchen, apparently unaware of the pressing danger. Thinking he could get rid of the men with medicine, Whitman told them he'd get the medicine if they calmed down and waited outside. He then removed a vial—the record is silent on exactly what it was—from a cupboard in the living room, and emerged into the kitchen where the men were and handed it over, carefully and calmly, explaining the dosage. By now John Sager and Mary Ann Bridger had stopped what they were doing and were watching the men carefully from across the room. After taking the medicine from Whitman, Tiloukaikt continued his tirade, angrily accusing Whitman of the deaths of so many Cayuse and refusing to leave. Tomahas, meanwhile, as though executing a prearranged plan, circled behind Whitman, drew a tomahawk out from beneath his robes, raised it high in the air, and brought it down hard on the back of Whitman's head.

John Sager lunged for a pistol on the mantel, while Mary Ann ran screaming from the house and circled back to the living room door where Narcissa was still barricaded with the children. Narcissa let her in and bolted the door again while Tomahas continued his assault on Marcus Whitman in the adjacent room.

Whitman crumpled to the floor in a rain of blows from the hatchet, unable to cover his head and sustaining numerous brutal injuries to his head and neck. He lost consciousness just as Tiloukaikt, seeing John reaching for the pistol, drew a musket from his robes and shot John Sager squarely in the chest.

And then all hell broke loose.

As the report issued from the house, a band of dozens of Indians burst from the yard and rushed the house and outbuildings en masse. It was an all-out attack, and they had been awaiting the signal: the gunshot. Tiloukaikt and Tomahas hacked at Whitman and John Sager until they thought they were dead—one of them slicing open John's throat and, inexplicably, stuffing his shirt into the gash—and then emerged outside to join the melee. Men, women, and children were running to and fro in abject panic, some running to escape and being cut down in a hail of gunfire, and others running to help and being met with the same assault. William Marsh, a recent arrival at Waiilatpu to care for his daughter and grandson, was hired to operate the mission's gristmill and had been operating the mill that morning. He charged from the mill but "got only a few steps" when he was cut down by gunfire, dying instantly in the grass courtyard. Judge Lucien W. Saunders, who was living on the mission with his family in exchange for teaching school, similarly ran from the school into the courtyard, and began racing to the emigrant bunkhouse where his wife was working that morning. He didn't get far either. He was tackled by two Cayuse wielding knives, wrestled to the ground, and stabbed to death.

In the stockyard, Jacob Hoffman, another emigrant, was butchering cattle when he heard the shot that hit John Sager. Two Indians had been loitering nearby, ostensibly waiting for a handout of beef entrails, and at the signal rushed upon him. Hoffman was holding an ax and did his best to defend himself, but he, too, was killed almost instantly, either by gunfire at close range or with the butchering knives.

The Indians' first prearranged priority, apparently, was to eliminate the men, which they did within a few minutes, those whom they found, anyway. The two who survived the initial attack, emigrants Nathan Kimball and Andrew Rogers, charged across the yard under a flurry of bullets and reached the house, pounding on the barricaded door until Narcissa Whitman unbolted it, and they spilled inside as she bolted the door behind them. They were bleeding profusely from gunshot wounds. Narcissa and the others bandaged the men as best they could.

With the help of Mary Ann Bridger and two other emigrant women, Mrs. Hall and Mrs. Hays, Narcissa had, meanwhile, dragged Marcus into the living room. They left the body of John Sager where he lay, his gaping neck a clear indication that he was beyond hope. Whitman was conscious, but just barely, and muttering to his wife about what she needed to do: keep the children safe. They positioned Marcus on a settee and bandaged his gashed head. He lay moaning but soon became incomprehensible and finally lapsed into unconsciousness.

Out in the yard, the Indians emptied the schoolhouse and the children huddled together, screaming in panic at the violence unfolding all around them. But someone was missing, Joe Lewis noted. There were only girls in the group, which meant that at least one young man was still unaccounted for: fourteen-year-old Francis Sager.

Francis had been at school that morning, and when he heard the shot that killed his brother, and Lucien Saunders had run from the building, he had ushered all the children up into the schoolhouse loft. He must have sensed that Lewis and the others were eliminating the men, so he hid from view when Lewis entered the school and ordered all the children down from the loft and into the yard. Lewis, not seeing Francis, began scouring the buildings, and finally lined up all the children in the yard with the apparent aim of summary execution. It was then that Francis, listening or watching from the loft, emerged to join his sister Matilda, who was eight years old, in the line. She was bawling hysterically, and he, not for the first time, began to comfort her. His actions likely saved the children's lives, but Lewis immediately grabbed Francis by the collar, dragged him from Matilda's grip, and, in full view of his sister and the other children, shot him in the head.

The scene inside the living room was similarly hysterical. Several children had been bathing in washtubs when the assault on Whitman occurred. They had run in a blind panic, stark naked, upstairs to join the others who were sick in bed. The living room was covered in blood from Kimball, Rogers, and Whitman, but Narcissa somehow maintained her poise and bandaged the men, urging them to stay upstairs to protect the children. Upstairs, Kimball must have known that the Indians would rush the living room next and so positioned the barrel of a gun—"a discarded musket"—so that it aimed at anyone attempting to ascend the stairs. The gun was useless, but only the pointed barrel was visible from below.

It was at this moment, after Marcus Whitman had lost consciousness, that Narcissa must have realized the futility of her predicament. The Indians' rage, however ill-conceived and misguided, was inescapable, and she was trapped. She walked to the door and looked outside. She would have seen the children huddled in the courtyard. She must have seen the body of Francis Sager lying close by. She would have seen the bodies of the schoolteacher Lucien Saunders and those of her friends Jacob Hoffman and William Marsh, slumped in the grass. And then she caught Joe Lewis's eye. He was staring at her from the yard, a pistol in his hands. Another Indian—the record is silent on exactly who—was standing nearby. He raised his musket and fired. A ball pierced the glass in the door's window and hit Narcissa in the chest, knocking her backward in a spray of blood. It was not a mortal wound; she recovered her composure yet again and was quickly bandaged and helped upstairs. And only just in time. The Indians broke down the door and raged through the house, destroying whatever they could. They set upon Marcus Whitman, who was either already dead or simply unconscious, and mutilated his face with a quirt.

Only the broken barrel of the gun prevented them from charging upstairs. Tamsucky, a Cayuse who the Whitmans had trusted, entreated them to descend, explaining that the Indians were preparing to set fire to the house if they did not. Their lives would be saved, he said. Whether she believed him or whether she had given up, Narcissa did descend the stairs, only to catch sight of her husband's mutilated body on the settee. She collapsed in hysterics.

Rogers helped her to a settee, and Joe Lewis then insisted that Rogers take one end of the sofa, and he the other, so that they could together carry her outside. Thinking Lewis was somehow offering to help, he picked up the other end, and they carried Narcissa through the front door and out into the yard. They only got a few paces, however, when Lewis set his end down and stepped away from Narcissa. A group of Indians in the yard then let loose with a volley of musket fire at Narcissa and Rogers, who were hit multiple times. Narcissa was dead. The Indians then rushed Narcissa's body and inflicted the same mutilation on her face as they had done to her husband. Rogers, meanwhile, lay bleeding and moaning in the grass, not quite dead, but mortally wounded. "[T]o the enjoyment of his attackers he struggled in the mud, suffering a lingering death that did not finally release him from pain until far into the night," wrote Erwin Thompson.

The standoff continued that night with Kimball and the children in the attic and the Indans downstairs and in the outbuildings. Kimball attempted to reach the river during the night to retrieve water for the children, draped in a blanket so as to appear to be an Indian as he moved in the dark. He had managed to reach the river, only to be discovered as he was recrossing a split-rail fence that bordered the yard. He was shot to death on the fence; his body remained slumped over the top rail, in plain view of the survivors the next morning. The children remained holed up in the attic all night and emerged the following day to a scene of idle confusion punctuated by brief bursts of violence against surviving males. Two more men, Crocket Bewley and Amos Sales, who had been sick in bed the previous day and had been left alone, were hauled outside and murdered after they had begun to taunt their captors with stories of swift retribution on the part of surrounding communities. Another man, James Young, was delivering logs to the mission the following morning, Tuesday, December 1, unaware of the events of the previous day, only to be ambushed by a band of Cayuse and killed in the road.

The events of November 29 and 30, 1844, became known as the Whitman Massacre, one of the most notorious events of the early Westward Expansion. But once the Indians had vented their anger, they now seemed not to know what came next.

"The Cayuse were exultant," wrote Erwin N. Thompson in *Shallow Grave at Waiilatpu*, the most definitive volume on the massacre. "They had destroyed what they believed had been the source of all their troubles and ills. With the death of the *tewat* and his haughty wife, good times would return and Waiilatpu would be free from wagon wheels and the unfathomable ideas of the whites."

The slaughter soon turned into a siege as the Indians, holding the women and children hostage, attempted to figure out their next step. It lasted thirty days.

Several people managed to escape. Emigrants Peter Hall, W. D. Canfield, and Josiah Osborn all slipped away in the night. Hall made his way alone to Fort Walla Walla, a military installation some twenty miles away, and then fled—not bothering to seek assistance for the fifty people still trapped at Waiilatpu. Canfield walked to another mission, Lapwai, some 110 miles away, which took him five days. Osborn had successfully hidden his wife and children beneath a loose floorboard in the house and saved his family by helping them slip out at night. They reached Fort Walla Walla the next day. The director of the fort, William McBean, was himself "no hero" and was careful not to extend himself on the part of the captives, but he did send word to the Hudson's Bay Company at Fort Vancouver, which set in motion an ambitious rescue mission.

"The Indians could not know," Thompson wrote, "that the Whitmans would become martyrs in the eyes of their countrymen and that a great revenge would be visited upon the tribe." Once given an excuse to act on their fears, the emigrants had no trouble justifying a bloody revenge that would have ramifications for decades to come.

The massacre at Waiilatpu was a media sensation. News of the killings spread to the communities in the Oregon Territory like a prairie fire, fueled by an already-fearful white population living in a constant state of anxiety amongst the Indian populations.

It also effectively cut the 1848 migration to a fifth of its 1847 size; just over one thousand emigrants ventured west that year while more than five thousand had done so in 1847. It fanned the dormant fear of Indians in white settlers into a blazing panic and precipitated a backlash of military and vigilante assaults on Western tribes that would continue until well into the twentieth century and morph into the stuff of Hollywood legends. News of the massacre also prompted the 1848 act of Congress, signed into law by President James K. Polk, that officially created the Territory of Oregon as part of the United States.

More immediately, however, the massacre and subsequent siege of Waiilatpu was followed by the so-called Cayuse War, which consisted of a two-and-a-half-year vigilante manhunt for those responsible throughout the region of what is now eastern Washington and northern Idaho.

The leader of the vigilantes, officially called "Oregon Volunteers" and organized by a swift act of the provisional legislature, was none other than Neal Gilliam, deposed general of the Independent Oregon Colony. The ever-loyal William Shaw, Gilliam's brother-in-law, and two of Shaw's grown sons, were by Gilliam's side in a fruitless search of the men responsible for the Whitman Massacre. Gilliam met an untimely end during the war, when he—a day after admonishing his men not to leave their rifles loaded—pulled a gun, barrel-first, from a wagon and was shot in the head when the trigger was accidentally tripped. Shaw transported Gilliam's body back to his family and arranged for Gilliam's funeral.

The five Cayuse ringleaders, including Tomahas and Tiloukaikt, were eventually captured, in 1850, given a hasty trial, and hanged at Oregon City. The hangman was Joe Meek, father of Helen Mar, who had died of measles (and lack of treatment) during the siege. Joe Lewis, the massacre's real instigator, however, quickly realized that the response to the massacre was one of overwhelming force and a tidy takeover of Waiilatpu was a delusion. He slipped away from Waiilatpu during the siege and disappeared. While Lewis wasn't brought to justice in frontier fashion, he didn't live long. He was killed in an unrelated gun battle on an Idaho horse trail.

The historian Herbert Howe Bancroft eulogized Gilliam thus: "Thus died an honest, patriotic, and popular man, whose chief fault as an officer was too much zeal and impetuosity in the performance of his duties; whose glory would have been to die in battle." John Minto would not have been so charitable of his characterization of a man he considered not only a racist but also a dangerously ineffective leader.

The siege itself was a harrowing ordeal. The multitudes of children sick with measles began to die, including the six-year-old Louisa Sager and Helen Mar Meek, both, apparently, from lack of medical attention. A few days after the massacre, Louisa had died in her sleep in the arms of her older sister Catherine. When Catherine awoke, she said, "I still sat looking at my sister. Her hands were thrown over her head, and she seemed to be in a sound slumber. Miss B. remarked, 'How nicely Louisa sleeps!' Laying my hand on her face, I found it icy cold. I lay my ear to her mouth, but the breath was gone."

The siege also included several rapes—when the Indians took several of the women and teenage girls as "wives." Catherine Sager, almost thirteen years old at the time, and although a favorite of one particularly aggressive Indian, escaped this fate, effectively hiding with the help of the other women each time he came looking for her.

The bodies were buried by a Catholic priest named J. B. A. Brouillet. This itself was a shocking event in the lives of the survivors, all evangelical Protestants who had been taught that Catholics were akin to the devil. Elizabeth Sager recalled that she was more afraid of this man than she was of the Indians at the height of the attack. The captors allowed Brouillet to enter the mission, bury the dead and administer a short service, and then leave.

Negotiations with the Indians were handled through the efforts of Peter Skene Ogden of the Hudson's Bay Company. It would be the company's mission to save the captives, the American settlers to avenge the attacks, and the Indians, according to historian Erwin Thompson, "to salvage as much as possible from their crisis." Ogden proved a successful negotiator. As a British subject, he enjoyed a neutrality that the Indians understood. He couldn't speak for the vengeful Americans, he said, who wanted to storm the mission and slaughter the captors, but he could advise the Indians how they could save their skins: by allowing the hostages to live.

"I give you only advice," he reportedly told them, "and promise you nothing should war be declared against you. The company has nothing to do with your quarrel. If you wish it, on my return I will see what can be done for you; but I do not promise to prevent war. Deliver me the prisoners to return to their friends, and I will pay you a ransom, that is all."

The Indians agreed and accepted Ogden's offer. He subsequently delivered 62 blankets, 63 shirts, 12 guns, 600 loads of ammunition, 12 flints, and 37 pounds of tobacco. On December 29, a bitter cold morning, the prisoners were released. Led by Ogden, a caravan of wagons and horses, carrying the fifty survivors and several escorts, emerged from the mission and slogged north along the muddy road to Fort Walla Walla. One of the escorts was Whitman's Indian friend Stickus, who agreed to attend the caravan and quell any last-minute misgivings the Cayuse may have had.

After our crossing of the Blue Mountains, we arrived in Walla Walla late in the afternoon, the temperature on a bank sign reading one hundred degrees. We promptly got lost in all the chain stores, pawnshops, and "Quick loans for car titles" stores but finally found the town's only "campsite," which the guidebook described as "Walla Walla's newest and best RV park!" after rumbling over a set of railroad tracks just north of downtown. Not surprisingly, the campground, such as it was, was nestled in the industrial section of town, behind a mini-storage facility and a grain elevator and appeared to have been carved out of this heavy industry zone only weeks before. The acres of shimmering asphalt, freshly applied and still a rich black, was rimmed by a few recently planted saplings and a few patches here and there of dazzlingly green sod. The RVs, and there were dozens of them, must all have had air-conditioning or their owners would have been broiled alive in this searing landscape.

As I pulled into the RV lot I stopped the car and looked out across the asphalt. Waves of heat dazzled my eyes. There was not a single tent in sight. Nor did there seem to be anyone around.

"Why did you pick this place?" I asked. The words just slipped out, and once I heard them come from my mouth, I wished I could swallow them back out of the car's stale air, where they hung like ugly proof of my jerkiness.

"Me? *You're* the one who needed to get to this shit-ass town!"

She was right, of course. She had only read from the guidebook while I was driving, and she had actually suggested that, since there didn't seem to be much in the way of actual parkland near Walla Walla, that we camp in the Umatilla National Forest in the Blue Mountains. But I had insisted that we scope the place out and consider its accommodations up close. Maybe the campground would prove a hidden jewel. Besides, we'd be in and out in forty-eight hours, I'd said. But I was hungry and therefore irritable, and the heat outside was obviously intense. I had to blame someone.

She was using that special voice I recognize when I know my folly has pressed her to the brink, though, and, justifiably, she was in no mood to accept my grouchiness. I suggested we step out of the car so the kids would be spared my flaying and not supply their own commentary, which is what always happened when she and I got into a "discussion" in the front seat.

We stepped from the AC of the car and were greeted by a whoosh of hot air. My eyeballs went dry instantly. I blinked to keep them moist and squinted in the glare. Standing on the black top, the heat was unbelievable, as though we were standing on a red-hot griddle. I could feel it warming the bottoms of my feet through the soles of my shoes.

I then put up a feeble defense about giving the town a chance, and how we could use a little break from primitive campsites, but even as I spoke I realized we couldn't stay here. The tent without shade reaches temperatures at sauna level, let alone in one-hundred-degree heat. Our visit would require that I leave Leah alone with the kids, since I needed to visit the Whitman College Library and the Whitman Mission, which is now a National Historic Site operated by the National Park Service. The college library houses original manuscripts and other artifacts belonging to the Sagers, Shaws, and Whitmans, which meant the kids and Leah would be left at this scorching patch of asphalt for hours at a time with no relief. What we had seen of the town did not seem promising for diversion, either. There was not even a pool at this place, which at least the last RV park we stayed at, in Cahokia, Illinois, had offered.

I suddenly hatched an idea. We would find a hotel with a pool. The kids could enjoy a few days of semiluxuriant frolicking, playing in the pool and eating at a few restaurants. But this was a complicated proposition: Leah doesn't like hotels; they depress her, the dingy carpeting, the fiberglass-like feeling of the bedspreads and curtains, and the fact that Oakley tends to come alive in a special way when he enters a hotel, tearing through the halls without regard to his "inside voice" and ferreting in the breakfast buffet like a starving pioneer child. But, thankfully, Leah agreed it was a better idea than staying at this place, and, once we got back in the car and tore out of the RV park, tires screeching on the asphalt, the kids were delighted.

We drove back into town and tried several hotels, only to be turned away each time. Each was inexplicably full. After the second or third rejection I finally had to ask a hotel worker: "Why are all the hotels in Walla Walla full? What's here?" This nasty little town seemed to offer no succor to the traveler, no natural attraction, just a patch of commercial enterprise amidst the rolling farmland.

He shrugged. "It's always like this," he said. "Weddings, baseball tournaments—and the wines." Walla Walla weddings? Walla Walla wines? Why would people come to this town in the middle of Washington's parched grasslands for recreation?

We did finally find a place, a miserable little Travelodge with a pool, presided over by a sneering young Indian man (from the subcontinent, not a Walla Walla native), who explained he only had one room left, a dark little hole beneath the stairwell that was evidently last used by a heavy smoker. There was a small swimming pool, and it was surrounded by a tall fence so Oakley could be kept in or out, depending on our circumstances. He happily ran my credit card $75. I began to wish I had remained with Henry Sager's ghost back on the banks of the

Green River in southern Wyoming. Returning to a city with the family was too depressing; we all thrived in the wilds.

Over dinner at a little brew pub down the block from the Travelodge we learned from a couple seated at the next table that Walla Walla is effectively making its case as a country retreat for Portlanders and Seattleites seeking their own Sonoma or Napa Valley experience. Walla Walla's fertile topsoil can grow just about anything, and the mild climate has proved rich possibilities for vintners who have set up trendy, oaken-lined tasting rooms. It's now a tony weekend hotspot for city folks to guzzle wine and wander the streets browsing expensive home furnishings.

Later that evening, we discovered the beauty of Whitman College, founded in the late-nineteenth century and named for Marcus Whitman. As we entered the campus, we were greeted by a bronze statue of Whitman with a quote chiseled into its stone base: "My plans require time and distance." (When I quipped to Leah that my plans, too, required time and distance, she just glared at me.) The campus of Whitman College was improbably lush and bursting with color, its brick and stone buildings shaded by mature leafy trees and bordered by gardens, green lawns, and hidden fish pools, standing in contrast to the brown fields of the surrounding countryside. I made a beeline for the library, only to discover that the archives themselves, where the full Sager and Shaw collection was housed, were shuttered until Monday. It was Friday, which meant we were no longer able to make a surgical strike in this town and would have to spend three nights here. We trudged back to the hotel where I asked the keeper to run my credit card for another two nights.

The following morning we trekked to the Whitman Mission site five miles away. It was promising to be another scorching day, so we got an early start. The buildings have long since disappeared; only the tall hill that the mission children enjoyed climbing still remains as a solitary original landmark. I met the park's ranger, a tall, skinny young man whose clothes didn't fit him well and with a nervous disposition—perhaps the result of spending so much time around such an unsettling place. When I explained that I would like to ask him a few questions about the site, and wondered whether he could show me around, he looked over his shoulder nervously and hemmed and hawed in a croaking voice—"Umm, well, umm"—and mumbled about it being something he could not really do. His reticence was odd: every other park ranger I had met was overjoyed to have an interested visitor and happily showed me around and shared his or her knowledge of their site, since so few visitors apparently care enough about the history, they said. He finally agreed, insisting on bringing a large sackful of history books lest I ask him a tough question, and he strode out to the original site of the mission buildings at a breakneck pace, with me trotting along behind, struggling to keep up. I noticed his pants didn't fit him well; they were far too short, so that his white socks appeared below his cuffs. With his agitated manner, gangly build, and enormous stride, I considered whether Ichabod Crane had returned to earth to serve more time as a park ranger on a haunted patch of ground in eastern Washington.

The Park Service had carefully reconstructed the footprints of the original buildings, so it was possible to envision the lives of the Whitman and Sager families. We wandered the footprints, the ranger nervously showing me where the children had been lined up, where Marcus Whitman had been when struck by Tomahas, where John Sager was when he was shot, and where Narcissa Whitman was standing when she was shot in the chest through the living room door. I stood on each of these places and looked around.

While he was speaking, the kids kept pushing the plastic buttons on the displays, and a loud canned baritone voice would boom from a speaker about the particulars of the massacre. "To your right, the gristmill was. . . ." Each time they did this, the ranger would give a nervous jump. He would then raise his voice to try to speak over the canned voice, nervously glancing at the children as they approached the buttons again. This went on for a few minutes until I realized the poor fellow was on the verge of nervous collapse. I thanked him for his time and released him. He was visibly relieved and took off at a trot, covering the one hundred yards to the visitor center in about three strides, and disappearing safely inside.

After he left I stood in the place where Narcissa had last stood at the living room door. Had the fog burned off, she could have seen the

Blue Mountains to the east, the curve of the Walla Walla River coming within about one hundred feet of the house, and seen where her daughter had drowned five years before. The river has since been rerouted—only a damp spot and a tangled grove of willows remains in a shallow dip in the landscape.

Finn and I ran to the top of Memorial Hill, as it is called now, huffing and sweating in the rising heat, beholding a magnificent 360-degree view of rolling wheat fields and mountains beyond, and then descended to the grave site. A large granite slab bears the names of all thirteen people who died on November 29 and 30, 1847. The locations of neither Alice Clarissa's grave nor the paired graves of Louisa Sager and Helen Mar Meek are known.

I purchased a bound copy of Narcissa's letters in the gift shop and read for the first time, that afternoon in the motel room, of exactly how she had lost Alice Clarissa. I was reminded of our experience with Oakley on Lake McConnaghy back in Nebraska, when he had slipped away from us for forty-five minutes and played in the water, Leah and I each thinking the whole time that he was with the other. Sometimes luck has a lot to do with the trajectory of your life.

We spent the rest of the weekend watching the World Cup on TV (in which the Frenchman Zizou Zidane head-butted an Italian opponent and France subsequently lost the match), playing in the pool, and exploring the paths, hidden gardens, and duck ponds of the Whitman College campus. We also discovered a climbing wall on an exterior wall of the college's gymnasium. And on Monday I trolled the library archives, discovering numerous original letters and several striking artifacts, including a brilliantly colored patchwork quilt that Catherine Sager had made when she was an old woman and living in Spokane. It was made of cloth scraps, a signature "crazy quilt" style. One of the patches was a ribbon from a country fair from 1912. She must have been deep into seventies when she made it. The archivist at the library explained that the Sager Collection, as it is called, was donated by the granddaughters of Catherine, Elizabeth, and Matilda, who all maintained an interest in sharing their story. It had been decades since the material had been gone over, she said, and she was in the process of putting the material into a modern archive. She had no idea, herself, what the collection included, and my visit proved to be a fascinating treasure hunt for us both as she brought the relics out one at a time, wearing her white gloves when handling the exhibits and making me do the same, delighting in the contents of old letters and photographs. She discovered an old photo of William Shaw, which must have been from the 1880s, since he was a very old man in the picture. His wide-set features had a severe bearing, but there was kindness in his eyes. Next to him sat an equally serious Sally Shaw, looking plump and healthy, though also a very old woman when the photo was taken.

I examined piles of Catherine's handwritten letters and diaries, including a handwritten biography of her father, which traced his life from his youth in Virginia and Ohio, to where he died on the banks of the Green River. It was written in the detached, Victorian voice that was her style, referring to her father as "Mr. Sager" and in another place, "the loving husband and kind father." Her mother was Mrs. Sager—never "mother." She also included a tribute to the siblings who died at Waiilatpu: her brothers, John and Francis, and her sister Louisa.

John, she wrote, rose to the responsibility of his station with aplomb. "At the early age of fourteen he was by the death of his parents left in charge of his five sisters. Young as he was he seemed to realize the importance of this charge. For three years a cross or impatien[t] word was never uttered to any of them. But in him we found ready sympathy in all our childish troubles."

Of Francis she wrote: "Francis was of a confiding nature—gentle and genial in his manners with a tenderness for others that could not bear to see them suffer. He had always been on the best of terms with the Indians, in fact seemed a favorite with them, spoke their language fluently and often spent the night in their lodges. . . . His picture will always remain in my mind as he lay in death. His head covered in curls, and a smile upon his face, he looked as though he might only be asleep."

She described the death of Louisa and the panicked delirium the three-year-old suffered when she realized her favorite brother John was dead. "She was devotedly attached to her oldest brother and learning of his death she wept in all abandon of grief, refusing all consolation—

making answer to all 'I want brother John.' She refused all nourishment and spent the time weeping and moaning." Louisa would die the following day.

It was at once troubling and comforting to hold in my hands the paper that Catherine had written on more than one hundred years before, and to read the stilted words that were awkward expressions of shattered love. Over the course of our journey, we had considered the landscape and looked for vague clues in the land that would have suggested the passing of the Independent Oregon Colony. But until now, when I read of the deaths of parents and young children, I hadn't felt the personal closeness. Here in this fluorescent-lit, climate-controlled room, wearing a pair of ridiculous white archivist gloves and handling this old paper and a tattered patchwork quilt—I was touching death and love at the same time.

20

THE VALLEY OF HOPE

THERE WERE AT LEAST TWO HEROES whose efforts saved the remaining emigrants of the Independent Oregon Colony of 1844 from almost certain disaster: Dr. John McLoughlin of the Hudson's Bay Company at Fort Vancouver, and the twenty-year-old John Minto.

Minto and his friends Dan Clark and S. B. Crockett arrived in Oregon City, Oregon, in a warm shower of rain on October 19, 1844, more than a month ahead of everyone else traveling by wagon. The three men had split up for their descent of the Columbia and cheerfully "renewed our bedfollowship" on arrival in Oregon City. But Minto had promised Wilson and Nancy Morrison, when he went on ahead before the wagon train reached Fort Hall in what is now eastern Idaho, that he would return for them with supplies and assistance, since his original bargain was to see the family past the Dalles, a patch of rapids that required a long portage, and the family's cattle over the Cascade Mountains and into the Willamette Valley. Minto would not let the Morrisons down.

Dr. John McLoughlin—known throughout Oregon Country as "The Doctor"—had arrived in 1824 as the Chief Factor for Hudson's Bay Company operations in the Pacific Northwest and quickly set up

Fort Vancouver on the Columbia River. The doctor personally purchased large tracts of land and oversaw platting of what became Oregon City, ground zero for the Oregon migration. A kindhearted but shrewd businessman, he lorded over Hudson's Bay Company's Western fur trade as manager of a territory that stretched from the Mexican border—what is now the northern border of California—all the way to Alaska to the north and eastward to the Rocky Mountains. He was a political genius, carefully cultivating friendships with everyone: trappers, Indians, and newly arrived emigrants who were keen to establish a government. But when emigrants began arriving in the early 1840s, McLoughlin faced a dilemma: Hudson's Bay Company was a British-owned (Canadian) company, and Great Britain had an equal claim to the territory the Americans were now seeking to gobble up, yet the emigrants arrived in desperate straits and needed his immediate assistance if they were to survive the first year. To the detriment of his job, McLoughlin chose to help those in need and regularly extended company credit, whether to purchase flour and other provisions, or to offer the use of company equipment, such as the stable "bateaus" that could transport people, wagons, and gear down the Columbia from the Dalles to Oregon City. As a result, McLoughlin would be fired in 1845, but he became a living legend amongst Oregon pioneers. He formally relinquished his British citizenship and officially became an American citizen in 1851, earning great wealth in the process from numerous upstart businesses that he helped capitalize. In 1957, one hundred years after his death, he would be dubbed "the Father of Oregon" by an official act of the Oregon legislature. A mural of McLoughlin taking Narcissa Whitman's hand and welcoming her to Oregon in 1836 hangs in the rotunda of the Oregon State Capitol.

As soon as the young men arrived at Oregon City, they quickly found work to support themselves. It would be some time before the Morrisons and the others who were proceeding all the way to the Willamette Valley that fall would arrive at the Dalles, so the plan was to work as long as they could, and at the same time consider how best to organize for a fleet of small vessels to ascend the river with sufficient supplies to bring the families the rest of the way to Oregon City—the end of the Trail.

The men were in ragged condition, "half famished," their clothes worn thin, and, worst of all, they had no money to organize such an ambitious rescue. But Oregon City was a bustling city in the throes of its budding prosperity: timber was being feverishly cut at new sawmills, the country's first wheat was being harvested, and everywhere was opportunity for a young man willing to work in exchange for shelter, three meals a day, and purchasing credit at the company store. The following day, Minto secured work as a cook for a work party that was building a barn for the wheat crop for Gen. M. M. McCarver, speaker of the provisional Oregon legislature and a man of considerable influence in the area. Minto cut a good deal—this was a trade not just for his own sustenance but for provisions for the emigrants who would soon arrive at the Dalles and need food and transportation downriver. He spent two weeks with the work crew, and they managed to build the barn, harvest the wheat, and store it all in the new granary. McCarver was well pleased with Minto's assistance and wrote a letter of credit for use at the Hudson's Bay Company supply store at Fort Vancouver.

And then the men spent the next month going from job to job as opportunities presented themselves. In one six-day period Minto and his two friends built five log cabins, which were required, as stipulated in the land claim requirements, to be at least sixteen feet square and with a pitched roof that met the walls no less than six feet from the ground. "We had no team help of any kind," Minto said, which meant they did the work with hand tools, felling trees, shaping the corners of the logs, and then manually heaving the logs into position. And then during the month of November Minto split rails of cedar fencing, some fifteen hundred of them, the result of which provided a great service to the emigrants whose large herds of cattle would need to be contained on arrival. While the work was onerous, Minto was energized by the experience, and admitted, "never have I felt such delight in being alive."

While at Vancouver (in what is now Washington State and not the Vancouver in British Columbia), Daniel Clark, still making his way to Oregon City, had briefly assisted the Hudson's Bay Company in unloading a ship, and had a curious incident that he relayed to John Minto on his arrival at Oregon City. Minto would delight in repeating the story about his friend for decades to come, at annual "Campfire Orations" and "Reminiscences," since he considered the experience to embody the spirit of American audacity.

After the ship was unloaded, Clark decided to inspect the vessel, an enormous sailing vessel that had likely come from Europe via Cape Horn. Being from Missouri, he had never seen an oceangoing ship, and was taken with its size, and thought, since no one was around, he'd have a look around. He climbed the gangplank and proceeded to inspect the ship from stem to stern, wandering the deck fore and aft, entering the cargo holds, the cabins, the crew's quarters, and finally ending up in the aft cabin, where he abruptly came face-to-face with the ship's master, who was busily writing in his log.

The captain was surprised to find a stranger wandering his ship and demanded an explanation: "Young man, who are you; and what do you want here?"

"Sir, I am an immigrant just come down the river," Clark stammered. "I do not wish to intrude, but I wanted to see the ship, as I never saw one before to recollect."

"Where do you come from and why do you come here?"

"We come from Missouri, across the Rocky Mountains; we've come to settle Oregon and rule this country."

The captain glared at Clark for a few moments, shook his head, and seemed to let out an exasperated sigh before answering: "Well, young man, I have sailed in every quarter of the globe, and have seen the most of the people upon it; but a more uncouth, and, at the same time, bolder set of men than you Americans I have never seen."

To Minto, an English immigrant who had, like McLoughlin, relinquished his British citizenship for a chance to be an American, this was the highest praise.

When Minto received word that the families were due to arrive at the Dalles in the first few days of December, he ingratiated himself with Dr. John McLoughlin, requesting a small load of supplies and the use of a bateau for the excursion upriver. The heavy boats were usually handled by a minimum of seven strong men, "six at the oars and a captain to steer," but taking the boats upriver at this time of year was not an event that people volunteered for, especially not if there was no money in the adventure, so Minto, Clark, and Crockett would have to attempt it alone. (Both Clark and Crockett were under a similar obligation as Minto, bound by their word to get their adopted families down the Columbia and the cattle over the Cascades.)

At nine o'clock in the morning on December 4, the men arrived at Fort Vancouver and asked to see the famous doctor. McLoughlin kept his white hair in a long, wild mane and grew his chops full and bushy. Daguerreotypes of the doctor show a piercing gaze, which belied the man's magnanimous spirit. He was sitting on his front porch that morning, and he called the young men over to him.

"Are you the young men who have applied for a boat to assist your friends down the river?" McLoughlin asked.

They were.

"Young men, young men," McLoughlin said (he had a habit of stuttering when he was excited), "I advise you, if you can, take your boat above the cascades and bring all the people down the cascades—not your own friends only, and I'll see, I'll see they are brought down from there."

This would mean committing provisions and time to an untold number of emigrants in various states of privation. They simply could not know what they'd find on arrival at the Dalles. But Minto agreed immediately.

And McLoughlin added, "Under our rules we are not selling goods just now; we are taking stock for the year. But you are, I think, going on an errand of mercy and shall have what you need." This was vintage McLoughlin—a display of the same spirit that would cost him his job six months later but earn him the devotion of generations of Oregonians.

McLoughlin also encouraged the men to write a letter home to their parents, since a mail boat would be departing that day for the U.S. East Coast, and another one would not be available for six months. (Minto spent two hours writing a letter home to his family in Pittsburgh, not receiving a reply until two years and seven months later, in July 1847.)

If Minto and the others lacked manpower, they didn't let it bother them. Traveling upstream on the Columbia River was an adventure, and they, once again, were thrilled at the prospect. They also had good luck, since their departure coincided with a Chinook wind, the powerful southwesterly that sweeps the Columbia River Gorge in winter and elevates winter temperatures to comfortable levels. They rowed the heavy craft into the stream, stepped the boat's heavy mast, and set sail in the warm breeze, which blew them upstream sixteen miles on their first day. On the second day, December 6, the men repeated their efforts, and the wind "freshened as the day advanced," Minto recalled, "covering the river with whitecaps and sending us forward faster than any six Canadian oarsmen could have done."

They reached the first set of rapids by afternoon, and then realized their dilemma. They couldn't portage the heavy boat over three miles of rough terrain by themselves, so they hatched an ambitious plan: they would sail the vessel upstream, through the rapids, steering around rocks that protruded the surface. "Then for more than two hours we had an experience rarely if ever had in passing up those rapids before the day of steam navigation on the Columbia River," Minto said. "Sometimes the current would beat the wind in force and we would be slowly carried downstream towards black rocks cutting the surface of the river like a knife, the current being truly terrific. Again we hung just above certain destruction had the wind suddenly failed, and disaster would have been almost certain any time the steersman attempted to turn or go across current. However, the strength of the wind prevailed, and we reached the upper portage before nightfall."

At the base of the upper portage they encountered another team of boatmen, and the men agreed to help one another. The following day they then began to drag the boats, first one and then another, upstream in the shallows, a voyageur practice called "cordeling," Clark and Crockett and the other men hauling from shore on a lead rope, and Minto standing in the boat and keeping it from grounding with a long oar. "The eight men who had hold of the cord succeeded in pulling me up, reaching the calm water of the landing above the cascades, and only a barrel or so of water shipped, and no damage done," Minto said.

The scene that greeted the young men was one of utter desperation. Families that had been traveling since May, a full seven months without reprieve, were now huddled around the banks of the Columbia River attempting to secure passage downstream from the handful of Indians and trappers seeking to make a few dollars, since a winter crossing of the Cascades with wagons was unthinkable. It would be several years before a road would be cut through these mountains. (And the leader of one of these expeditions would be John Minto.)

Minto found Nancy Morrison and her six children, ages 1, 3, 5, 9, 10, and 13, among the huddled masses, and she quickly related their recent experiences. The last month had been the hardest ever. All were barefoot, despite the chill weather, and Minto learned from Nancy that the day before she had traded her last dress, except for the one she was wearing, to a group of Clatsop Indians for a peck of potatoes (about fifteen pounds) to feed the children. Their provisions were now completely exhausted. One of the men had gone off that morning to hunt ducks, but he had not returned, and they'd had nothing to eat all day. Meanwhile, Wilson Morrison had continued overland with the family's cattle and was at that moment experiencing the first of the winter's heavy snows. Minto immediately reported back to the boat crews and asked that he take from the supplies his entire share of the crew's provisions—so that he could turn it over to Nancy—leaving him with nothing to eat for the next week. Nancy took Minto's provisions, which amounted to a small portion of flour, meat, and potatoes, gratefully, and only later did Minto discover that she had distributed what little there was to everyone in her midst, not just her children, but to other families also. Minto did not hear what Nancy said to the others: "John knows who his friends are." She would not forget his selflessness.

For his part, Minto was devoted to Nancy Morrison, seeing in her the same attributes of the strong women who were the real backbone of the overland migration and the subsequent founding of Oregon. At an Oregon Pioneers Association reunion in 1890, he recalled, "She was no complainer, while sociable, not an excessive talker. She was at this time in the prime of life, and thinking for words to characterize her in her relations to her family and others, those of Proverb XXI: 25 come to my mind, 'strength and honor are her clothing.'"

Minto noted that Nancy Morrison quietly opposed the journey to Oregon, at least initially. "The movement was against the judgment and feelings of Mrs. Morrison; she told me so in so many words," Minto said, "but never alluded to the subject again until she had been several years in Oregon, and then she told me she was satisfied with the change on her husband's account; but she believed he himself was not."

Her quiet strength was typical of mothers at the time, Minto observed: "[T]here is something in womanhood which enables the wife and mother to bear up better than man in the direst extremity of privation. This woman"—Nancy Morrison—"whose traits I am trying to portray, was a natural captain of womanhood. There was no crying or wringing of hands or tearing of hair. She may have prayed; she certainly watched; and yet worked her way manfully through the difficulties of her surroundings with the courage of a brave man and the gentleness of a lady." A lady she may have been, but she was a tough lady when she had to be. When she and her children descended the rest of the Columbia, she threatened to throw someone overboard for excessive use of foul language. The language quickly improved. The journey was not without incident. Martha Ann Morrison, who was fourteen at the time, recalled that the little vessel they were in was forced ashore during a storm.

> Mother and the smaller children crouched near the fire which was built after repeated efforts and all night we were exposed to this December storm, with no protection except an old quilt which was thrown over the children. . . . We were now reduced to no change of clothing, and no chance of getting anything, for even with money we could buy nothing in the way of dry goods. Father then had $21.00. Ten dollars of this was paid for flour at Oregon City. We made patched dresses of all colors—even our stockings were many-colored. Out distress at being barefoot was painful.

That the Morrisons began the journey as one of the wealthiest families, driving a large herd of cattle and two wagons stuffed with provisions and equipment, and should have their fortunes reduced to such extent, was not surprising in retrospect, considering their character. Neither Wilson nor Nancy Morrison allowed anyone to go hungry when they still had provisions to share. They were barefoot and clothed in rags, but their generosity was infectious and informed the spirit of the new communities around the Willamette Valley.

Since Minto promised to aid everyone and not just the Morrison family, he had to leave Nancy Morrison here, at the upper portage of the Cascades, and continue upstream to the Dalles, which, prior to construction of a hydroelectric dam in 1957, was a thunderous, precipitous waterfall that marked the end of the overland journey. Nancy Morrison and the children were able to secure passage on another boat, allowing them to arrive in Oregon City a full week ahead of everyone else. When Minto, Clark, and Crockett arrived at the Dalles, they loaded the running gear—wheels, axles, and harnesses from three wagons—and seventeen emigrants into the bateau. The boat was loaded to the gunnels, and the weather was terrible for their descent of the river, but they succeeded in their journey, arriving safely at mouth of the Willamette on December 29, where they were invited, all twenty of them, to have dinner and spend the night aboard the brig *Chenamus*. The master of the vessel, a fellow Minto remembered clearly, was John H. Couch, a native of Newburyport, Massachusetts, who was loathed by the Hudson's Bay Company for his indomitable, entrepreneurial spirit—and who would go on to become one of the founders of the city of Portland, Oregon.

The officers of the ship offered their bunks to the women and children, and "we were treated with the best supper the ship's larder could furnish." The Morrison family, less Wilson Morrison, and the others arrived in Oregon City on December 30. On New Year's Eve, they returned the bateau and its gear to "the generous Dr. McLoughlin," Minto recalled, who "assisted in expressing the joy in our arrival by dancing the old year out and the new one in on the puncheon floor of a new log building finished that day."

Wilson Morrison left his cattle herd at the Dalles that winter and joined his family at Oregon City in the first few days of January. While most settlers found claims in the mild Willamette Valley, Morrison chose to press all the way to the mouth of the Pacific, spending the winter with their friend Solomon Smith some twelve miles west of Astoria and then settling a claim on the Clatsop Plains, just inside the mouth of the Columbia River. Minto helped the Morrisons and recalled the misery of the last leg of the trip: "It rained almost incessantly, and sometimes we were windbound on the voyage, in exposed conditions, and had to endure the pitiless storms of wind and rain where dry fuel could not be had."

Minto spent the remainder of the winter of 1845 working at a sawmill and in March returned with Wilson Morrison to retrieve his cattle herd, as he had promised. On the first of March, Minto hired a canoe, and with a five-dollar gold piece for his expenses, set out upstream again to retrieve the cattle. Minto had been ordered to drive the cattle, some eighty head, to Washougal, now in the state of Washington, and leave the herd in care of a man with the historically unfortunate name of George W. Bush, a black man married to a white woman who had undertaken the overland journey in 1844 intent on becoming a landowner. (The territory of Oregon, to Minto's chagrin, would initially outlaw ownership of land by blacks, but the state of Washington allowed it; Bush was aware of the pending restrictions and consequently settled in Washington, where he settled a claim of 640 acres.)

"Leaving the cattle in Mr. Bush's charge, as ordered," Minto recalled, "I made my way to the Clatsop Plains, and reported what I had done to Capt. Morrison; and, considering I had fulfilled my verbal agreement made just about one year before"—it was now mid-March 1845—"returned to Hunt's mill and worked there until about the middle of June when, with others I came to Oregon City to cast my first vote as a citizen of Oregon under the Provisional Government; my ballot being cast for George Abernathy, first Governor of Oregon."

William and Sally Shaw spent the winter of 1844–45 at the Dalles Mission on the Columbia River because of the illness of their son Thomas, who was close to death from typhoid. Shaw must have, again, heeded the voice of caution in his head when he chose to remain at the Dalles. He had just delivered the seven Sager orphans to the Whitmans, and the flightiness of Henry Sager must have hung heavy in his mind. He would take no such chances, even if the urge to arrive at the end of the trail must have tugged at him that winter. Thomas Shaw recalled, referring to himself and his family in the third person: "Rev. A. F. Waller, who had charge of the mission at that time, seeing their plight, offered them half of his own house as an abode for the winter and generously gave them of his medical supplies, and to this kindness Thomas said he owed his life. The family had great respect and love for Rev. Waller and felt no praise was too great for his self-sacrifice and devotion to his God and fellow men."

Thomas recovered, of course, and that spring they all—Shaw and his three sons, while Sally and their daughter Mary kept house—worked at Fort Vancouver, cutting shingles for the Hudson's Bay Company. That fall, they settled a claim near Salem, taking possession of 640 acres of land on October 23, 1845. William Shaw served one term on the Oregon provisional legislature. The Shaw children all made similar land claims, in 1850 and 1851, when they were married, since a man could only complete his full claim with a wife, in whose name 320 acres were written. (Thomas Shaw, like his father, served on the Oregon legislature, and eventually became a judge.) William Shaw's dream, nurtured by the tales of Capt. Benjamin Bonneville's adventures in the limitless West—to see his own children achieve the same success he had found on the early frontier of Missouri—was achieved.

And the Shaws remained pillars of their community. While they were no longer young (Shaw was nearly fifty in 1844) when they arrived, they nonetheless regained the prosperity they had built in Missouri, planting vast wheatfields that yielded a healthy annual profit. The Gold Rush cramped their initial luck, however, but the good karma they had established paid off, as detailed in the following story by their son Thomas, written when he was an old man:

> When gold was discovered in California and all the able-bodied men left the Willamette Valley, in 1849, the Shaw brothers were no exception and went with the grand rush. The father and mother, who were affectionately called Uncle Billie and Aunt Sally, were left alone on the farm. Some grain had been put in by the boys before they left and they expected to get back by harvest time, but the lure of the precious metal was too strong and they did not get back in time. Uncle Billie was past sixty at this time and had not been well all summer, so naturally they wondered how they were to get their grain cut and harvested. There were only old men and young boys left in the country to do the work. One morning, very early, Aunt Sally heard a rap at the door and looking out saw a lot of young boys gathered at the door. The leader

> asked if she would give them their breakfast. She said, 'Certainly, boys, but are you not out pretty early?' He motioned toward their grain field and she was astonished to see all their grain cut, bound and in the shock. The lads had done the harvesting in the small hours of the morning, so as to do their own work later in the day. This shows the affection in which this family was held in the neighborhood in which they lived.

After his family recovered their health at the Waiilatpu Mission in October 1844 with the Whitmans, the Reverend E. E. Parrish settled a claim, planting many acres of fruit trees, in what would become Marion County, Oregon, a place that continues to bear his name: Parrish Gap. Shortly after arrival he ran for, and was elected, to a judgeship in the provisional government. "We have abundant cause for thanksgiving to God," Parrish wrote in 1863, almost twenty years after his arrival.

Like his colleagues Shaw, Morrison, and Minto, Parrish was possessed of an egalitarian spirit and was cautious about exerting religion too much into everyday life. He was one of the founding board members of a nonsectarian college, the Jefferson Institute, incorporated in January 1857. Together, Edward and Rebecca Parrish raised their six children in Oregon. He died in October 1874, just a few weeks shy of his eighty-third birthday. Rebecca Parrish died in 1880 at the age of seventy-six. They left behind eighteen grandchildren.

The four surviving Sager girls never lived together as a family again after the massacre at Waiilatpu. They grew up, each of them married sons of emigrants, and scattered throughout the Northwest. Henrietta Louise, the youngest, who was born on the Trail, was killed in a strange shooting accident at a mining camp in California by a man apparently attempting to shoot her husband. She was twenty-six years old and had been estranged from her three older sisters for most of her adult life.

But the three others, Catherine, Elizabeth, and Matilda, retained a close bond throughout their lives and were proud of their heritage and of their family's strange story. They identified with what they dubbed their father's "stout-heartedness." That their childhood was tragic only added to this view. They returned to Waiilatpu fifty years after the massacre and oversaw the dedication of a memorial to the thirteen people who died on November 30, 1847.

When she was sixteen, Catherine married Clark Pringle, who came west with his family in 1845, and together had eight children. They lived on a farm near Salem, Oregon, and Clark eventually became a Methodist circuit rider. She remained a "serious, pious" woman and referred to her adulthood as "sober married life," according to historian Erwin N. Thompson. She died in Spokane, Washington, at the age of seventy-five.

Elizabeth lived in six different foster homes between 1847 and 1855, including a summer with the Parrish family. She became a schoolteacher at sixteen and then married William Fletcher Helm, the son of an 1845 emigrant. They had nine children. She died in 1925 at the age of eighty-eight. Shortly before her death she told the president of Whitman College that she still possessed the family Bible that accompanied them on the westward journey in 1844.

Matilda was only eight years old when the massacre occurred. She was raised by a stern missionary, William Geiger Jr., but of the three seemed to be the only one with a sense of humor, despite the fact that, after marrying at the age of fifteen to an emigrant named Lewis Hazlitt and having five children in quick succession, she was widowed in 1863. She married again, only to be widowed for the second time a year later, but in the process she and her husbands had developed a string of successful businesses. She married a third time—this time for good. She died at the home of one of her daughters in Reseda, California, in 1928—the last of the Sager children—at the age of eighty-four.

Throughout their adult lives, the sisters guarded the family story jealously, frequently giving lectures on the subject and correcting what they were felt were hyperbolic popular treatments of the story. They resisted moving the mass grave to a location on the Whitman College campus so that it would be safer from agriculture, and opposed a plan in the 1890s to build a memorial there, saying that a monument to Dr. Marcus Whitman and the others was "in the heart of the people." But they supported the idea of purchasing the Whitman property and establishing a home for orphans there, to be called Narcissa House, a plan that never materialized. The sisters finally agreed to a compromise on the memorial site: a monument would be built, but the graves would remain at the mission site. The remains were exhumed and reinterred in 1898 at the mission site beneath a marble slab that now bears the names of all who died in the massacre.

John Minto was later credited by nineteenth-century historian Herbert Howe Bancroft as being the "leader" of the expedition that saved the lives of the Morrison family and the many others in their train after they arrived at the Dalles and the Cascades with no way to descend the last part of the river to Oregon City. But Minto rejected this categorization. "Minto was in no sense a leader," Minto wrote in 1890 to the Oregon Pioneer Association's eighteenth annual reunion. "We were three boys, I may say, in age and experience; boys, I am proud to say, who did things when action was a virtue; but all the provisions we took back with us were only what we could buy and pay for—not ten dollars worth, I am quite sure." Maybe so, but Oregon did not forget John Minto. He went on to serve four terms in the legislature once statehood was achieved. He fought against—and defeated—early attempts to make Oregon a slave state, at one point, during debate on the proposed legislation, jumping to his feet and issuing a fiery rebuke: "Mr. Chairman . . . I wish to say here and now that no resolution that this meeting can pass shall force me to vote for slavery, when I have a choice of voting for freedom."

He explained later: "I had been constrained to listen to much talk in justification of secession and boasting of readiness to fight for it because the boasters had been born in a slave state. As for me, I had no birthright in any," since he was born abroad. "I had assisted to give the title of Oregon to the United States, to which Government my fealty was pledged in almost the same terms as my marriage vows. . . . When I lack courage to defend my wife, I may fail to support my pledge of citizenship; but till then, I am the enemy of every enemy of the United States, ready to act in her defense, 'by word or pen or pointed steel.'"

Lastly, he challenged an assembly of fellow legislators, who would soon vote to support his oratory, to consider all they had accomplished in the name of the United Sates: "[C]ast your eye north, or west or south, as far as you can see and much more, the United States has secured by gift the soil in liberal portions for citizens' homes. Then tell me, where's the coward that would not dare to fight for such a land? What security of tenure have you for your homes but the integrity of the United States?"

On July 18, 1847, after serving in the Cayuse War under William Shaw and Neal Gilliam, whom Minto unabashedly despised, Minto asked Wilson Morrison for the hand of his eldest daughter, Martha Ann. Martha Ann was only sixteen at the time, and the proposal shocked Morrison, who muttered something about her being so young and needing to be in school.

But Nancy Morrison settled the matter by telling her husband: "Well, if a day's wages will support a home, John Minto's wife will have one, for I know there is not a lazy bone in him." Nancy Morrison also knew who her friends were.

John and Martha Ann Minto were married on July 8, 1847, and would eventually settle a claim near Salem, Oregon (part of which exists to this day and is still known as Minto Island), have seven children, and enjoy a marriage that lasted almost sixty years. Minto briefly went to California during the Gold Rush, but came home after only a few months, with enough "yellow dirt" to start a seventeen-acre fruit orchard on his claim. He also became a successful sheep farmer (and was the first to import merinos into the territory), earning a position as the representative for the U.S. Department of Agriculture for the Pacific states on sheep husbandry.

Minto fervently believed that the founding of Oregon as an egalitarian state was at the heart of the settling of the territory, rejecting the idea that "a patriotic motive and the establishment of republican government was an afterthought," as so many would later assert. He considered it an "insult" that he and others should be seen as mere "hunter recluses like Daniel Boone."

"Common reason will not apply to Mr. Morrison's or Mr. Shaw's conduct in selling rich farms in Missouri to come to Oregon," he said in an article published a few years before his death. Unlike Morrison and Shaw, who were both staunch Republicans, Minto was a lifelong Democrat, committed to the ideal that government "must represent to the fullest degree the rights of man and the greatest good for the greatest number," according to one historian. The land claims were an added bonus, Minto thought, but the spirit that settled Oregon was one of equal opportunity, a fair start in a fertile land—for everyone.

John Minto's name is etched in stone—flanked by those of Sacajawea and Samuel K. Barlow, an 1840s pioneer who established what became known as the "Barlow Road" through the Cascades—in the Oregon House Chambers at the state capitol in Salem. When Minto died in 1915 at the age of ninety-three, his friend John Gill, a former Oregon legislator who shared a devotion to Robert Burns poetry with Minto and served with him in the House, published a eulogy to Minto in the Oregon Historical Society newsletter.

"[T]he news of his death was a shock to the whole commonwealth," Gill wrote. "I walked alone in the sunset up the beautiful path through the park to the Statehouse; fed the leaping trout in the fountain, as we two had often fed them; went into the silent halls where every step resounded, sat a moment in the chair he had commonly occupied when he came thither, and thanked God as I walked back alone amid the darkening shadows of the trees, through which the winter stars were shining, that it had been my unspeakable privilege to be the friend of John Minto."

EPILOGUE

> I wonder if ever again Americans can have that experience of returning to a home place so intimately known, profoundly felt, deeply loved, and absolutely submitted to? It is not quite true that you can't go home again. I have done it, coming back here. But it gets less likely. We have had too many divorces, we have consumed too much transportation, we have lived too shallowly in too many places.
>
> —WALLACE STEGNER, *ANGLE OF REPOSE*

WE SPED THROUGH THE COLUMBIA RIVER GORGE along U.S. Highway 84, following the water that John Minto and the Morrison family had traveled by bateau 162 years before on their final leg to the end of the Trail, covering the one hundred miles from the Dalles to Portland in about an hour and a half. It had taken them a week. The snowcapped peak of Mount Hood appeared in brief snatches as we sped west, but mostly the highway stays along the water's edge, the cliffs and tall bluffs of the Gorge providing a majestic passage to the coast. The barrenness of eastern Oregon—the sage and tufted grasses—soon turned to Douglas-fir and spruces as we approached the Cascades. We sped past the exits to Portland, now just another city crushed under the weight of sprawl, saw signs for Oregon City and Salem, and joined the narrow two-lane, Route 26, that dead-ends at the Pacific Coast Highway. The trees got larger, the air cooler, and colored a deep green. Ferns flanked the narrow roadway.

Soon we spilled out, and the sky opened up—and there was the sea.

We found Oswald West State Park by accident. A parking lot on the side of Route 101 bears a small sign, and stopping to investigate we learned that we would have to leave our car at the highway, load our gear into a wheelbarrow, and descend a steep path to the campground, which was hidden from view by the trunks of trees that were larger around than our car and rose skyward hundreds of feet, their tops lost in the heavy limbs. We loaded the wheelbarrow and hiked down into the ravine and were soon swallowed by the immensity of the forest. We had driven here in a car, and we were awed. To have walked two thousand miles and discover such fecundity must have brought the early pioneers to their knees.

We set up camp beneath a Sitka spruce with a trunk ten feet in diameter. These were old-growth trees, the same ones growing here when the Independent Oregon Colony settled Oregon. They could have sat beneath these same trees. And if the ghosts of the pioneers are anywhere, they are here in the murky shadows of these giants—and in the thunderous breakers of the Pacific.

The following day it poured rain, but we played on the beach with the rest of the vacationers, who were similarly undeterred by the wet weather. I learned that the mascot of the University of Oregon is the duck, and saw several raincoats with the goofy logo. We watched people pull razor clams from the sand using long steel tubes; and soon the surfers, sporting reckless facial hair, multiple piercings, and indifferent expressions, appeared in their wet suits and spent the day playing in the waves.

We spent four days amongst the trees at Oswald West, hiking the Pacific Coast Trail to Cape Falcon; climbing the steep, fern-fringed trail up Neahkanie Mountain in a thick, briny fog; and playing in the cold waves. Finn rated the campsite with six stars, the highest ever. Jonah caught a snake and Raven found a purple starfish. Oakley made friends with all the neighbors.

On the last day, a Saturday, we gathered some mussels from the tide pools and built a driftwood fire on the beach. So far, the beach had been fairly empty, the few visitors being those who were camping in the twenty-odd sites of Oswald West. But by 10:00 a.m. the rain had stopped, the sky cleared to reveal a brilliant blue, and the beach was suddenly full of day-trippers from Portland, an hour-and-a-half drive to the east. We could smell their shampoo and laundry detergent. Their clothes were clean and brightly colored. They spread fresh towels on the sand and waded in the water, squealing at the cold. When the water boiled, I plunked the mussels into the pot and clapped on the lid, and soon the shells opened up and showed the pink fleshiness inside. I spilled the pot onto a flat rock and Leah and I started in, cracking open the shells with rocks and slurping out the insides. I wasn't wearing a shirt and my skin had the coarse feel of accumulated sun and salt; Leah's hair looked so crazy that I burst out laughing. The kids were climbing on the rocks above us, and we watched them for a few moments before calling them to eat. Oakley was stark naked and was crawling around in the sand making cat noises. Jonah's shaggy hair covered his eyes, and he peered from behind his fringe with a hungry look. Finn's expression was haggard. Raven was so tan that her skin, usually a tawny brown anyway, was a deep bronze. Her curly brown hair was blonde at the tips. When I called them for lunch, which for them consisted of a few sad-looking leftovers of cheese and crackers and some raisins, I suddenly realized how we looked to this pack of weekenders: half-naked and eating our steamed mussels and meager provisions with our fingers around an open driftwood fire. We looked like the emigrants must have when they fetched up at Oregon City in December 1844—mannerless and savage. But we were happy.

It was time to go home.

ACKNOWLEDGMENTS

This book was a group effort by a great number of people to whom I owe heartfelt thanks: Tom McCarthy at Lyons Press for believing in this project enough to give it life; Jim Sollers for his remarkable illustrations and proving, once again, that art and reality can indeed be one; Candy Moulton for her gracious assistance with Oregon Trail history and especially for her welcoming spirit while we were at the mercy of the Wyoming trail dust; John Schaffner for his poems and inspiring trail-side performance; Ben Kern and Rod and Doris Henderson for allowing us to join them on their Overland Trail adventure; John Stevenson for the impromptu lesson on skinning and tanning a rattlesnake hide; John Mark Lambertson at the National Frontier Trails Museum in Independence, Missouri; Jackie Lewin at the St. Joseph Archives; Richard Anderson and the State of Wyoming for allowing us to camp at Independence Rock; Levida Hileman for her assistance on the history of Independence Rock; Jim Henderson for his trail sleuth-work; Whitman College curator emeritus Larry Dodd for his help on early map sources; Professor Roger Miles of Whitman College for his help deciphering the spirit of the Second Great Awakening; Janet Mallen at the Whitman

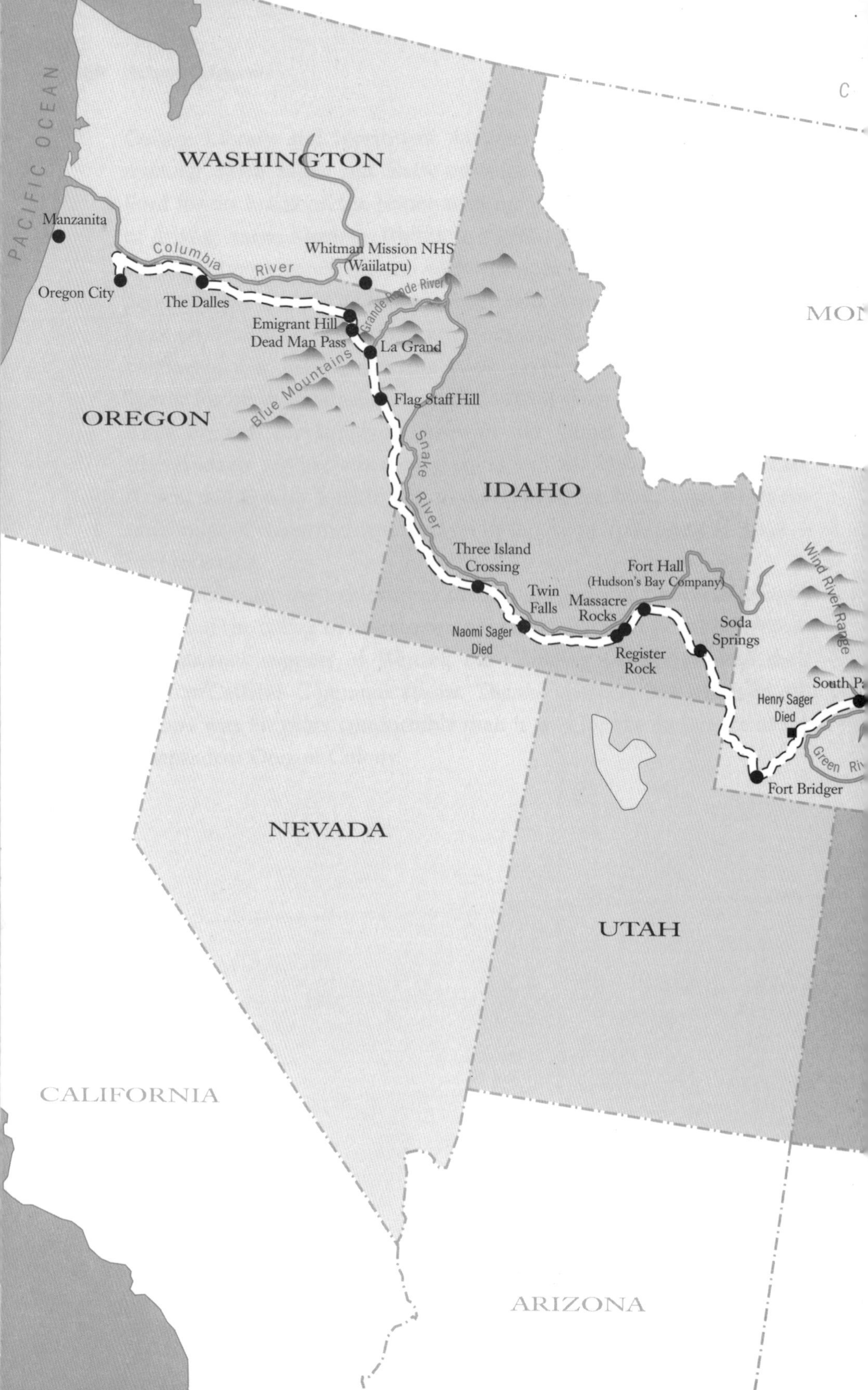

PACIFIC OCEAN
WASHINGTON
Manzanita
Columbia River
Whitman Mission NHS (Waiilatpu)
Oregon City
The Dalles
Grande Ronde River
Emigrant Hill
Dead Man Pass
La Grand
Blue Mountains
Flag Staff Hill
OREGON
Snake River
IDAHO
Three Island Crossing
Twin Falls
Naomi Sager Died
Massacre Rocks
Fort Hall (Hudson's Bay Company)
Register Rock
Soda Springs
Wind River Range
South P
Henry Sager Died
Green Ri
Fort Bridger
NEVADA
UTAH
CALIFORNIA
ARIZONA